# GETTING THE *MOST* FROM YOUR GAME AND FISH

*A Complete Field Manual for the North American Sportsman*

WRITTEN AND ILLUSTRATED BY

## ROBERT CANDY

*Alan C. Hood, Publisher*

Putney, Vermont

*DEDICATED TO — my late wife and personal secretary, Penny, a real participating sportsman herself when time allowed, the mother of my four children, and a great "hunting and fishing widow." She graciously put up with my crazy hours and tremendous accumulation of valuable junk associated with all my outdoor activities. In short, she made it all possible.*

Getting the *Most* from Your Game & Fish

Copyright © 1978 by Robert Candy

Copies of *Getting the* Most *from Your Game & Fish* may be obtained by sending $18.95 per copy to:

Alan C. Hood, Publisher
P.O. Box 1
Putney, VT 05346

Price includes postage and handling. Quantity discounts are available to dealers and non-profit organizations. Write on letterhead for details.

Manufactured in the United States of America.

**Library of Congress Cataloging-in-Publication Data**

Candy, Robert, 1920-
    Getting the most from your game & fish/Robert Candy ; illustrated by the author.
        p.    cm.
    Reprint. Originally published: Charlotte, Vt. : Garden Way Pub., c1978.
    Bibliography: p.
    Includes index.
    ISBN 0-911469-01-X (pbk.) : $16.95
    1. Game and game-birds, Dressing of.   2. Fishes, Dressing of.
3. Trapping.   4. Taxidermy.   5. Cookery (Game)   I. Title.
SK36.2.C36 1988
799.2—dc19                                                      88-8265
                                                                      CIP

Published by Alan C. Hood, Publisher, Putney, Vermont
10 9 8 7 6 5 4 3

# CONTENTS

SECTION VI

## KITCHEN TIPS

# PREFACE

For some decades hunting and trapping have been forms of outdoor recreation for most participants. The time when these endeavors were pursued solely to secure food and clothing generally has passed, except during times of emergency and in the few true wilderness situations that still exist, where hunting, trapping and fishing continue as ways of life even today.

These pursuits, now mainly recreational, often are misunderstood, largely because they entail the taking of life. The *sport* is all *before* the kill, and yet without the kill the challenge is unfulfilled. Furthermore, a certain amount of dying is necessary to sustain life. It is too bad that the reverence of living is not balanced by a comparable understanding of death. Each is a part of life.

Sportsmen should not have to apologize for their recreation unless they are that minority of slob fishermen, hunters, trappers. But we have hikers, campers and drivers, too, who fall into the slob category, spoiling everything they touch or do, who run roughshod over everybody and everything.

The opponents of hunting and trapping often are people well-intentioned but poorly schooled in the ways of the natural world they are trying to protect. They do not realize that "preservation" usually is diametrically opposed to sound "conservation" — that *wildlife cannot be stockpiled*. The preservationists often lack proper judgment from lack of exposure to nature. Unfortunately, they do not study wildlife enough to learn what really goes on in the natural community.

We all are sentimental about animals to varying degrees, but sentiment can destroy reason and becomes dangerous when people believe only what they *want* to believe.

There is no paradise for wildlife. Considerable tragedy and suffering are common in the wild, for every species has its sicknesses, debilitating parasites and continuous threats of death — even without the intervention of man.

But people have greatly compounded wildlife problems. People (and these include the anti-hunters and anti-trappers) have been most cruel to wildlife by their mass destruction of wildlife habitat — the places where wild animals, birds and fish must live, find shelter, obtain adequate food and reproduce. We have taken the best and pushed wildlife into the corners. Their needs are the same as ours: good soils, clean air and water, shelter and space. Often what we leave is fit for neither man nor beast.

We have eliminated most of the large predators and hardly tolerate those which are left when they interfere with our lifestyles. So now we, who have sorely upset the balances of nature, must help nature if many wildlife species are to survive in the future. Hunting, fishing, and trapping laws protect the futures of different species, and an important function of these laws is to provide for cropping the annual reproduction. Man, though very inefficient when compared to his wild counterparts, has become a necessary predator.

Hunting, trapping and fishing regulations are also designed to give everyone an equal opportunity to share in the "harvest." And that's what it really *is*, since *wildlife is a renewable resource.*
The allowable limits and quotas are adjusted upward when a local wildlife population becomes too great for the habitat that supports it — or when it creates too much competition for other species. Quotas are lowered or a closed season is set when the survival of a particular species is endangered.

Without this artificial culling, to reduce wild populations in a planned way so they better fit the existing wild habitat, some species become too numerous, too strong for others to cope with, and the whole wildlife community soon is out of balance. Then some species disappear. The dominant species thrive — but only temporarily, until disease, famine and other disasters occur.

One alternative is to let nature take its course. But *natural* culling often waits too long to take effect, and then is too drastic. All or nothing, boom and bust, is the rule in wildlife populations when nature is left to its own devices. Notice I did not say "her" devices, for Mother Nature is no lady.

Bambi, Bugs Bunny, Flipper, Sammy Bluejay, Lassie, and hundreds of other delightful fictional characters on television and in print make for enjoyable entertainment. Unfortunately, most parents do not point out to their youngsters that the entertainment is just that. Without their ever realizing it, too often the fiction becomes fact in the minds of many children and adults. The Bambi syndrome and others like it have put substantial roadblocks in the way of the sound wildlife management that is so sorely needed.

Actually there is little 'natural balance in nature" left, because people have upset the natural world so badly. We can, however, work with certain of the natural checks and balances to help sustain healthy wildlife. And *killing* usually is part of the control system.

Often when nature takes its indiscriminate course, there is long and large-scale suffering. When man steps in with well-calculated management controls, results usually are more expeditious, there is less overall suffering, and benefits accrue to man as well as to wildlife. Some controlled killing, even though it is poorly understood, must remain as a necessary tool to guarantee the future of much wildlife.

Although mainly for personal interests, hunters for decades have done more for wildlife conservation and protection than any other group. They have poured millions and millions of dollars into securing prime wildlife habitat for everyone to enjoy. They find healthy outdoor recreation while attaining the kill, and then they make full use of it. Wildlife prospers from their regulated actions and voluntary taxes. Can much fault honestly be found in this system?

Those who hunt, trap or fish as *sportsmen* would help themselves and our important natural resources by explaining these things to the uninitiated. It is only through common understanding that a more-or-less balanced and desirable environment can survive.

R.C.

"Game," in the title of this book, is used in its broadest sense, as opposed to the current usage employed by various fish and wildlife agencies. They break game down into categories — game animals, game birds, furbearers, unprotected species, and even varmints.

I use the dictionary definition of game as animals taken by hunting for their skins or meat. And for this book I consider trapping simply a regulated form of hunting. No "varmints" are mentioned because in my mind there *are* no unwanted species.

*Asterisks (*) that appear in the text indicate methods, equipment, or procedures that are illustrated, usually at the end of the chapter or section in which they are described. See index for specific items and page numbers.

# INTRODUCTION

This book is a show-and-tell reference for the new or relatively new sportsman (man, woman or youngster) who wishes to make better use of fish and wildlife taken.

Included are practical dressing procedures; field care of meat and fish, skins and furs; and their preparation for final home use or professional handling. Oldtimers should find some new techniques, and the army of "sportsmen's widows" perhaps will gain greater understanding of their husbands' other love.

This book is for the *sportsman*, no matter what his level of skills may be. And in case you wonder what the well-earned title of sportsman means, I'll tell you: Sportsmen (either sex) fully appreciate that today's trappers, hunters and fishermen usually enjoy their activities on someone else's land, and they respect that privilege.

Sportsmen understand the interrelationships that sustain healthy wildlife and aquatic communities. They only take what is legal to take and what they can use without hurting the resource for future generations. When they take a life, they know why they take it. They strive for quick kills and have a reverence for the purposeful order and beauty of nature, death being a part of it.

My friends share my basic philosophy: To appreciate the outdoors fully, you have to feel a part of it. But you cannot appreciate the whole experience without the basic skills. Worrying about how to act and what to do should not have to be part of the adventure.

For example, a woodsman can learn all he needs to know about a compass and map reading in one evening, yet many hunters carry compasses and don't know how to use them. It is a pretty foolish outdoorsman who does not carry one — and a more foolish one who does and has no confidence in it.

I have been blessed in my lifetime with knowing a lot of people who *sincerely* enjoyed the outdoors. Some undoubtedly were much better woodsmen than others. Some excelled in one skill while others did in many. I have learned from all of them. And when I stop learning I'll be heading for the happy hunting grounds. Many thanks to all of them.

I hope *our* experiences in the outdoors will make *yours* more enjoyable, make the recollection of adventures more fun, and make the use of the harvest more profitable and rewarding for you.

# EFFICIENT RECREATION WITH BIG GAME

# CHAPTER 1

# BEFORE THE HUNT

The comedy of errors I want to relate here may illustrate some things you should consider before you go on your next hunt. Other basic points about equipment and game regulations follow.

Fort Falls and I had hunted together on several occasions. We were visiting down at Tilt's General Store in Freedom, N.H. one fall day when we met Harry. He was home from the Service and wanted to go deer hunting with us. After getting the high sign from Fort, I agreed to take him along, though neither of us had hunted with him before. Harry was a tall and lanky, amiable kid. I say "kid," though he was only a half-dozen years my junior.

Traditionally the New Hampshire deer season is a long one. We locals (and I was one by only a few years) hunted the first of the season hard, went back to work in mid-season, and then nearly panicked towards the end if we didn't have our deer. By that time it was really cold — often with a crunchy crust on the snow.

I had fallen prey to that pattern before, so this year I was working on the front end of the season and decided to stay with it, like the out-of-state hunters. They always come up with a better success ratio because they stay right with it.

Fort stopped by my house that evening with an idea he wanted to try. I had no rifle and had been hunting with a 12-gauge pump and rifled slugs. When my wife, Penny, went along she used a Remington Sportsman, a three-shot 20-gauge. I didn't particularly like using a shotgun for deer in this big country, but I was just getting my business started, building a house, and had a young family. I could wait.

Fort's idea was to borrow Penny's 20-gauge with the slugs, for he was thinking about buying one. I could use his .303 rifle.

Shortly after lunch we picked up Harry and headed for Durgin Hill. (All of the "hills" in Carroll County really are small mountains.)

A short board meeting in the alders, before we hit the base of the mountain, determined that we would guide on each other and hike up to the top, line-abreast. Serious hunting would begin on the other side. Already we knew that Harry was not the greatest woodsman in the world. (He would be noisy walking down the center of Route 16.) We decided to put him in the middle, to guide on Fort or me at either end.

Just as we broke up, Fort asked me if I had brought along any bird shot, and I obliged with some 20-gauge sixes. Partridge season was open, along with the deer season, and we had some good cover to pass through on the way to the top.

We took the line, and I had no difficulty telling where Harry was, even if I couldn't see him. The dry leaves, hidden sticks and his shuffling gait announced our progress to any and all game in the vicinity. I wasn't very optimistic.

About a third of the way to the top I looked across and saw Fort bring the shotgun up. Then he sort of came to port arms, and up went the gun again. Then he went to a partial port arms, and up again. I couldn't figure what was going on, so I froze. Harry was a little behind the line. The next thing I knew, Fort took a couple of careful steps. Then Bang, Bang, Bang! He was empty.

There was a crashing sound ahead of us, and I knew a deer was cutting across above me. Up went the rifle. I was ready for it if it came to the opening in the hardwood sprouts.

"Hey, Fort, wh'ud ya see?" yelled Harry. The sound of the running deer changed abruptly, straight up the mountain. I cussed softly and went over to see my buddy.

Fort hadn't been very optimistic either about our chances of seeing deer with Harry along, so he had put a number six in the chamber, followed by two slugs. Then when he saw the deer in good range above him, he had to decide whether to jack out the bird shot and get to the slugs, or sting the deer and try for a difficult jump shot. That's what he was doing when I saw his strange antics. He had settled for the latter course and was suckered into the curse of the automatic — three shots as fast as they can go, without benefit of careful aiming between. He looked pretty sheepish.

"I may have hit him on the second shot," Fort volunteered. "I think he bunched up, but he took off like a runaway freight."

We moved up and went over the area very carefully without finding a fleck of blood or hair. He had missed clean. We continued uphill to the ledges.

A few days before I had bird-dogged while Fort took a stand, so now it was my turn. We whispered and Harry got the word as we stood on top of an outcropping surrounded by fat white pines and acres of running juniper that wouldn't quit. I was to stand there while they circled down the east side through a stand of beeches. It was a good nut year, and a well-used trail to the beeches passed almost under the outcropping we were on.

Suddenly I felt a wind shift, and I told Fort I would do better across the way on another hump. The deer trail passed between the two. I would give Fort the OK sign if things shaped up when I got there.

I left, circling back down the side of the rocky knoll. I had gone twenty-five yards when I came to the trail. And there lay a ten-point buck flat on the trail. His head was outstretched, chin on the ground. He was lying on his belly with all four legs stretched to the rear as though he had been dragged there. His eyes were closed.

I flipped the safety off the .303 and moved in. Standing at the ready, I called to Fort. He had taken a ten-pointer the year before, and when we were kidding I had told him I would drag his deer out — if he got another ten-pointer this year.

"Come get him, Fort. It's another ten-pointer like last year's," I yelled. The knob where I'd left them was hidden by broad pines, and the wind was blowing briskly now. I nudged the big deer's shoulder with my foot. Not a whisker moved. I gave him another shove, and then I saw the plowed groove on top of the pelvis.

I wasn't about to blast that deer with Fort so close. He might want the head mounted, for it surely was a beauty. "C'mon," I yelled.

Patience has never been my greatest virtue. I hate to wait too long for anything. I rattled the deer's rack with the rifle barrel and nothing happened, so I stepped to his rear, put on the safety and rested the rifle butt on the ground beside the deer. My left hand gripped the barrel just down from the muzzle. Using the rifle as a cane to steady myself, I bent over the hindquarters to examine the wound. I spread it apart. And then lightning struck.

The deer jumped to his feet right under me. The rifle was flopping on one side as I held onto the muzzle as hard as I could to keep it aimed away from me. I had one leg half over the deer's back and tried to get the rest of me up on his back. With my free right hand I reached forward and grabbed a fistful of hair and hide. The big buck was a wild bronc, kicking and jumping. I was coming down on him (way out on his rear end) when he started up again, and as I started up again, he lurched out from under me. All I had was a fistful of hair when I landed about five feet up in a pine. I switched ends of the rifle as I fell to the deck. The deer was hightailing it downhill through the juniper. I jumped up and ran to get a shot, caught a foot in the juniper, and touched off one hasty shot as I disappeared into the dry green prickles.

That shot brought my friends on the double. Mad? Boy, was I mad! I ranted while they laughed like fools. Then I began laughing too. How stupid can anyone be? I kept seeing those *closed eyes.*

We had no trouble trailing the big buck's route through the dusty junipers down to the beeches, but then his tracks blended with a lot of others and we lost him. One thing was sure, he was in good shape. I could attest to that. A week later, twelve-year old Franklin Davis shot that deer not three hundred yards from my front door. I went over to see it. The earlier wound was nearly closed.

I settled for a four-pointer that year, but I became famous around the area. I'd be ashamed to tell you some of the things I was accused of doing in the juniper patch — all in good fun, of course.

Perhaps if we all had had our heads screwed on tight, things would have been very different. We had a greenhorn with us and hadn't counseled him at all. Fort and I both were using firearms that were strangers to us — I well remember fighting the safety on that .303 when the deer was disappearing. And there was no excuse for my not taking action when the deer was lying there with its eyes closed. I've never made that mistake again.

Most frustrating or downright disastrous outings come from three main causes, I think. Lack of planning fouls up more trips than anything else.

Second, some people want to be experts overnight. Now I know many highly qualified outdoor people, but I don't know one *expert* on the out-of-doors. Certainly I am no expert, and I know full well that I can never be one — nor can anyone else. The field is much too broad. Some may be expert in one area or in part of one of the disciplines, but people just don't live long enough to acquire expertise in all aspects of the out-of-doors. Knowing this should create a healthy humility, but alas, such is not often the case.

The third major problem for many, particularly noticeable when the affluent society appeared, is that people own equipment and do not know how to use it. While only the best is good enough for some, thousands of other outdoor people with very little besides a lot of common sense enjoy themselves much more and are more productive.

## Checking the Basics

No matter where you stand on the economic ladder or the level of your outdoor experience, the following points are basic to most outdoor activities, pursued away from civilization. They are particularly important to consider *before* you go hunting.

### GAME LAWS AND REGULATIONS

Hunting, fishing and trapping have their own laws and regulations, and these rules are not set arbitrarily. If everyone understood the various demands of the many species in the animal kingdom, and the delicate balances and interdependencies between them, and also knew and understood the needs of the plant world that directly or indirectly provide animals with their food and shelter and still more about air, water and soils that are basic to life support systems — we still would need such laws. It's because all of us are a little greedy — some more so than others.

Adequate enforcement, then, has to be carried out to be sure the laws are kept, for people cannot be trusted to use good common sense all the time, even when they *do* understand the principles behind the laws. We have hunting, trapping, and fishing regulations partly to give everyone an equal and sporting opportunity to share in the outdoor harvest.

You should gain thorough knowledge of these laws of the state, province or country where you intend to hunt, trap or fish *before* you leave home.

**Licenses and permits** are required for hunting, fishing and trapping. The license period often begins and ends on the calendar year *or the fiscal year,* and sometimes there are special licenses for special seasons. Some places demand special stamps or permits for certain species, even after a general hunting or fishing license has been obtained. Check it all out carefully *beforehand,* and enjoy yourself without worrying about forefeiting valuable vacation time, additional money, your reputation, or the trophy you might be fortunate enough to get.

**Tagging game** frequently is demanded by wildlife agencies to keep things honest and get accurate data for future management. Usually, the tag must be put on the animal *immediately* upon taking it, *before* moving or dressing it, and the tag cannot be removed until the carcass is cut up for consumption.

To prevent losing the tag on a large mammal during the "drag," or in transport on the highway, secure the tag *inside* an ear,* if this is allowed. Check the local law or special instructions on the permit first for the particular animal being taken. Sometimes, the tag has to be attached to a different part of the anatomy.

If a paper or cloth tag is to be put inside an ear, first make a small neat slit through the ear cartilage about an inch in from an edge near the bottom of the opening. Push one end of a string or soft wire through a hole in the tag, and then through the ear slit from the inside. Pull it out enough for tying, and wrap the rest of the string or wire around the outside of the ear, pulling it together, cradling the tag *inside the roll.* Tie the ends of the string, or twist the ends of the wire together securely. The tag so protected will not rub, rip or blow off even under the hurricane conditions it gets subjected to when flying down an interstate on top of a car.

The so-called "box-car" tag can have its metal strap run through an ear too, if this is allowed. The barrel or box part should be *inside* the ear. The strap is wrapped around the ear and its end pushed into or through the barrel to lock it in place. Test it to be sure.

And while we are on the subject of tags: Some tags are already on the quarry before a hunter or fisherman takes it. Occasionally a deer may have a numbered collar on it; a turkey, a colored streamer; a duck or goose, a metal band around its leg; and a bear, a small radio transmitter attached to it. Even fish may have one sort of tag or another, brands or clipped fins, to identify them.

All these identifiers are used to gain more knowledge about different species of wildlife. Be sure to return the various devices to wildlife agencies with details of the hunt and the prize you have taken. If you see birds dyed strange colors, or find numbers on a fish (resulting from a cold brand put on it at an earlier age), give information on when, where, how taken and other pertinent details that might be of interest to the biologists. This cooperation will help the future of your sport.

**Sex and identity** of game are asked for at checkpoints or reporting stations. The feathered head and one wing often must be left on game birds until they are cut up for consumption, or a tail also may be required for age determination.

From an Alberta summary of big game regulations: "IMPORTANT — If you remove testicles and penis, leave the entire scrotum* intact on hind quarter. Meat will not be tainted. Note: If you skin your game, scrotum must remain attached to meat on a piece of hide." (Scrotum: Sac containing testicles.)

Requirements such as this give some idea of how closely you should check local regulations where you hunt. They may tell you how you must hunt, how and what to do when transporting game, and even how you must dress your game. None of the requirements is difficult to abide by if you know what is expected of you ahead of time.

BASIC FIELD EQUIPMENT

You should evaluate your equipment long *before* you go afield. Plan carefully, and you won't find yourself unprepared and in the middle of a bad scene that easily could have been avoided. Little things can make a big difference — like a good pocket stone for putting an edge on a knife, an extra hank of rope, a small sifter or canvas cover for a pack basket (if you trap), an extra compass and even a few clean rags. If they are not with you when you need them, all sorts of problems may occur. Think ahead. Do you have enough salt? Don't be afraid to use a pencil and paper. Then remember to *use* the checklist *before* you cut the umbilical cord to civilization.

Every hunter should know his firearm intimately, and be able to clean and strip it completely. Take care of it and keep it in fine working order. Become proficient with it. Sight in your rifle before using it for hunting. Pattern your shotgun at various distances. Know what can be expected from your firearm and the shells you intend to use in it.

Bow hunters should get needed muscles in condition to pull to full draw and practice shooting as much as possible the year around. Check your bow for limb alignment. Then look for fine lines or cracking of fiberglass and laminated wood. Keep broadheads razor sharp. Check for warped or bent arrows. Inspect the bow string for nicks or frays and replace it if needed. Buy an extra string to keep with you as a spare. You get the idea.

**Knives** are the first thing that comes to mind in the equipment line when anyone thinks of dressing game. I have seen hunters use all kinds of knives to dress and skin out deer — army bayonets (one of them with the blade sharp as a razor on *both* sides), "bowie knives" heavy enough to cut elephant hide, and various crude to beautifully engraved "hunting knives." Actually, what is a "hunting knife"?

By my criteria, a hunting knife is any bladed tool I choose to carry that will do the job relative to the hunting I am doing at the time. Actually, I carry two.

The first* has a five-and-three-quarter-inch, heavy, narrow

blade of fine Finnish steel, a smooth bolster and a smooth, hung-over, one-piece wooden handle through which the tang passes. The end of the tang is rivited over a small, thick washer at the top of the handle. The blade-end fits snugly inside a friction-type, reinforced leather case that hangs flexibly from my belt. I've used it more than forty years, but not very often for dressing and skinning animals. I save it for heavy work like building blinds, rough-working a large piece of wood, splitting kindling, opening cans, cutting cattails — and a thousand other things.

When it comes to dressing and skinning, I have found a strong but light, four-inch, fixed-blade hunting knife completely satisfactory. My preference from experience, however, has been a quality, brand-name, three-bladed folding pocket knife. I can put a fine or wedge edge on the blades without much trouble. The blade keeps that edge for a reasonable length of time.

My favorite combination of blades is usually termed a "Stockman's Knife."* When closed, the knife measures four inches overall, and I've had no trouble dressing and skinning deer using one that measures only three-and-a-quarter inches closed.

I use each of the three blades differently for various operations. General cutting calls for the long-pointed "clip" blade, the largest one, on which I keep a fine edge as sharp as I can get, full-length.

For making initial cuts in skinning, I use the "sheepfoot" blade with its turned-down point. I keep that one more wedge-edged, but sharp full-length, too.

The third, "carving" blade has a double-convex curved tip, quite rounded. I lightly drag the rounded tip, the outer third of the working edge, across a stone (any stone) to dull it intentionally. With the dull tip I can *push* the hide from the carcass in somewhat stubborn spots. And I can use only as much of the sharpened two thirds of the blade below the dulled tip as needed to cut stubborn connecting tissue without risk of accidentally cutting the hide. I also can use the sharp two-thirds of the blade for shaving fat or muscle beginning to hold to the hide rather than the carcass.

My working knife by "Case"

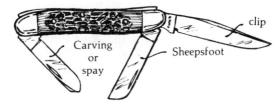

Carving
or
spay

Sheepsfoot

clip

There is a family of jury-rigged skinning tools that hardly can be called knives, since they are really spoons.* Don't laugh until after you have given them a try. For deer and other big game, a big serving spoon is called for. A relatively cheap stainless spoon or one of the regular steel not too heavily chromed is better than the more expensive, heavily chromed or quality stainless steel spoons. For smaller skins try one made from a cheap stainless steel teaspoon. The milder steel of the less expensive ones can be touched up to a wedge-edge much easier. Experiment with different type handles to best suit your hand and techniques.

You will soon learn that much of the skinning operation is done simply by pushing hide from the carcass with the heel of your hand or the pod of a thumb.

**Fire starters** are good insurance even if you never need them. For normal uses you can carry paper safety matches inside a folded plastic sandwich bag. For further protection of your matches, there are many fine, waterproof match cases for sale. If you do not mind the jingling sound coming from your pocket when you least want it, then select one of the well-made metal types. But carry a bandanna in a pocket with such a case, to separate it from pocket change or other potentially noisy "important stuff."

If your budget is tight, or if you forgot to buy a commercial match case, try these ideas. I will guarantee you will get fire from your matches when you need it most. You will never have all your matches go up in a flash along with getting a very painful thumb with these,* and if you happen to go swimming with them, don't worry. Your matches and tinder will stay dry and do a good job when you crawl out of the water.

Some night before the season, lay out these things on the kitchen table: a pound or less of block paraffin, a box of strike-anywhere wooden matches, a clean tin can (with its top removed) that will fit with room to spare in a larger saucepan (also needed), a spool of sewing thread (any kind or color will do), a bottle of model airplane dope or fingernail polish (clear brushing lacquer works well), a newspaper and a pair of scissors.

First select a dozen wooden matches that have good solid tips and a thick layer of the lighter colored material on the striking end. Lay them paired together with the top of the wooden shaft of one lying next to and immediately below the hard igniting head of the other one.

Take the paired matches,* now in head to tail relationship, and wind the sewing thread over itself close to one of the heads to secure the thread to the matches. Then tightly spiral wrap the sticks down to the other match head. A few overhand knots will finish the wrapping off so the thread will hold without loosening. Break or cut off the thread about an inch from the match bundle. Do the same with the other matches.

Now take the quick-drying lacquer and dip the head of one match into it, deeper than the height of the phosphorus coating, just a little way up on the shaft. Quickly wipe the excess off with your fingertips or a cleansing tissue. You want the whole surface of the head covered, but very thinly. Do the same on the other end of the paired matches. Then treat the other matches.

Next cut strips of newspaper as long as the width of a page (of a full-sized newspaper), and wide enough to extend a half inch beyond your matches. Place one set of matches at an end of a single paper strip with about a quarter inch of paper extending out from the matches. Roll the matches tightly in the paper using the full length of the strip. Press the loose end of the paper against the matches to keep it from unrolling. Then wrap the roll with the thread as you did earlier when pairing the matches. Tie it off in similar fashion and leave about *four inches* of thread hanging. Do the same with the other sets of matches.

Fill the saucepan about a third full of water and put it on the stove to heat. While the water is heating, pare or cut off enough paraffin from the block to about half fill the can.

Bring the water to a boil. Then lower the heat and put the can with the paraffin in it into the hot water. Before long the paraffin will turn to a clear liquid. *Be careful* not to slop the paraffin onto the burner.

Pick up each roll by the hanging thread end and dip it into the liquid paraffin. Lift it out and place it on the extra newspaper. While the wax is cooling, push the overage of the paper at both ends into and over the head of the match inside. The wax will hold the crimp at each end like the end of a shotgun shell. Give the roll another dip or two to build up the wax coating on the outside. Before the last dip has cooled, cut the thread off close to the roll and wipe a finger over it to lose the thread end in the soft wax. Smooth both ends of the roll the same way. If a void is evident at either end over the head of the match, fill it with soft wax and smooth it off with a fingertip.

You can carry these loose if you want, but I like to wrap a turn or two of narrower newspaper around four to six rolls and dip all of it in paraffin once more. This holds the bundles together in a unit that is no bigger than a shotgun shell. It is an easy matter to pick a roll from the packet with a thumbnail. Keep these matches for emergency use, or when bad weather dictates their use for easier fire starting.

To use one of the matches — and you have two chances with each roll — peel down the paper *below* the head of the match with a thumbnail. Your kindling, squaw wood or basic fire to be lighted should be all built before striking the match. Strike it on any hard, dry surface and *hold the match nearly horizontal* when the flame shows. Then put the whole roll under the fire sticks laid for the fire. The paraffin-soaked paper and wooden shafts of the matches make an instantaneous, hot flame of good size which lasts long enough to get a fire going quickly under very adverse conditions.

An alternate method* for making waterproof matches is accomplished by starting the same way. A small plastic or cardboard box *slightly longer* than the tied head-to-tail matches is used. About an eighth inch of paraffin is spooned into it. Bundles of matches then are quickly floated on the paraffin, keeping them parallel to the sides of the box and spaced evenly apart from each other. A space of about an eighth inch between the outside match and the side of the box should be maintained at both sides. When the paraffin has cooled, repeat in layers until you have a sufficient number of match bundles encased. Pour a final thin layer on top. Be sure the whole paraffin block is hard. You can put it in the refrigerator for a while to be sure. Then either leave the box as part of the unit or break it away to attain a solid paraffin block with match bundles protected inside it. To get a match bundle out, use the point of a knife, and save the chips to help the fire along as it is started.

**A first aid kit\*** can be worth its weight in gold if you need it. Since many friends neglect to carry one, mine has been called upon several times. A good working first aid kit is not necessarily one purchased as a unit off the drugstore shelf. Most of those have more of a particular item than you need, yet leave out a lot of things you should add to make it complete. Many have nice painted steel cases that may be fine for your auto but not in a pocket or a pack.

I strongly recommend buying materials separately at the drugstore and tailoring them to fit your demands. The overage can be used to supply the home medicine cabinet.

All the following items will fit easily inside an aluminum, single-bar soap box with piano hinge back and snap cover. A rubber band around it, to be sure it stays closed, isn't a bad idea.

1. ADHESIVE TAPE. Take it out of the nice dispenser and neatly wrap a fair amount around a smooth hardwood tongue depressor, building a flat roll with edges even. When you have enough, cut the wood depressor off fairly close to the tape.

2. GAUZE. Get a small one-inch roll. Remove it from the box and lightly wrap and tape it inside thin plastic. It can be used for bandage or to make your own pads (with adhesive tape) for minor cuts or burns. Commercial bandages of this type also are good, a few of each size is all you need. They take up very little space.

3. ASPIRIN or other similar pills for headache, fever or pain can be left in the small twelve-pill hinged box.

4. HEARTBURN or acid stomach pills of your own choosing should be included too, just in case your own cooking or a friend's creates problems. I doubt that you will need a whole roll. Take only what might be needed. Covering the outside of the roll lightly with frosted transparent tape helps to fight humidity deterioration of the pills, and you can label it.

5. HALAZONE TABLETS. Pills for water purification in case of emergency are good to have on hand. Incidentally you can boil out the chlorine taste. Boiled water by itself is not too appealing, but anyone can remedy that: Just pour boiled water back and forth a few times between containers and you will be amazed at the change. You put the dissolved

oxygen you boiled out back into it. Remember that the next time you heat snow to make water — a tedious job, and check page 34 for purifying water.

6.  ANTISEPTIC OINTMENT. A small tube keeps much better and with fewer problems than a glass bottle with liquid. Most ready-to-buy kits have a tube large enough to serve a family for months.

7.  BURN OINTMENT. Again just a small tube. If you get a major burn, you'll probably either head to a hospital or "buy the farm" before you get out of the woods. Seriously though, burns are bad business. Work to avoid them, and be sure you know proper treatment. Burns often result in serious infections if carelessly treated.

8.  COMPRESSES. A few assorted small compresses kept in their individual, sterile packets are sufficient. One very important item that will have to be carried separate from your mini-kit is a large compress in case an axe ends up in your foot, or there is some other serious accident. The sterile wrap can be further protected by aluminum foil neatly wrapped over it with the ends folded over and taped. I've had occasion to use this item, and it always surprises me that more hunters and fishermen do not carry one or more in their basic gear. If doctor-type compresses are hard to come by, women's sanitary napkins work fine and can be purchased in grocery stores.

9.  TRIANGULAR BANDAGE. If you wear a good-sized bandanna as a sweat band on your head or around your neck to keep the snow or rain out, you will have one with you. Otherwise, one can be jury-rigged from a T-shirt or a sling improvised from a shirt with a few safety pins.

10. SAFETY PINS. Carry an assortment, but don't overdo it.

11. NEEDLES AND THREAD. The needles can be helpful in removing splinters or blisters (and be careful of that one), but I find I use them more for ripped pants or coats. Either way, they are small and useful. The needles can be carried with a razor blade in the block with the paraffined matches. A *small amount* of #50 thread is wrapped around a piece of tongue

depressor. Melted wax over it secures the end and often helps when sewing canvas or other heavy cloth.

12. COLD REMEDY. I cannot remember getting a cold from my outdoor escapades, but I have been known to go duck hunting in horrible weather with a bad cold. On these adventures I went well-prepared, and was considerably improved on my return. I never really knew whether to credit the outdoors or the medicine. Maybe it was the combination.

    To be on the safe side, take remedies that you have confidence in. Long-range types you take twice a day have worked fine for me. I also recommend some antiseptic throat lozenges for a possible sore throat. Take the various pills out of the large containers, but if they are sealed individually, take only as many as you may need *still sealed*. Put the various pills into individually taped, plastic packets with a label on each, and then put the collection into a plastic bag to keep them all together.

13. RUBBING ALCOHOL. Take only a small amount in a sealed, flexible plastic tube — the type fishing snaps and swivels come in. The alcohol can be used for itches or for sterilizing purposes.

14. VASELINE. Carry a small tube for everything from chapped hands to sunburn and rust prevention.

15. SOAP. A *small* bar of hand soap, hotel-size, can be used for general washing of wounds or general sanitation. Don't underestimate its value.

16. SOAP (yellow naphtha type). This is one of the best precautions against irritation from poison ivy, poison oak or the like. Bath soap will spread the oily, toxic substance, but the the naphtha will cut it and wash it away. Take a small piece from a large bar of laundry soap. Lightly wrap it in plastic and tape it closed.

17. KEROSENE. This is chigger or tick repellant to be carried only where needed. Use a small, flexible plastic tube or pill bottle with a screw cap, and seal it.

It does no good to have all these things with you if you don't know when and how to use them. Do your studying at home. You don't need a doctor's book in the bush, but you should have basic medical knowledge carefully stored in your head. Take a mini-idiot card in your kit if you need it, until you have things down pat.

**A compass,** though small, can bring peace of mind and help you avoid unnecessary problems, serious injuries or even death.

Do not look for a cheap model. You can make a compass for almost nothing by giving a sewing needle pushed through a cork a sharp blow on one end and floating it in a cup of water, but it is not very practical to carry in your pocket. A very fancy one is not needed either for practical woods use, where most of us are not concerned with running survey lines. In most circumstances an eight-point card, marked every forty-five degrees is adequate, and certainly a sixteen-point card is plenty, with N, NNE, NE, ENE, E and so on. It is impossible to walk in the woods to a line of so many degrees. You will do well to hold the general line of one of the sixteen points or somewhere between them with periodic checking.

Liquid dampening of the needle is a big help in practical use. The sealed liquid steadies the needle. The north end of the needle (really the south end of the magnet) and the card's cardinal points marked with night-glow paint are worth considering. A rugged case also is important. I like all of these things in my compass, but beyond these, the simpler it is the better.

One word of caution concerning the tiny inset compass in a gun stock, with just the arrow. It will tell you where north (magnetic) is, and you can figure out the rest, but too many people think this takes the place of a regular compass. During the war, these little compasses could be concealed efficiently even if the enemy stripped you, and they had another name before they got to be "gun-stock compasses." When recovered under wartime conditions, one could be used to work your way toward a cardinal point to find your own lines if they extended far enough. For smaller-scale traveling, however, it is not that practical for most people.

I cannot resist mentioning a prime consideration when using a compass — *think big!* Few people, even those who brag about how far they travel in a day, ever walk off a map. If you come out by compass to the road where your car is parked, what difference does it make if you are a half mile or so one side or the other of it? Don't try to remember every twist and turn you make. Concentrate on what you are doing and enjoy yourself. When it is time to go home, head in the general direction of the car and you won't be far wrong. Of course, if you haven't studied the map or the lay of the land *before* you go in, you may face some major problems.

Without going into "orienteering," the science of map and compass use, you should know and be able to do these things with confidence from memory: set a course, set a back-course, and set over a course when you have to go around a large obstacle; walk in a relatively straight line in the woods once a course has been determined (you don't go along with compass in hand in front of you); keep a straight course across flat snow, open marsh or desert with scarcely any landmarks; know what to do at night — and there are more. I hope I have whetted your curiosity enough to dig it out. Remember, *you* are never lost, it is the *place* where you want to go that gets lost.

People often brag that they never carry a compass, and they have never been lost. An old Maine guide made the same claim. He may not have been lost, but he was in serious doubt for three days once until another guide with a compass found him.

**A flashlight.** Another important piece of equipment for the *day pack* is a small flashlight. Check laws to be sure one is legal. A two-cell light with a red-glow hood and alkaline batteries is fairly light and dependable. This item is handy if you go out early, or are caught out late getting back to camp, and also serves other normal uses. *Not many deer carry a flashlight* . . . it is a good safety measure during low-light hours. Disposable lights no larger than a pack of cigarettes and nearly the same weight are also good. Caution: Most of the disposable kind do not grow dim when the charge weakens. They remain at full brightness and then quit cold. Plan accordingly.

YOUR PHYSICAL CONDITION

Your physical condition also is important. Know your physical limitations, and get into condition *before the hunt,* if you cannot stay in condition all the time.

## LIFESAVER MAYBE — COMFORT FOR SURE.

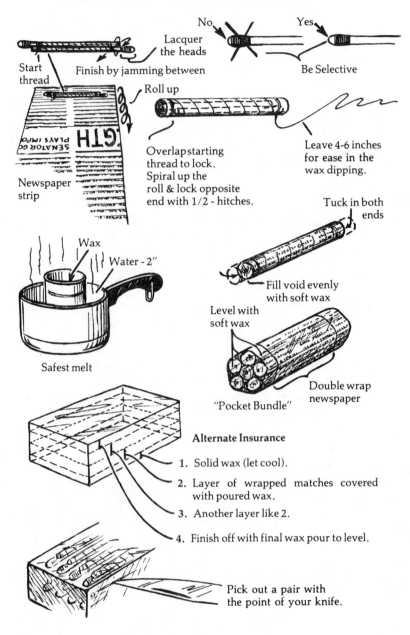

No

Yes

Lacquer
the heads

Be Selective

Start
thread

Finish by jamming between

Roll up

Overlap starting
thread to lock.
Spiral up the
roll & lock opposite
end with 1/2 - hitches.

Leave 4-6 inches
for ease in the
wax dipping.

Newspaper
strip

Tuck in both
ends

Wax

Water - 2"

Fill void evenly
with soft wax

Level with
soft wax

Safest melt

Double wrap
newspaper

"Pocket Bundle"

**Alternate Insurance**

1. Solid wax (let cool).

2. Layer of wrapped matches covered
   with poured wax.

3. Another layer like 2.

4. Finish off with final wax pour to level.

Pick out a pair with
the point of your knife.

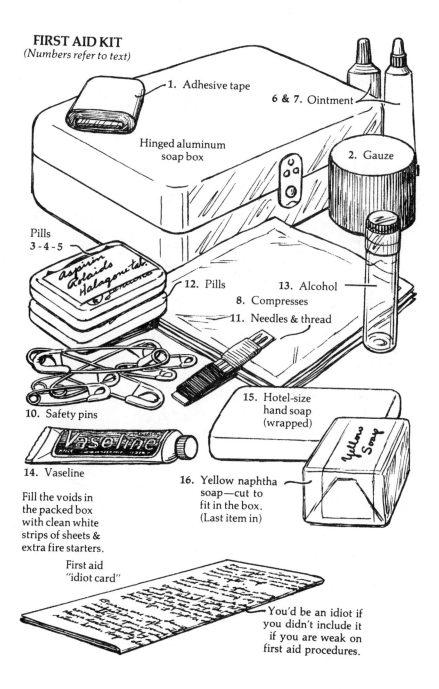

**FIRST AID KIT**
*(Numbers refer to text)*

1. Adhesive tape

6 & 7. Ointment

Hinged aluminum soap box

2. Gauze

Pills 3 - 4 - 5

*aspirin Rolaids Halogen tab.*

12. Pills

13. Alcohol

8. Compresses

11. Needles & thread

10. Safety pins

15. Hotel-size hand soap (wrapped)

*Yellow Soap*

14. Vaseline

16. Yellow naphtha soap—cut to fit in the box. (Last item in)

Fill the voids in the packed box with clean white strips of sheets & extra fire starters.

First aid "idiot card"

You'd be an idiot if you didn't include it if you are weak on first aid procedures.

23

## TAGGING THE TROPHY

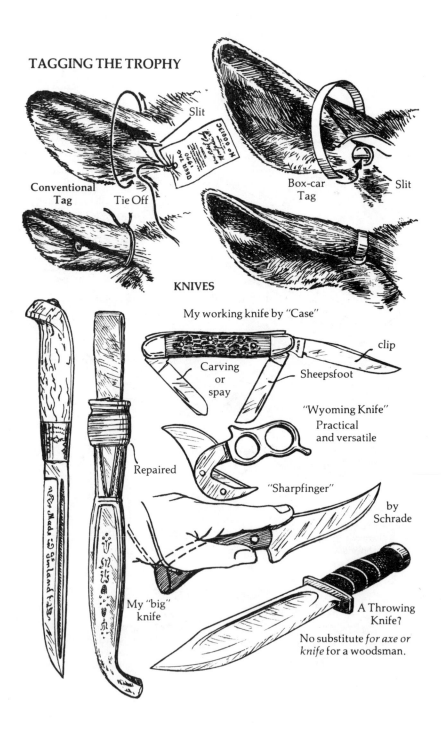

Conventional Tag

Slit

Tie Off

DEER TAG
1990
Nº 0003C

Box-car Tag

Slit

## KNIVES

My working knife by "Case"

Carving or spay

Sheepsfoot

clip

"Wyoming Knife"
Practical and versatile

Repaired

"Sharpfinger"

by Schrade

My "big" knife

A Throwing Knife?

No substitute *for axe or knife* for a woodsman.

## STAINLESS SPOON SKINNER

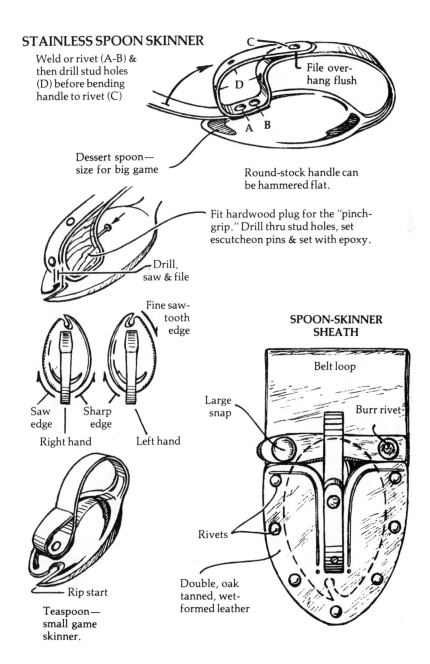

Weld or rivet (A-B) & then drill stud holes (D) before bending handle to rivet (C)

File over-hang flush

Dessert spoon— size for big game

Round-stock handle can be hammered flat.

Fit hardwood plug for the "pinch-grip." Drill thru stud holes, set escutcheon pins & set with epoxy.

Drill, saw & file

Fine saw-tooth edge

Saw edge | Sharp edge

Right hand | Left hand

Rip start

Teaspoon— small game skinner.

### SPOON-SKINNER SHEATH

Belt loop

Large snap

Burr rivet

Rivets

Double, oak tanned, wet-formed leather

25

CHAPTER 2

# FIELD DRESSING
# YOUR DEER

With but slight variations, any hoofed animal can be dressed much the same way — horse, cow, sheep, goat, antelope, caribou, elk, moose or one of the thousands upon thousands of deer — white-tailed, black-tailed and mule — taken every year by North American hunters.

Domestic animals usually are skinned out cleanly in one operation and under optimum conditions. Such is almost never the case with the hunter working in the field. He usually has to take care of the hide and meat at the point of taking, during the transport to a place of temporary storage or to a vehicle, during the trip home, and at home.

Improper care at any point can spell ruination for the meat or hide or both, and bring unnecessary disaster to an otherwise great trip. It is one thing to hunt and not be productive, but it is a whole different ball game to have been successful and then lose the prize through carelessness.

Since the deer is America's number one big game animal, and since so many people hunt it, and since you asked me along by reading this book, I'll kibitz on a white-tailed deer hunt in the Northeast. Okay? Special problems will be covered later for other locales.

## Kibitzing On Your Hunt

A single shot shatters the quiet of the forest. That one shot is all you have. The deer whirls around and disappears into the whips. Now you force yourself to wait, taking not a step from the stand where the shot rang out. You wait by the clock.

Five minutes later, you quietly make your way down the corridor where the bullet sped, alert to any sound or movement ahead — nothing but the distant chatter of a squirrel.

You worry. You see the scarred duff where the buck turned and crashed headlong into the brush. Down on a knee you study every leaf and stick in the area. Not even a fleck of crimson. You glance again at your watch and steel yourself to wait once more. Thoughts and scenes from past hunts race through your mind. Remembering the careful alignment of the sights on the neck of the trotting buck, you're hopeful. The quick twisting jump — had you missed? Or much worse, the nagging thought of a crippling shot. Conditions aren't good for easy tracking. You wait again.

Five minutes pass. Anxiously, you gingerly pick your way into the brush. The buck's first few jumps are easy to see, where his grouped feet, landing and pushing off in the dead leaves, tumbled them. On third jump you see the tell-tale sign — a large red splash colors the dull crisp leaves. You listen. Nothing — only the pounding in your ears. One final pause to be sure. Let him lie down. Let him lie down, you tell yourself.

The final push is made quietly. Scarlet flecks show an intermittent trail. The track reveals the gallop turned to a trot, then a shuffling walk, and there, twenty-five yards ahead at the base of a small hemlock, is your deer. He's down and still. The rifle comes up. Off goes the safety as you cautiously move in. You circle your buck, a nice six-pointer. His head is down, his eyes *open and glazed.* The moment of truth. He's dead. You have your buck.

But there is no great hurrah . . . not yet. The finality of the deed is apparent. What a beautiful creature, even now. You bend over him, and with glove removed, you run your hand over the sleek gray-brown hair on the shoulder. You double check the points of his polished rack. Sobering thoughts turn to satisfaction as your mind rationalizes to the positive and blots out the negative. You answered the challenge, took him in his prime. He should go 150-160 pounds dressed. That much venison won't be hard to take. And there'll be a sizable piece of buckskin. You'll put that to good use. The small rack will make a fine handle for your knife, toggles for a winter jacket or buttons for a buckskin vest.

*Sportsmen-hunters* of both sexes, young and old, the world over, experience similar emotions. Only the details vary. Man's reverence for life wrestles with an inborn sadness for death. Both emotions are important to thoughtful people and completely normal. Nothing is wasted in nature, not even the deer that die on the winter range, but making use of the deer you take to provide food and useful items is, you might say, "Good for body, soul and peace of mind."

Enough of this. There is work to be done, and you know it. The *sport* has ended. Put that tag on the deer, right now. Be sure it is filled out, if that is required.

STARTING THE FIELD DRESSING

Some hunters feel that the throat should be cut as the first order of business, the jugular opened to bleed out. Do it if you must, but it isn't necessary. It makes an added mess, may catch on sticks during the drag out, and can spoil a good trophy — or at least make more work for the taxidermist. You will soon have the whole body cavity open anyway for much more complete drainage while the blood is still warm and fluid.

Put the deer on its back on a fairly smooth level spot where it will not slide or roll by itself as you work on it.* Elevate the head slightly. With the belly up, the entrails settle in the body cavity below the cut you are about to make.

If the deer is a buck, many hunters cut off the scrotum first, but in some areas, this is prohibited by law (see Chapter 1, p. 11). Some claim the meat will taste strong if the testes are not immediately removed. Maybe it would have some effect, but all body functions have stopped. In any event, the scrotum is no problem, or laws making it mandatory to keep it attached to the carcass never would have been allowed.

It really doesn't matter which end you start at, so if you want to "cut 'em off" (and the laws allow it), do so. When the deer is a doe, however, why not try it from the front end,* as I prefer to do? For one thing, the rib cage up front holds the hide and muscle away from the entrails below, and there is much less chance of piercing viscera at the start. If you *do* start up front, make the starting slit into the body cavity immediately behind the midpoint where the ribs join together.*

There is only one correct way to make the belly cut, whether it be up or down the middle, and that is from *underneath* in the body cavity. The muscle, tissue, and hide is cut from *below,* up through.

Once the starting slit (about two to three inches long) is carefully made through the parted hair at either end into the body cavity, stand astride the carcass facing the direction in which the cut will be made. With knife in one hand, bend over and put the index and second fingers of the free hand through the opening made in the belly. With palm forward, hook your fingertips* up under the sheet of fat and muscle over the belly. Separate the fingers slightly, and then place your knife blade (edge-up) between the fingers with the unsharpened back of it resting at the juncture of the two fingers.* With a little practice, the fingers will lead the sharp blade along a straight center line, cutting *upward* from the body cavity. The primary purpose of the fingers, however, is to keep the innards away from the point of the blade so they will not be pierced.

There are a couple of other good reasons for using this procedure. Cutting hair dulls the edge of a knife rapidly. This method cuts the hide from underneath, and the attached hair at each side of the cut parts automatically as the incision progresses. There is practically no cut hair to get on the meat.

**The genitals** of a buck should be cut off or skinned out when the body cavity is opened from the midpoint juncture, extending from the center of the rib cage to the genitals. Leave attached if required by law. Then on a buck cut the hide close to and completely circling the anus.* *Include* the vaginal opening with the anus as a unit on a doe.* You usually will find considerable suet-like fat under the hide in this area. With your knife, carefully circumscribe a cone around the anus, diminishing internally, but deep enough to completely free it without slicing the intestines (and tube, if a doe) attached to it. The apex of the circumscribed cone is directed under the pelvic arch.* Try not to cut into the meat at each side.

It is a simple matter with a buck to free the anus and pull it out six or eight inches from the carcass with the intestine attached.

With a doe there is an added step: The anus and vaginal opening are freed as a unit. Pull it out far enough to get an index finger between the vaginal tube and the intestine. Then with a "piggin" string (a foot-long piece of stout twine) tightly tie off both tubes close to the body.* Wrap another turn and tie off tightly again. Now cut off the tubes close to the hide, an inch or so outward from the string tie-off.

Grasp the exposed intestine (on the buck) close to the carcass, and pinch it together with the fingers of one hand while the other hand grips the intestine adjacently outward and slides down it to the free end,* the anus. Any "deer berries" held in the last segment of the tract thus will be voided outside the carcass. You can tie it off with a short string, but I usually don't on a buck. Cut off the opening of the anus, and let the section of voided intestine hang.

REMOVING THE INNARDS

Turn and straddle a hind leg of the deer at one side. Finish and clean up the cut from the belly to the circular cut made at the anus. Now with the whole topside (belly) open, reach in *behind and under** the exposed innards. The bladder, a translucent bag, lies close to the forward part of the pelvic arch. It may be filled or empty. Carefully slide your hand under it, palm up, and feel for the tubes to the rear of it that extend under the pelvic arch, and which you cut off earlier at the other side of the arch. Grasp them between a couple fingers, palm up, and pull everything forward and toward you, rolling the carcass to that side. Trapped blood and the innards, still attached up forward, will roll out of the body cavity over the flank. The free end of the voided intestine (and the vaginal tube) will pull through the pelvic arch with the entrails.

Now move to the front end of the belly incision, and you will find quite a void there, once the rumen (the food storage bag, the big first stomach) is pushed aside.* The gullet (esophagus), however, is still attached. It passes beyond the exposed and still-attached liver lying tight against a smooth, pinkish, membranous sheet — the diaphragm.*

**The diaphragm** covers the lungs and heart. Reach in front of the rumen and grasp the gullet as far forward as you can. Pinch it loosely and stroke it toward the rumen pushing any mash-type food that may be in it into the rumen. Cut the voided gullet off close to the liver, and roll out the exposed entrails to the rear of the liver. Now the body cavity is mostly clear. The liver lies on one side smoothly against the exposed diaphragm.* The small grayish organ on the other side, that looks somewhat like a little liver, is the spleen. Trim it out and a small breech will be made in the diaphragm. Gently lift up the liver and make a couple of two-inch cuts in the diaphragm close to and at each side of the backbone. These cuts, and the breech where the spleen was removed, will allow trapped blood ahead of the diaphragm to pour out and be voided from the body cavity. Roll the carcass to help clear the fluids.

At this point your deer is field dressed *for northern climates.* Hunters of the North woods find it expedient (without causing harm to the meat or edible organs) to leave the diaphragm in place to hold the heart, liver and lungs ("lights") in place during the drag back to camp or car. The kidneys still remain at each side in the back, too.

**If the weather is warm,** it would be a good idea to take out the liver — standard practice in the South — and then neatly cut out the whole diaphragm at its juncture with the rib cage. Remove the heart, and massage it to remove all blood from its passages. Wipe or wash the heart and liver, and wrap them separately in clean cloths which you should have with you. Then pull out the kidneys. Carry the edible organs back to camp in a daypack or a porous cloth (muslin) bag which can be dampened when you come to clear water. I always hate to see plastic in contact with meat or fish. In short order, slime develops under the plastic and deterioration starts, except under ideal conditions.

You're not done yet, when the weather is warm. The lungs, remaining gullet and windpipe deteriorate quickly in warm temperatures. Run spread fingers inside the rib cage along the ribs from the sides of the rib cage to the backbone. Your fingers will slide under the lungs. Lift them out cleanly. Reach up the throat and pull back on the gullet and windpipe, cutting them off as far up as you can reach. You can finish the job — removing the tongue and what is left of the two pipes — when you get back to camp.

An exception should be noted that often is encountered in the Southwest when mule deer or other big game is taken in arid areas where sand or fine dust is common. Under these conditions, do not open up any more of the carcass to the elements than is necessary. Don't cut the throat and keep the belly cut to a minimum.

In this situation, start at the *hind end.* * A cut just even with the front of the knee of the hind leg, about two feet long, should be sufficient. Chances are the weather will be warm, so strip down; there will be quite a reach to take care of things up forward. This special situation is discussed further on page 40.


DISPOSING OF THE INNARDS

What you do with the innards depends on many things. If you are deep in the woods, let birds and other wild scavengers make use of them. If you are close to civilization, kick out a shallow grave and tumble them into it, covering them over with the duff kicked out. Press it all down firmly and no one should be bothered. Innards present an offensive sight to people, but are really only another instance of "natural pollution." That night, skunks or raccoons may undo your efforts, but they will probably clean up their mess.


THE PELVIC ARCH

Some hunters, no doubt, will take issue with my not having cut through muscle to expose the pelvic arch so it can be separated and the tubes lifted out.

I do not recommend cutting the muscle or breaking the pelvic arch on any deer in the field, unless it has to be quartered to pack it out. But if you disagree, here is how it is done.* On younger deer, you will find a cartilaginous juncture on the median line where the two sides of the pelvic arch are joined together. Cut through the cartilage. Don't attempt to cut through the bone with your knife. On older deer, you will find a belt axe is needed, but a folding saw* does a much neater job. I used to break the arch until I learned better. I'll tell you why I no longer do it: The pelvic construction of a deer, including both muscle and bone, is rather lightly put together for an animal of its size. Lateral movement of the hind legs of a deer is not a characteristic motion, and muscles that keep the legs in parallel planes with the body are relatively weak. This is why we get "split" or "splayed deer" in the wild when they are forced to travel on ice-covered snow. Their rear legs sometimes slide apart, one to each side of an icy hump perhaps, and the deer literally falls apart internally at the pelvis. It never can get up on its hind legs again, and dies a lingering death. When a hunter cuts the muscle over the pelvic arch and then breaks the arch itself, he creates the same results.

If you do not cut through the muscle and the arch, the legs stay together much better when the deer is being dragged. Sure, you can tie the hind legs together at the feet and hocks, but even then, there is a lot more flopping around on the drag out with the arch split open. The hind legs tend to catch in everything along the way, especially when pine needles or slippery leaves are on the ground during a downhill run. Why not let nature's design help you as much as it can?

If the animal is an older, mature deer or one of the larger species, you will have to saw or chop through the arch to split it. Any deer, or even a moose, can be handled as first described, if it can be hauled out intact. When skinning and quartering are necessary to pack out the hide and meat, use a hand saw on the bones.

CLEANING THE BODY CAVITY

Another point that is argued is cleaning the body cavity after you have gutted the deer. In northern climates, I use plenty of clean snow to wash and wipe it out, or I dunk and slop it well in the first pool of a clear running brook I come to. I figure that amount of blood is natural pollution of minor impact. The poolgrade of streams where I hunt is so great that the tumbling water purifies itself in a very short run anyway — oh yeah?*

A very good hunting companion of mine in the North Country has been telling me for years *not* to wash out a deer because the meat will spoil — but it hasn't yet. Furthermore, when my wife wants to cook the meat, she does not appreciate dried clots of blood and hair glued to it. Believe it or not, I have seen hunters of my friend's school-of-thinking wipe out the body cavity with handfuls of dried leaves, moss and ferns. Need I say more?

In areas where water is not up to drinking standards,* you have to *plan ahead*. Take along some good-sized, clean wiping cloths. Towels or Handi-Wipes work fine. Carefully wipe all the blood and hair from the meat *as soon as the carcass is gutted*. Work from the throat back to the hindquarters methodically and meticulously. There still will be a coating of natural meat fluids on the surface that dries out quickly, protecting the meat from immediate attraction of flies or fast bacterial deterioration.

## DANGER — WATER UNSAFE!

Ever hear of "lamblia"? It is but one of several classes of a species of intestinal bacteria known for many years to cause very serious sickness in humans. As new classes were discovered, the species name "Giardia" came into general use.

This one-cell flagellate swims by its multiple, whip-like tails, and may eventually attach itself to the wall of an intestine. When a human, wild mammal, bird or even amphibian ingests unpotable water, these bacteria often go into the body too.

An infected animal's droppings containing the bacteria often fall into or near water where rain can wash it into a water source thus causing it to become polluted. Severe sickness caused by giardia was long blamed on other causes.

With human populations exploding worldwide, and since so many humans live or find recreation in the outdoors, the danger of running afoul of giardia is very great. For example, neither you nor I can feel safe now drinking out of what may seem to be pristine streams or ponds. No thinking outdoor person should poo-pooh giardia. Be sure of your drinking water (tested) or use purification tablets per instructions, or *boil the water for at least 5 minutes.*

## LACING THE CARCASS

If the weather is cold, and dust, or fine sand are common, there is another, more comfortable way to prepare the carcass — but again, you have to plan ahead. Make a normal or only slightly shorter belly cut and proceed as outlined earlier. Reach into your day pack and take out the thong-needle* you made to accommodate the one-eighth-inch braided nylon line (decoy line will do) that you also brought in good supply (twelve-foot minimum). After the body cavity has been wiped clean, and the body temperature has lowered some, make a series of small holes through the hide about an inch back from the edges of the belly cut, at both sides, and full length. These holes should be about four inches apart. Lace the incision as you would a boot, to just pull the cut together (not too tight) to keep out dirt, and tie it off. Be sure to tie the hind legs together at the hocks and feet to reduce excess strain on the hide in the laced pelvic area.

With this method you will sacrifice a narrow strip of hide along each side of the belly cut, if the hide is tanned. But the same holes can be used later to toggle the hide in stretching and drying it.

**Caution:** When a carcass is laced, at camp or at the car, just as soon as possible, open the cavity up and place spacer sticks* to keep it propped open. Wipe out the body cavity carefully with a damp rag once more and again when the deer is hung. For road travel in hot, dusty country in particular, bag the deer* propped open. Put a sealed bag of ice cubes in the cavity as soon as you can purchase them.

Now that the deer is tagged and field-dressed, the next job is getting it into camp or to the car.

## WHERE THEY'RE AT

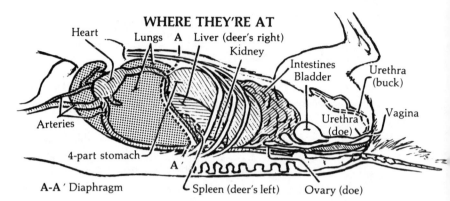

Heart — Lungs **A** — Liver (deer's right) — Kidney — Intestines — Bladder — Urethra (buck) — Urethra (doe) — Vagina — Arteries — 4-part stomach — **A'** — Spleen (deer's left) — Ovary (doe)

**A-A'** Diaphragm

In cold weather — leave kidneys, liver, diaphragm and everything forward of it in place until ready to hang. Breech diaphragm low and cut artery for bleedout.

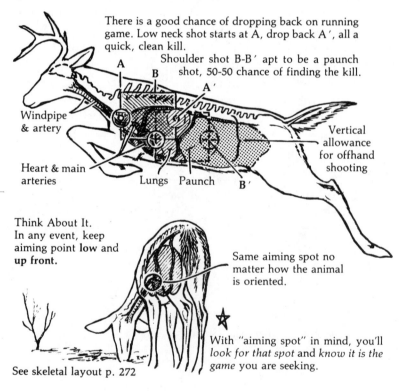

There is a good chance of dropping back on running game. Low neck shot starts at A, drop back A', all a quick, clean kill.

Shoulder shot B-B' apt to be a paunch shot, 50-50 chance of finding the kill.

**A** **B** **A'**

Windpipe & artery

Vertical allowance for offhand shooting

Heart & main arteries

Lungs   Paunch   **B'**

Think About It.
In any event, keep aiming point **low** and **up front.**

Same aiming spot no matter how the animal is oriented.

With "aiming spot" in mind, you'll *look for that spot* and *know it is the game* you are seeking.

See skeletal layout p. 272

# FIELD DRESSING BIG GAME

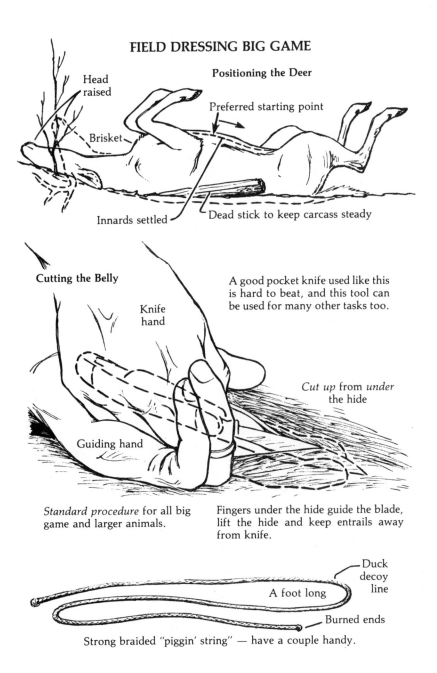

**Positioning the Deer**

Head raised

Preferred starting point

Brisket

Innards settled

Dead stick to keep carcass steady

**Cutting the Belly**

Knife hand

A good pocket knife used like this is hard to beat, and this tool can be used for many other tasks too.

*Cut up* from *under* the hide

Guiding hand

*Standard procedure* for all big game and larger animals.

Fingers under the hide guide the blade, lift the hide and keep entrails away from knife.

Duck decoy line

A foot long

Burned ends

Strong braided "piggin' string" — have a couple handy.

# USEFUL ANATOMY

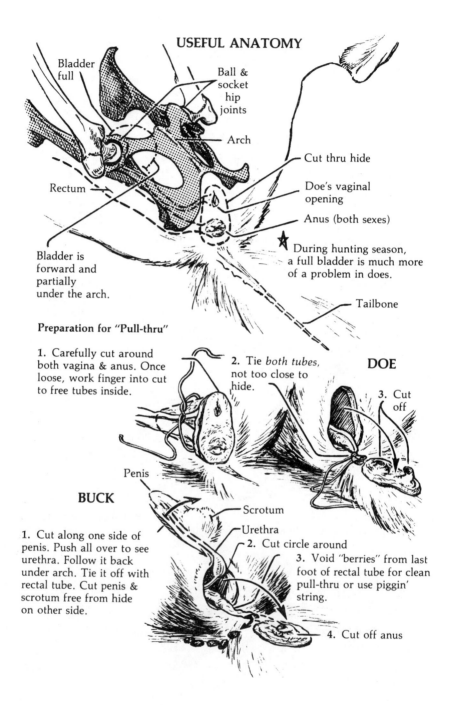

Bladder full

Ball & socket hip joints

Arch

Rectum

Cut thru hide

Doe's vaginal opening

Anus (both sexes)

Bladder is forward and partially under the arch.

★ During hunting season, a full bladder is much more of a problem in does.

Tailbone

**Preparation for "Pull-thru"**

**1.** Carefully cut around both vagina & anus. Once loose, work finger into cut to free tubes inside.

**2.** Tie *both tubes,* not too close to hide.

**DOE**

**3.** Cut off

Penis

**BUCK**

**1.** Cut along one side of penis. Push all over to see urethra. Follow it back under arch. Tie it off with rectal tube. Cut penis & scrotum free from hide on other side.

Scrotum

Urethra

**2.** Cut circle around

**3.** Void "berries" from last foot of rectal tube for clean pull-thru or use piggin' string.

**4.** Cut off anus

38

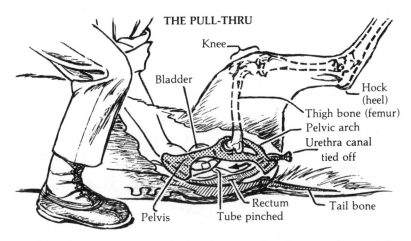

## THE PULL-THRU

Knee

Bladder

Hock (heel)

Thigh bone (femur)

Pelvic arch

Urethra canal tied off

Pelvis

Rectum

Tube pinched

Tail bone

Lift up on bladder, work fingers back and under arch to loosen urethra & anal canal (tubes) then pinch them between extended fingers and pull all back.

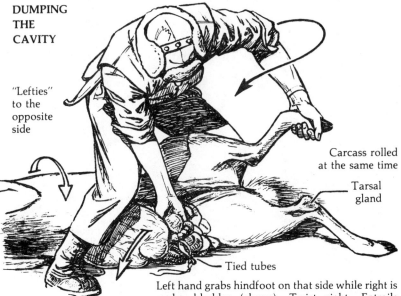

## DUMPING THE CAVITY

"Lefties" to the opposite side

Carcass rolled at the same time

Tarsal gland

Tied tubes

Left hand grabs hindfoot on that side while right is under bladder (above). Twist right. Entrails dumped over flank.

## PELVIC ARCH SEVERED ONLY WHEN QUARTERING

(Wait until final butchering by choice)

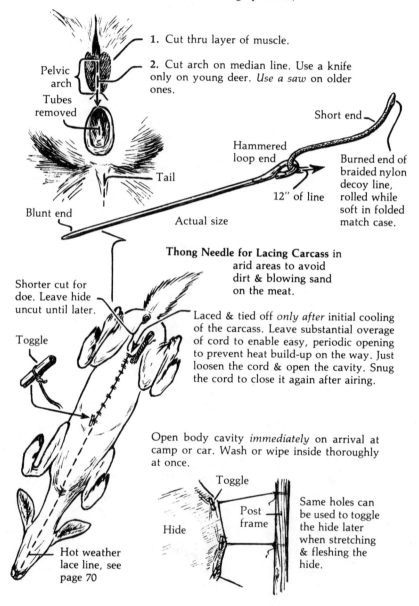

**Pelvic arch**

**Tubes removed**

1. Cut thru layer of muscle.

2. Cut arch on median line. Use a knife only on young deer. *Use a saw* on older ones.

Short end

**Hammered loop end**

Tail

12" of line

Burned end of braided nylon decoy line, rolled while soft in folded match case.

Blunt end

Actual size

**Thong Needle for Lacing Carcass** in arid areas to avoid dirt & blowing sand on the meat.

Shorter cut for doe. Leave hide uncut until later.

Toggle

Laced & tied off *only after* initial cooling of the carcass. Leave substantial overage of cord to enable easy, periodic opening to prevent heat build-up on the way. Just loosen the cord & open the cavity. Snug the cord to close it again after airing.

Open body cavity *immediately* on arrival at camp or car. Wash or wipe inside thoroughly at once.

Toggle

Post frame

Hide

Same holes can be used to toggle the hide later when stretching & fleshing the hide.

Hot weather lace line, see page 70

**Leaving a Head for Mounting "in the Hide"**

**1.** Ascertain the cape line desired (p. 88) & cut the line around.

**2.** Proceed based on the at-home or at-camp skinning of the head. Estimate the lines* & don't cut *hair* making the Y-cut on males or the single back-of-the-neck cut on females. See pp. 88-89.

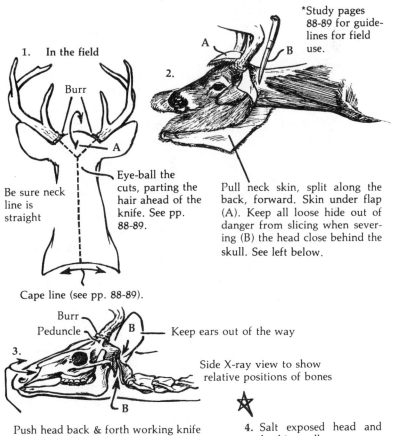

*Study pages 88-89 for guide-lines for field use.

1. In the field

Burr

A

2.

A    B

Be sure neck line is straight

Eye-ball the cuts, parting the hair ahead of the knife. See pp. 88-89.

Pull neck skin, split along the back, forward. Skin under flap (A). Keep all loose hide out of danger from slicing when severing (B) the head close behind the skull. See left below.

Cape line (see pp. 88-89).

Burr
Peduncle    B — Keep ears out of the way

3.

Side X-ray view to show relative positions of bones

B

Push head back & forth working knife between back of skull and 1st vertebrae, cut carefully.

**4.** Salt exposed head and neck skin well as soon as possible (see text).

CHAPTER 3

# THE LONG TRAIL BACK

Getting a deer back to camp is a lot of work, but it's all part of the game. Make two or more trips if you hunt alone, or get some help if the deer is a big one. This is especially important if you are not in tip-top physical shape, or if you work most of the time in an office, or if you are over forty. You may *think* you are not getting older — just getting better — but who are you kidding?

Dragging a deer is standard procedure in the North Country, whether there is snow or not. In many areas where there is heavy hunting, it is probably the safest way too — though that thought seldom comes to mind. Rarely in northern climates are deer ever moved from the kill site to camp or to a vehicle any other way. The one exception is a modified form of drag, the "travois" (covered separately later), used when a really big deer is taken well back in the puckerbrush.

Some hunters these days carry heavy plastic sheeting (6 mil or heavier) to tie under the deer for skidding it out. It makes for easier skidding, and *is* pretty tough material, but you need brakes on the carcass when it starts downhill on pine needles, dried grass or slippery beech leaves. Gravel also tears up the plastic after a while, and sharp dry sticks can pierce it or bring things to a grinding halt.

METHODS FOR DRAGGING

**The simplest form of drag** is only assured by shooting a buck with a good rack — not always in the cards. You will have sore shoulders and blisters on your feet if you drag a deer far this way, but the system *is* simple. You just grab an antler and start pulling.

**Drag ropes** are carried by almost all deer hunters in the North. Ten or twelve feet is long enough for anyone dragging a deer, buck or doe. If there are two people, however, things work better with two such ropes attached, one to a customer. More hunters should try that idea. Two people on one rope does not always work very well.

Using the rack on a buck to truss up the drag is easy.* Dragging a doe, however, sometimes is a different story. In no case should any animal be dragged by a hind leg or legs *against* the grain of the hair. I saw it being done once, and offered a suggestion. It was greatly appreciated.

Dragging a doe by a front leg isn't a whole lot better either. I find the easiest way to drag a doe is to truss the forelegs with the muzzle or jaw.

Once the drag line is secured to the deer, there are some options for the other end that are worth trying. Why not learn from a team of horses? They have been pulling things for a long time. A stout stick with the rope securely knotted about the middle so one hand can pull each side of the knot, makes a fair whiffletree. One problem is maintaining an even pull with both hands. And it is nearly impossible for two people to pull evenly, with one each side of the knot, though it is often tried.

The pull is evened out better when two lines come from the deer to the *ends* of the whiffle. This way there is less pivoting at the handle. It is less tiring for an individual, and better for two people if only one rope is available. Truss the deer with the *center* part and you won't have to cut the rope to get two haul lines.

Moving from the horse-drawn team to the dog team, we find an even better solution — the shoulder harness — good if you planned ahead and have one or more with you. A single loop works fine with one person, two loops even better, as shown, or one shoulder loop to each person (on the inside shoulder) if two people put their shoulders to the task. If the trail is narrow, this system works fine since the draglines can be of varying lengths and still take advantage of full pulling power. If you have more company, give each one a line, like a fan-rigged dog team. If they all have the shoulder loops, there won't be much grunting and groaning.

If two hunters work together, the load can be divided: one can pack out skinned hindquarters, liver and heart on a pack frame, while his companion can easily drag the head, neck, forequarters and full loin with the hide still attached.* The skinned hindquarter hide is rolled hair-in, and is brought forward and tied inside, against the loin.

## METHODS FOR CARRYING

**Rucksack style*** over the shoulders is the method sometimes used by hunters in the South and West, when they take a small deer (dressing out a hundred pounds or less). The load can be lightened somewhat without having deer bones crunching against yours, if the forelegs are skinned and the back legs sawed off below the hocks. Some rope is needed to keep things together better.

There are many variations, but it is a traditional carry, and that means something to some people. If used today, however, a bright coat or vest should be secured around the body of the deer for safety reasons and *checked periodically* to be sure it stays in place.

**Caution:** Any time big game is carried off the ground, it is just good common sense to tie a bright coat or large piece of fluorescent orange cloth around it. Since current hunting laws in many places demand so many square inches of orange be worn by hunters, some lame-brained hunter dangerously could reason: "If it ain't orange, it's gotta be a deer," — and it is! Think about it.

**A pole carry*** for deer is common in many areas where two hunters work together. The opposite feet, front-front, rear-rear, are bound together *below* the foot joint. A stout pole then is passed through the arches formed between the bound feet, and it is shouldered. The head is usually trussed up to the pole or forelegs to keep it from dragging. A bright coat or cloth is laid over the belly and secured down each side, for safety.

**A litter carry*** is a variation of the pole carry. Such a litter, using a heavy canvas cot cover slipped over a couple poles (one on each side), can be made easily and quickly for carrying all kinds of things, a deer included. One good use for it is carrying boxes of food and other supplies into a camp that has to be approached on foot. Two people easily can carry a lot more this way — as well as irregular-shaped things — than by using two pack frames. Short cross-poles lashed between the carrying poles a foot or two in from the ends often help when carrying boxes or hardware.

**Canoe transport** of deer or other big game often is a much easier way to go than all backpacking. It is important to distribute the weight evenly in the canoe, and to keep it low. This can be better and more easily accomplished, especially when portages are to be negotiated, by skinning and quartering* all or part of the animal.

**Horse transportation** is great when it can be used, but not many horses will carry game, unless they have been trained to it. A lot of horses in a pack string either get so flighty it is dangerous to have them carry game, or they flatly refuse. Nearly all horses are scared to death of bears, dead or alive. Many will rear or bolt when they come to a spot on the trail where a bear has urinated or left a scat.

If a buckboard can get into an area to pick up a downed giant, however, things come out pretty rosy. Before you leave civilization, check out the possibility of getting a horse or tractor with a stone-boat drag, or a horse and buckboard into the area you plan to hunt.

**The travois*** is a combination litter, drag and buckboard all rolled into one, and *you* are the horse. It works as well today as it did for the American Indian and the French explorers, who allegedly borrowed the idea and gave it the name. The travois was the Indian's moving van when it came time to set up housekeeping in a different area. All of the family's worldly goods were secured to the travois hitched up to a horse, and off they would go.

It is a good piece of jury-rigging for a hunter to file in the attic of his mind. You will be surprised how well one works, and find out that you are much stronger than you think you are. When you take big game way back in the puckerbrush, and you don't have a horse — make a travois.

It is really a wheelless wagon. The design can vary, but basically you provide two tough, green-pole shafts, just stout enough and long enough to do the job at hand. The poles for the shafts should match as closely as possible. The tip-third should be fairly limber when loaded. The butt ends are forward.

The travois works fine in almost any kind of country. The poles should be somewhat stouter for rocky or shale situations to cope with the greater abrasion on the tips, longer than normal in soft bog or marsh locations, and about as shown for normal woodland conditions.

Depending on the load and your preference, the apex can be truncated forward with shafts held apart by a lashed-in-place crossbrace* for a shorter rig. Greater width between the shafts up forward, relative to their length, also is a result. The sharp-pointed apex with the butts lashed together* is longer but much more rigid when it needs to be. For long hauls, shoulder straps,* a hip strap and a tump line can be rigged separately or in combination*.

While the construction of a travois does not demand a great deal of rope, it is one more occasion when you will be way ahead of the game to have an extra hank of it in your day pack, and to know some basic knots. Nylon rope stretches, but the knots will not slip if you tie them right. The stretch in the line can play to your advantage, as it gives a clamping action in a bight or when it is laid over itself under tension. It will not rot, and it has tremendous strength for its diameter.

When cutting any of the synthetic ropes, immediately burn* the end to prevent fraying. It is a good idea to take a light, inexpensive cigarette lighter along, whether you smoke or not, for just such use. And *keep it dry*. Save your matches for emergency use.

Advantages of the travois are that you can carry a considerable load fairly easily and the spring in the poles acts as a shock absorber over rough country. The travois saves wear and tear on game so carried,* and it can be rested easily. You can avoid the weight lifting act each time you stop by setting the forward end at natural traveling height* against a tree, downed log or ledge. Then step out of it, get the kinks out of you, and step back in when you are ready to go again.

When packing the travois, distribute the load to balance as you would in loading a trailer to be pulled behind a vehicle, keeping a proportional weight on the "tongue and hitch," according to your physique. Use the skids of the travois to advantage. You want partial weight on the shafts, but all of that weight eventually will be transmitted to your legs.

Keep the head of your big game forward with hind legs dragging behind when you put it aboard.* Thus, any contact of the animal with the ground will be *with the grain of the hair.*

Plan for the rack on antlered game. There has to be room for you to pull without a tine of the rack jabbing you now and then. One solution to this problem, if time allows, is to dress out the game beyond normal field dressing. If a head mount is planned, cape the hide *leaving the head in* (explained and illustrated at the end of Chapter 6), and pack that on your back. That way, the rack can extend up or back* and won't bother you on the move. the rest of the carcass with hide on and legs attached can be lashed on the travois.

## DRAGGING TRUSSES

Rolls over on its side during the drag. Downside antler is rockered up and travels easily.

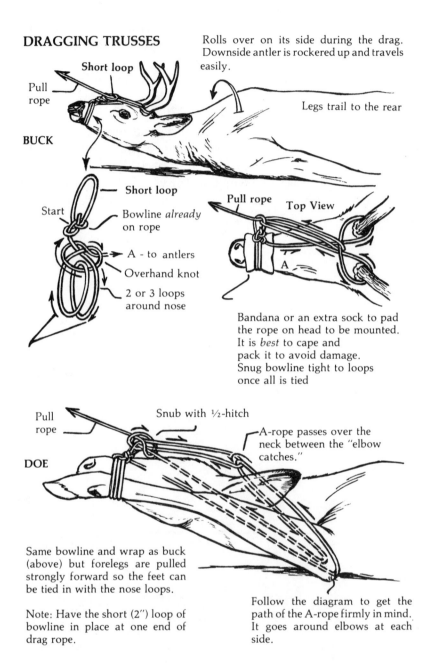

**Short loop**

Pull rope

**BUCK**

Legs trail to the rear

**Short loop**

Start

Bowline *already* on rope

A - to antlers

Overhand knot

2 or 3 loops around nose

Pull rope   Top View

A

Bandana or an extra sock to pad the rope on head to be mounted. It is *best* to cape and pack it to avoid damage. Snug bowline tight to loops once all is tied

Pull rope

Snub with ½-hitch

**DOE**

A-rope passes over the neck between the "elbow catches."

Same bowline and wrap as buck (above) but forelegs are pulled strongly forward so the feet can be tied in with the nose loops.

Note: Have the short (2") loop of bowline in place at one end of drag rope.

Follow the diagram to get the path of the A-rope firmly in mind. It goes around elbows at each side.

# DRAGGING TECHNIQUES

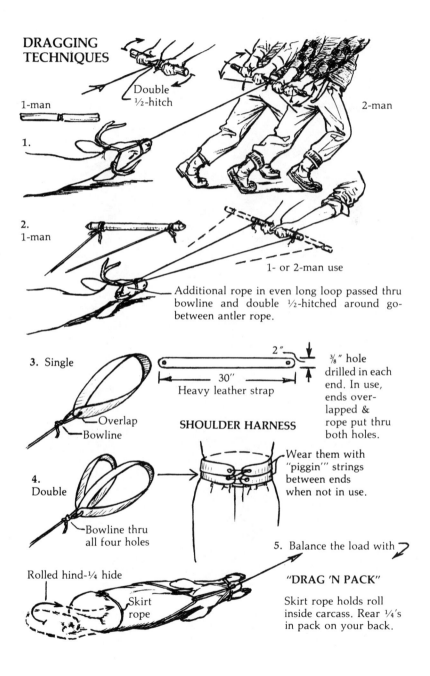

Double ½-hitch

1-man

2-man

**1.**

**2.**
1-man

1- or 2-man use

Additional rope in even long loop passed thru bowline and double ½-hitched around go-between antler rope.

**3.** Single

Overlap
Bowline

2″

30″
Heavy leather strap

⅜″ hole drilled in each end. In use, ends over-lapped & rope put thru both holes.

**SHOULDER HARNESS**

**4.**
Double

Bowline thru all four holes

Wear them with "piggin'" strings between ends when not in use.

**5.** Balance the load with

"DRAG 'N PACK"

Rolled hind-¼ hide

Skirt rope

Skirt rope holds roll inside carcass. Rear ¼'s in pack on your back.

## CARRYING BIG GAME

**1. RUCKSACK CARRY.** Only for small big game. Most variations tend to slip, stretch or are downright uncomfortable.

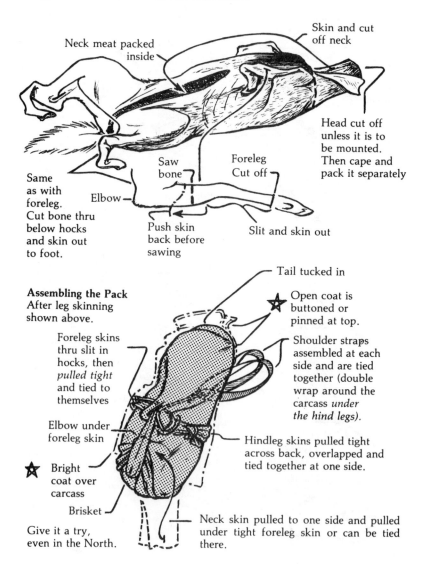

Neck meat packed inside

Skin and cut off neck

Head cut off unless it is to be mounted. Then cape and pack it separately

Same as with foreleg. Cut bone thru below hocks and skin out to foot.

Saw bone

Foreleg Cut off

Elbow

Push skin back before sawing

Slit and skin out

Tail tucked in

**Assembling the Pack**
After leg skinning shown above.

Open coat is buttoned or pinned at top.

Foreleg skins thru slit in hocks, then *pulled tight* and tied to themselves

Shoulder straps assembled at each side and are tied together (double wrap around the carcass *under the hind legs*).

Elbow under foreleg skin

Hindleg skins pulled tight across back, overlapped and tied together at one side.

Bright coat over carcass

Brisket

Give it a try, even in the North.

Neck skin pulled to one side and pulled under tight foreleg skin or can be tied there.

50

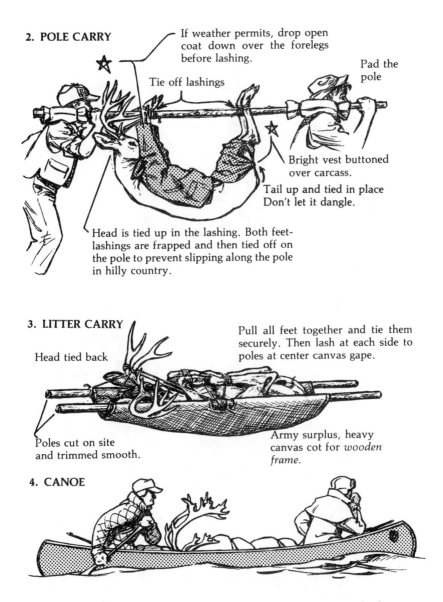

**2. POLE CARRY**

If weather permits, drop open coat down over the forelegs before lashing.

Tie off lashings

Pad the pole

Bright vest buttoned over carcass.

Tail up and tied in place Don't let it dangle.

Head is tied up in the lashing. Both feet-lashings are frapped and then tied off on the pole to prevent slipping along the pole in hilly country.

**3. LITTER CARRY**

Head tied back

Pull all feet together and tie them securely. Then lash at each side to poles at center canvas gape.

Poles cut on site and trimmed smooth.

Army surplus, heavy canvas cot for *wooden frame.*

**4. CANOE**

Whether portages are to be encountered or not, divide the carcass for better balance and ease in handling. *Keep the load low.*

## THE TRAVOIS

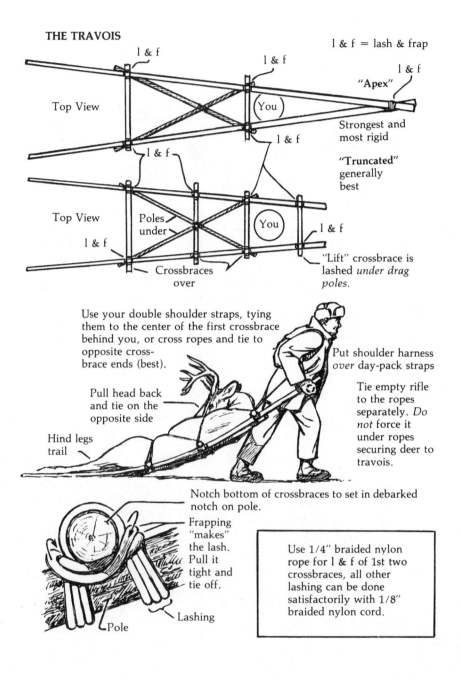

l & f = lash & frap

l & f    l & f    l & f

**"Apex"**

Top View

(You)

Strongest and most rigid

**"Truncated"** generally best

l & f

Top View    Poles under

(You)    l & f

l & f

Crossbraces over

"Lift" crossbrace is lashed *under drag poles.*

Use your double shoulder straps, tying them to the center of the first crossbrace behind you, or cross ropes and tie to opposite cross-brace ends (best).

Put shoulder harness *over* day-pack straps

Pull head back and tie on the opposite side

Tie empty rifle to the ropes separately. *Do not* force it under ropes securing deer to travois.

Hind legs trail

Notch bottom of crossbraces to set in debarked notch on pole.

Frapping "makes" the lash. Pull it tight and tie off.

Lashing

Pole

Use 1/4" braided nylon rope for l & f of 1st two crossbraces, all other lashing can be done satisfactorily with 1/8" braided nylon cord.

**Burn Whipping** (synthetic rope)

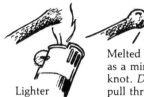

Lighter

Melted ball acts
as a minor jamb
knot. *Does not*
pull thru easily.

Tapered end for
*easy pull-thru,* by
rolling in matchcase
when melt is soft.

**Caution:** Avoid burning yourself, especially out in the puckerbush. Let the end cool before using the rope and be careful overmelt doesn't drip on you.

Rest travois at travelling height. Step out of it, work out the kinks, rest, then step into it again, mount shoulder straps and you're on your way again.

Head and cape in day-pack, antlers point back — no jabbing

Harness straps over day-pack straps

**Short Model**
2 crossbraces only, carcass divided

Light line ties neck skin down

"Lift" cross-brace, 1/4" lash ropes.

Neck meat inside body cavity

2 braces

CHAPTER 4

# HANGING THE DEER

One way or another, your deer finally gets into camp from the kill site. Toward the end of the trip it seems to double in weight, but that's normal. Once in camp, there is more work to do to protect it until it goes out to satisfy mandatory reporting requirements or to take home.

## Hanging the Carcass with Assistance

Eager hands usually are available to assist in hanging the deer. Most camps optimistically have a *meat pole* in place — a rugged plank or stout, trimmed pole secured horizontally and high enough to hold the suspended deer completely off the ground. Too often it is just that — a pole. Where predators may investigate the camp at night while hunters sleep, a ladder and a considerably higher pole generally are used.

Whether hung head-up or hocks-up depends largely on local custom, personal choice or whether a head mount is desired or not. In either position, the deer hangs vertically so the carcass will drain and cool properly.

### MEAT POLES*

The best meat pole for a base camp is one that is in place *before it is needed.* It should be stout enough to carry the most optimistic number of deer it might be called upon to handle — the normal complement of hunters based there, assuming they all got lucky within two days.

A small set of blocks-and-tackle cannot be recommended too highly. One often-ignored item to go with them, however, is a movable means for securing the upper block to the pole,* and the means to transfer a deer from the blocks to the pole* when another deer comes into camp and also needs the blocks-and-tackle. Again, planning ahead saves time and makes the work easier.

S-hooks* are available in various sizes and weights at most general or hardware stores. They can be used as is, or eye-hooks* can be made from them by pounding one half of the "S" or squeezing it shut in a vise to form an eye. File off some of the edge of the square-cut rod at the open end — for easier insertion under a tendon or for placing over a rope under strong tension. Have enough of these eye-hooks in camp, allowing *two* for each expected deer and a few extra. They can come in handy for a lot of other uses around camp, too.

**The block loop** is a removable, loose-fitting loop — double or triple if necessary to support the deer weight demanded — to go around the meat pole to hold the upper block. Secure a heavy ring at one end and a heavy eye-hook at the other. The welded steel ring (about two inches in diameter) is attached by knotting or splicing the rope. the upper block hook can be attached readily or removed from the ring. This makes it easy to remove the blocks-and-tackle when not in use.

**Hock-loops,*** two for each deer, also can be made similar to the block loop. Make them ahead of time. These loops are used when the deer is transferred from the blocks and also can be used to hang a deer head-up,* if you so desire. In either event, make these loops long enough so when they are positioned on the pole, the hook and ring when interlocked will be *even with or a little below* the hocks of a deer — when it is pulled up to the meat pole as close as possible with the blocks-and-tackle. The transfer then is quite simple when you have a ladder.

Permanent iron hooks* can replace the rope loops if desired.

Either meat pole shown can have all the loops removed easily when there is no weight on them to store for the next season.

A hock-spreader* is unnecessary if you hang a sheep, antelope or deer by a hind leg, but when hanging by both hind legs, the usual way, it is standard. A pole between the hocks keeps the rear of the carcass open for quick cooling. Why not let the hock-spreader serve both purposes, lifting the deer and keeping the carcass open? A shaped board or limb of a tree of sufficient length and strength can be used to support your deer — with plenty of rope on hand and a lot of straining. When either of the meat pole systems shown is combined with the accessories noted, things will go much easier.

These hock-spreaders can be made between seasons and be ready when you need them. Made of green hardwood or three-quarter-inch pipe, they will serve you for years, be ready when you need one, and work efficiently with much less effort and rope.

In both examples, the rope(s) for securing the legs to the spreader is left attached to the spreader at each end. It is a simple matter to throw a loop or two around each leg and snub it on the inside with a *drop hitch*. There will be no slipping, tipping or dropping a deer off the support. Furthermore, the blocks-and-tackle are readily attached and detached, or the weight shifted to the supporting hock-loops on the meat pole, freeing the blocks for the next deer.

Each end of the hock-spreader* is pushed through a slit made in the void of the gambrel. If you feel you must remove the tarsal gland (see p. 67) be sure you do not cut the heavy Achilles tendon.*

One end of a heavy S-hook or the open side of an eye-hook is inserted in each hock *first*. Then the spreader is positioned and the respective leg lashed in place. The blocks-and-tackle are hooked through the center eye-bolt or closed S-hook for raising or lowering the deer. Once up at the meat pole, the hooks or rings on the hock-loops hanging from the pole engage the waiting hooks in the hocks, and the weight of the deer is transferred to them as the blocks are lowered, detached and moved to accommodate the next deer.

A **ladder** is another useful piece of camp equipment that makes the job of hanging deer easier. It can be made on location ahead of the hunting season, such as on a "woodcutting" weekend. The ladder should be long enough to reach safely above the meat pole and the eaves of the camp. If stored properly between seasons, it should last for years, but be sure to check it carefully every year before it is used.

CONSIDERATION OF HEAD MOUNTS
WHEN HANGING DEER

When a head mount *is* desired, the deer should *be hung by the hocks*\* to avoid damaging the hair around the head with the rope.

Before the hanging, some hunters cut out the *tarsal gland* or *paint brush* in each hock, before placing the spreader pole between the hocks. They claim there's a risk in handling the deer and getting musk on the meat, though usually during hunting season there is more urine on the paint brush than musk. I don't bother with these glands, because I cut the skin above them when it comes time to skin the legs. Nothing has ever run down the legs from any of the leg glands, and they have never caused a meat problem for me or anyone I know. (See page 67.)

If a head mount is *not* desired, and if temperatures are somewhat above freezing, it is important to open up the rest of the carcass with a knife and saw.\*

Note: It still needs doing if a head mount *is* desired. First you must cape and skin the neck and head — as detailed later. Then proceed as detailed here.

Cut through the brisket, the front of the rib cage, and up the throat along the center line almost to the tip of the lower jaw. Remove the tongue and what's left of the gullet and windpipe. Wipe it all clean. The tongue should be trimmed, washed and wiped clean if it is to be eaten later.

Once the deer is hung, there is usually another round of story telling and admiration, as the group rests and looks over the deer. Then stout *cavity spreader sticks*\* are cut and placed at intervals across the opening of the carcass at the neck, forequarters, belly and hindquarters so the meat can cool quickly.

# Hanging the Carcass — Solo

Occasionally you will need to hang a deer, or other animal of comparable size, all by yourself, when away from camp at a "fly-camp" (back-packing camp). With a lot of grunting and groaning and a little jury-rigging, eventually you can get the job done, and the bigger and stronger you are, the easier it will be. Some optimists carry a small set of blocks-and-tackle with them in a day pack when they hunt, but even the small sets have a lot of rope you can't use for anything else, if you want them to work when you need them. They are good, but you may be carrying a lot of extra gear for nothing — for a long time. I like them in a base camp, but not on my back.

**A walking tripod*** demands much less rope, does a very satisfactory job, and the rope also is available for other uses — hardly true for the blocks-and-tackle. The tripod is a set of three matching poles lashed and frapped at the top ends. Frapping* is important to get the flexibility needed.

The trick in using this loaded rig is to get it all in motion at the start. Pointing the bottom (butt) ends of the poles, and making heel-holes to set the "even-poles," helps to avoid kick-outs once things are in motion.

Judgment in selecting the poles is fairly critical. Some flexibility in the poles is all right, but not too much. A lot depends on the availability of poles in the area, the kind of wood, and whether it is green or dried. Twelve- to fourteen-foot poles, about three or four inches in diameter at the butts are a good average size for a big deer. The *lever-pole* can benefit from a crotched or notched top to keep the rope from slipping down.

A roll-up type pocket saw stretched between a humped-up green stick,* a light pruning saw that pivots into a protecting wooden handle,* or that easily packed "aluminum slat" — the Sven saw* — all pack well and do a good job in cutting such poles. They double on bone, too, when needed.

Secure the deer up short to the lashing as shown. A bowline over one of the "even-poles" will suffice. Lay out the tripod relative to the deer as illustrated. It is helpful to grunt a little at the start to get some height established at the center. Place a prop* under the lashing, if needed, to let you get back to the lever pole. Then you and the lever pole start moving in steadily.* Never lift the end of the lever more than an inch or two above the ground. Once up part way, you can rest and attack the project in spurts.

When the tripod is up with the deer hanging, the tripod legs can be moved fairly easily to adjust it. The same general principle can be used in other situations when you find you aren't strong enough to lift something by yourself. For big bear, elk or moose, however, forget the tripod.

## MEAT DELICACIES TOO OFTEN IGNORED

When the deer is finally hung, some hunters think the immediate work is done, go into camp and call it a day. It is surprising to me how many fail to make use of the delicacies they've dragged out.

**The heart** of a deer makes great sandwiches, and is usually held in high esteem even by those who normally do not eat the heart of other animals. (Boil it for five minutes, let it cool, then slice it.)

**The tenderloins**, if not removed when the deer is hung, will be shriveled and dried by the following day. In a couple of days, they will be hard, and later they will have to be trimmed away.

Look inside your hanging deer and you will see two narrow red strips of meat running lengthwise along each side of the backbone. These are the tenderloins.* Slip a finger under the forward end closest to the ribs. Lift up to pull the meat away, or use a knife judiciously if needed. Once loose, they usually will strip right off the carcass with a steady pull, or cut them off where they build onto the hindquarter meat. Handle these two pieces of meat with loving care, and be sure they are on the menu soon!

**The kidneys** are next after you have taken care of the tenderloins. Remove the exposed kidneys from their protective fat at each side of the backbone. Prepare them when the rest of the fellows are out trying to get their deer. Boil the kidneys well, changing the water, and serve them sliced without fanfare. Probably everyone will relish them.

## CARING FOR THE CARCASS

If the meat is hung outdoors in the shade, it should be wiped again if necessary, and a light, loose-fitting cloth bag pulled up over it. Some hunters wrap the carcass in cheesecloth, like a mummy. Flies may still be a problem, however, since air should pass through the thin cloth layer. White vinegar can be brushed all over the exposed meat, or fine black pepper rubbed all over it to help keep the flies away.

A special refrigerator type bag* takes care of cooling and flies. The bag packs easily, and it can be laundered for use year after year. It is simply a take-off on the smaller, easily packed refrigerator for back-packing and tent camping, shown after Section IV, Fish.

If things were normal, your deer has been field dressed, hauled to camp where supplemental dressing was accomplished, and it has hung on the meat pole a day and a half. Now it probably is time for it to be taken down, reported and hauled home on the car.

In warm weather, skinning the carcass won't wait (details are in Chapter 7), and better cooling of the meat will result. If the head is to be mounted, it, too, should be skinned out carefully. All of the hide's skin side should have fine table salt* rubbed generously into it. Fold the edges inward on all sides to keep in the brine that soon forms when the salt works on the hide. Then loosely fold or roll up the hide with the hair on the outside of the neck. Protect it from flies, and put it in a cool dry place. Take it to the taxidermist, or plan your own tanning schedule.

If the weather turns really warm, nothing short of leaving camp and heading to a cold storage locker with the deer is recommended.

*Pickling salt is coarser, but works very well, especially on larger animals. Rub it hard into the green (wet) hide.

# CHAPTER 5

# ROAD TRANSPORTING
# OF DEER

You cannot delay it any longer. You have to take that deer, one way or another, down the road on a motor vehicle — sometimes only a few miles, but for many a trip of several hundred. Don't blow it now, after you have done so well up to this point. Most states and provinces have laws regulating the transportation of game — small as well as big game, and every hunter should know the laws, as mentioned in Chapter 1. One set of circumstances may hold true for commercial common carriers and another for a private car. Importation laws, covering the taking of game across state, provincial or international boundaries, also should have been checked carefully *before the hunt.*

## Packing the Meat

If the meat is to travel far and arrive in fit condition to eat, some extra-careful planning is in order. One problem can be getting enough ice for proper packing, especially en route. A lot of outfitters or guides include such service as part of a package plan — but check it out anyway. I know fellows who think nothing of traveling with a box trailer full of meat from the Canadian Maritime Provinces to Michigan, and others who bring back big rainbows and cohoes from Michigan to Vermont each year. The secret is in the planning.

Most of the insulation you need, if you are taking the meat or fish with you, should be planned for the *top* and *bottom* of the container. Why the top needs good insulation is readily apparent, but a lot of sportsmen forget the terrific, concentrated and continuous heat coming from the road surface of the highway even when the sun is not shining, but the traffic is heavy. If you can arrange for dry ice, it lasts longer, but it is becoming increasingly difficult to find. If you should find some, DON'T put it in close contact with game of any kind, or it will "burn" (dehydrate) it. Put several layers of newspaper between it and the game being transported.

Any kind of foamed plastic, "peanuts," buttons or puff-pocket sheeting used for general mailing (to keep things from getting broken) provides good insulation, and don't underestimate newspapers — but keep them dry. Plastic bags or quilts lined with newspapers can be made from building "membrane sheeting" purchased at any building supply store or lumber yard. Plan for easy access (for inspection) when you lash down the load.

**Well-dressed game travels best.** Some of the best woodsmen and guides I have known have been Indians. They are great people and fine companions. But don't expect the meat to be packed right just because an Indian did the job.

I can remember a lot of half-rotten snow geese arriving at home from a trip to James Bay in Ontario, yet an elegant hindquarter from a big caribou arrived in perfect condition from a trip to Alberta. A fast field dressing with muddy marsh grass packed in the belly of a goose (with a primary flight feather skewering the skin together over the grass) is *not* recommended for long distance travel, even by air. The carefully cleaned and wrapped hindquarter came through beautifully.

Work with your guide or outfitter and get to know him. Ask questions, and your odds will be better. As a last resort, protect your investment and do the packing yourself. At least then you will know who to blame if something goes wrong. That's some satisfaction — or is it?

**Covered meat and hides travel best.** Open meat should be protected from flies and road grime. How often have you seen deer tied to the top of a car, or worse still, on a fender, close to the hot engine, the belly open from stem to stern as it flies down the highway — or directly over the engine in rear-engine cars?

The hair or fur on animals thoughtlessly transported usually is filthy upon arrival, and the meat is probably a mess, too. But, it doesn't take much planning to throw in an old sheet or bedspread to wrap and tie around the object of all the time, effort and money you have spent. Making the muslin bags, mentioned earlier, costs nothing by comparison, and they can be washed and used over and over again.

**White vinegar or ground black pepper,** also mentioned earlier, can be rubbed over the surface of exposed meat to help keep flies away. When the meat is washed later, you won't taste anything different. The muslin bag does an even better job, but use both where flies may be a serious nuisance. Incidentally, you rarely need to carry glass with you for anything these days. The world of plastic has taken over and makes things much lighter for the backpacker, too. A soft plastic, watertight jug should be used for taking along the vinegar.

Conditions may change drastically between your hunting area and home. You cannot adjust to that situation unless you have planned ahead and have the needed items with you.

## Car-Top Transportation

Often car-top transportation becomes a problem without a hunter realizing it. Car-top game should be wrapped or bagged and the *body cavity propped open.* In warm weather, the bag can be wetted periodically, and evaporation by the strong wind of the slipstream, even though it is warm, will keep the contents cooled much more than you may imagine. When you stop, park in the shade, and wet the cloth again before continuing your trip. Don't overdo the wetting, however. You don't want excess water on the meat. A sealed bag of ice cubes laid in the cavity works well, too.

**Knots and ropes** have always played important roles in the out-doors, and will continue to do so, even with the availability of shock cords and their various fasteners. Any hunter or woodsman should learn a certain number of basic knots, know what they will do and won't do, and be able to tie and untie them quickly without reference to diagrams. Knot know-how will help when tying a deer (or anything else) on the car, and it will eliminate the need for having yards of rope and knots on knots.

I admit that I like to tie knots, to splice, and to work with rope. The one knot I probably use most I call a "drop hitch." I use it for tying canoes on cars, tying boats up temporarily at a dock without cleats, tying down canvas when I know I will need to get it off quickly, and even nailing down a sheet on a sailboat (which isn't good seamanship).

This knot* is only a half hitch with a loop pulled under it and the "bitter-end" (free end) left hanging. It becomes a "drop hitch" when a second loop is formed by *dropping* the free end through the first loops and snugging it up to the rope passed through. The second loop thus is formed — the lock loop. This knot will stay tied under tension or not, and it can be untied quickly even under strong tension by grabbing the lock loop and pulling the free end back through. Keep pulling, and the remaining loop disappears, the knot is untied and the rope is free.

Another way of locking this knot (when the main part of the rope is standing clear) is to take the first formed loop and bend it around the standing part, pushing the loop under itself to form a doubled-rope half hitch around the standing part. The last formed half hitch will not tighten under strain on the standing part, and yet it keeps the original knot from slipping. To untie it easily, push the double loop back through and give a sharp tug on the end of the rope.

A third variation is to use a smooth dowel, toggle or belaying pin passed through the loop, which is snugged against it by pulling on the free end of the rope. Stress on the standing part of the rope may tighten the knot, but pull the pin from the loop and a tug on the free end of the rope frees everything.

**Caution:** When using any form of drop hitch, be sure the whipped ends of the rope to be pulled through are smooth and painted, and DO NOT have them a greater diameter than the ropes. Roll the *burned* ends while still soft on a hard surface, to keep the same smooth diameter as that of the rope.

I would also recommend as basic the *square knot, sheet bend* and the *bowline* which is only a looped sheet bend), *clove hitch, double half hitch* (which can be difficult to untie), the *timber hitch* (very easy to undo after heavy stress is relieved) and basic lashing and frapping. A Boy Scout or one of their handbooks will show them all to you in detail.

# MEAT POLES AND TRANSFER

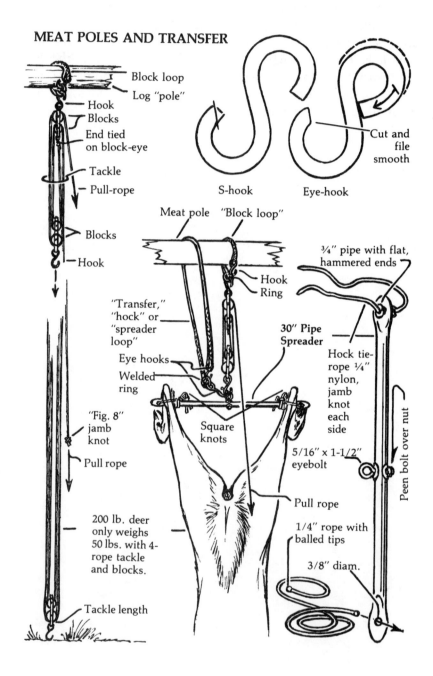

Block loop
Log "pole"
Hook
Blocks
End tied
on block-eye
Tackle
Pull-rope

S-hook

Eye-hook

Cut and
file
smooth

Blocks
Hook

Meat pole    "Block loop"

Hook
Ring

¾" pipe with flat,
hammered ends

"Transfer,"
"hock" or
"spreader
loop"

30" Pipe
Spreader

Hock tie-
rope ¼"
nylon,
jamb
knot
each
side

Eye hooks
Welded
ring

"Fig. 8"
jamb
knot

Square
knots

5/16" x 1-1/2"
eyebolt

Pull rope

200 lb. deer
only weighs
50 lbs. with 4-
rope tackle
and blocks.

Pull rope

1/4" rope with
balled tips

3/8" diam.

Tackle length

Peen bolt over nut

# THE GAMBREL JOINT OR HOCK

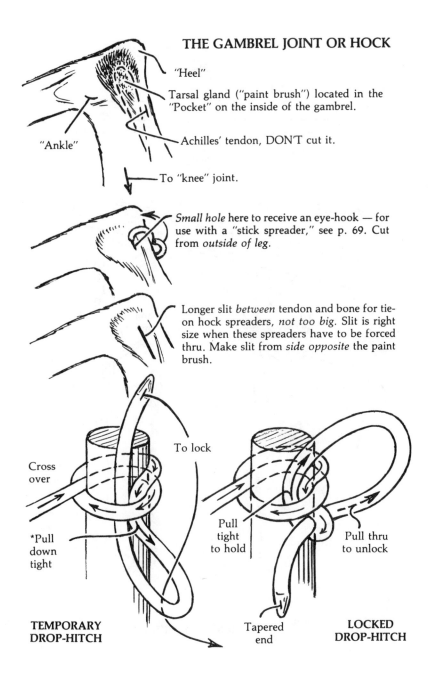

"Heel"

Tarsal gland ("paint brush") located in the "Pocket" on the inside of the gambrel.

"Ankle"

Achilles' tendon, DON'T cut it.

To "knee" joint.

*Small hole* here to receive an eye-hook — for use with a "stick spreader," see p. 69. Cut from *outside of leg.*

Longer slit *between* tendon and bone for tie-on hock spreaders, *not too big.* Slit is right size when these spreaders have to be forced thru. Make slit from *side opposite* the paint brush.

To lock

Cross over

Pull tight to hold

*Pull down tight

Pull thru to unlock

**TEMPORARY DROP-HITCH**

Tapered end

**LOCKED DROP-HITCH**

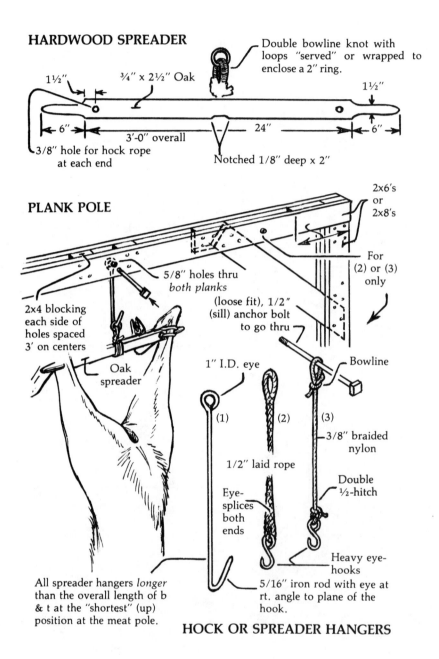

# HARDWOOD SPREADER

Double bowline knot with loops "served" or wrapped to enclose a 2" ring.

1½"

¾" x 2½" Oak

1½"

6"

3'-0" overall

24"

6"

3/8" hole for hock rope at each end

Notched 1/8" deep x 2"

# PLANK POLE

2x6's or 2x8's

5/8" holes thru *both planks*

For (2) or (3) only

2x4 blocking each side of holes spaced 3' on centers

(loose fit), 1/2" (sill) anchor bolt to go thru

Oak spreader

1" I.D. eye

Bowline

(1)

(2)

(3)

3/8" braided nylon

1/2" laid rope

Double ½-hitch

Eye-splices both ends

Heavy eye-hooks

All spreader hangers *longer* than the overall length of b & t at the "shortest" (up) position at the meat pole.

5/16" iron rod with eye at rt. angle to plane of the hook.

## HOCK OR SPREADER HANGERS

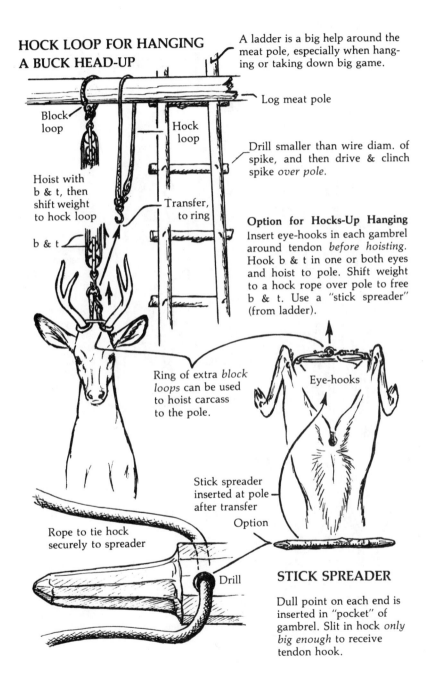

## HOCK LOOP FOR HANGING A BUCK HEAD-UP

A ladder is a big help around the meat pole, especially when hanging or taking down big game.

Log meat pole

Block loop

Hock loop

Drill smaller than wire diam. of spike, and then drive & clinch spike *over pole.*

Hoist with b & t, then shift weight to hock loop

Transfer, to ring

b & t

**Option for Hocks-Up Hanging**
Insert eye-hooks in each gambrel around tendon *before hoisting.* Hook b & t in one or both eyes and hoist to pole. Shift weight to a hock rope over pole to free b & t. Use a "stick spreader" (from ladder).

Ring of extra *block loops* can be used to hoist carcass to the pole.

Eye-hooks

Stick spreader inserted at pole after transfer

Option

Rope to tie hock securely to spreader

Drill

## STICK SPREADER

Dull point on each end is inserted in "pocket" of gambrel. Slit in hock *only big enough* to receive tendon hook.

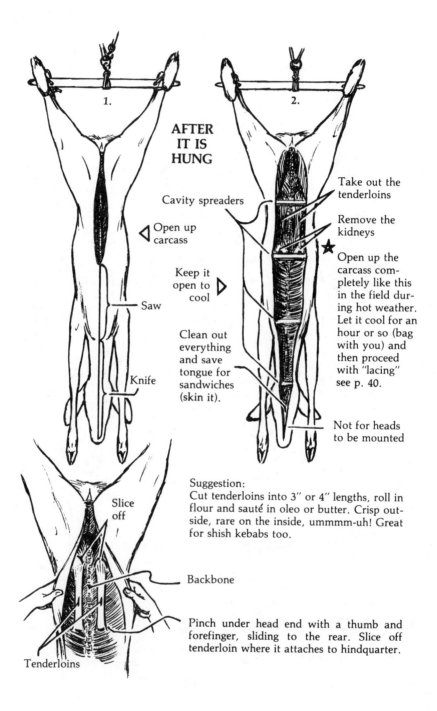

**AFTER IT IS HUNG**

1.

2.

◁ Open up carcass

Cavity spreaders

Keep it open to cool ▷

Saw

Knife

Clean out everything and save tongue for sandwiches (skin it).

Take out the tenderloins

Remove the kidneys

★ Open up the carcass completely like this in the field during hot weather. Let it cool for an hour or so (bag with you) and then proceed with "lacing" see p. 40.

Not for heads to be mounted

Slice off

Backbone

Tenderloins

Suggestion:
Cut tenderloins into 3" or 4" lengths, roll in flour and sauté in oleo or butter. Crisp outside, rare on the inside, ummmm-uh! Great for shish kebabs too.

Pinch under head end with a thumb and forefinger, sliding to the rear. Slice off tenderloin where it attaches to hindquarter.

70

## WALKING TRIPOD

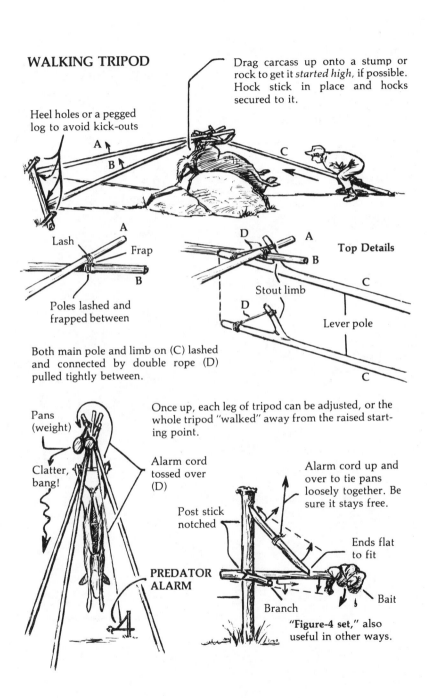

Drag carcass up onto a stump or rock to get it *started high*, if possible. Hock stick in place and hocks secured to it.

Heel holes or a pegged log to avoid kick-outs

A

B

C

Lash

Frap

A

B

Poles lashed and frapped between

D

A

B

**Top Details**

Stout limb

C

D

Lever pole

C

Both main pole and limb on (C) lashed and connected by double rope (D) pulled tightly between.

Pans (weight)

Clatter, bang!

Once up, each leg of tripod can be adjusted, or the whole tripod "walked" away from the raised starting point.

Alarm cord tossed over (D)

Post stick notched

**PREDATOR ALARM**

Alarm cord up and over to tie pans loosely together. Be sure it stays free.

Ends flat to fit

Bait

Branch

"**Figure-4 set,**" also useful in other ways.

## TEMPERATE WEATHER (not too warm)

1. Skin it
2. Cool it in a bag in the shade

Top of muslin bag open for loading, closes with drawstring or folds over and pins to keep out flies.

A half dozen utility sponges tied or pinned on, helps to keep bag wet longer. (Bunches of clean rags can be substituted.)

Legs cut off below hocks, and at "wrists" on forelegs.

**Procedure.** (Muslin bag works for hanging and travelling.) Soak it and press out excess water before pulling it over carcass.

Soak sponges or rags and secure them to bag in dripping condition.

Hang bag in shady and breezy place where predators won't get at it.

Bag stays in camp or car until needed for hanging and cooling.

Allow width and length to accommodate a big racked buck.

Both ends squared and cut full.

Zipper belly side

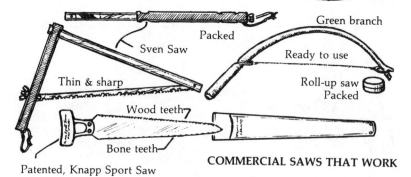

Packed
Sven Saw

Green branch

Ready to use

Thin & sharp

Roll-up saw
Packed

Wood teeth

Bone teeth

**COMMERCIAL SAWS THAT WORK**

Patented, Knapp Sport Saw

## UNBLEACHED MUSLIN
## TRAVELLING BAG

1/8" braided nylon cord in hem tightens and ties around hind legs.

(Allow for a good rack)

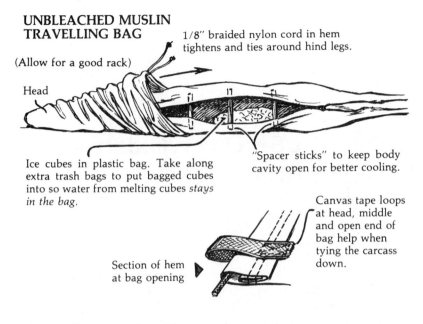

Head

Ice cubes in plastic bag. Take along extra trash bags to put bagged cubes into so water from melting cubes *stays in the bag*.

"Spacer sticks" to keep body cavity open for better cooling.

Canvas tape loops at head, middle and open end of bag help when tying the carcass down.

Section of hem at bag opening ▶

## PACKING "QUARTERED" MEAT requires extra attention

1.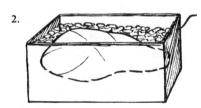

Carefully wipe down meat and wrap it in cheesecloth or clean sheeting.

2.

Pack in corrugated cartons and completely surround it with insulating material. Crushed newspapers work O.K. Wrap all in plastic sheeting and pack in ice.

### "BLISTER WRAP"

3. Use plenty of insulation *on top* of the iced boxes. Tie tarp over and provide for adequate drainage for the melt water.

CHAPTER 6

# AND THERE'S MORE WORK
# TO DO AT HOME

Instead of going directly home from deer camp and finishing the work at hand, some hunters cannot resist the temptation of taking the deer over to show Cousin Jack, and then Uncle Charlie, and then to the V.F.W. (that stop alone is very time-consuming). I'm sure some deer go by the board just being shown off all around the county.

## Final Hanging

After or during the accolades at home, the deer should be hung again, usually in a protected spot like the garage or barn. Space at the freezer locker may have to be rented if the weather is warm. In any event, the hide should be stripped from the carcass as soon as it finds a resting place, unless the job was done earlier.

How long the meat should hang before it is cut up is a personal matter. I'm not one to let it age until the meat turns as dark as an old crow's, and I don't want it to freeze and thaw either. In cold weather, a few days to a week at most from the time of kill is long enough to let even an old buck hang, according to my way of thinking.

The time is pegged even closer in a technical report on mule deer from the Agricultural Experiment Station of the University of Wyoming in Laramie. Although talking strictly about mule deer, it raises many valid points that probably could and should be applied generally to white-tailed deer as well.

On the point of aging, a careful, controlled testing — *two weeks was too long*. "Seven days at 38° F. may have been sufficient aging time to make all deer acceptable in tenderness."

In addition, it is probable that this *shorter* aging period would improve texture of the meat. Less weight loss due to carcass shrinkage, less trimming loss, less bacterial growth on the surface of the carcass, and less bacterial growth in gunshot areas are also advantages of a shorter aging period. Some hunters complain that venison fat turns rancid after a few months in frozen storage. A shorter aging period will increase the time fat can remain in frozen storage without becoming rancid.

Other interesting areas of this Wyoming report settled several things for me:

Metatarsal glands were saved from deer and placed on top of beef roasts during cooking. Although a distinct odor was present during cooking, no differences between flavor of beef roasts with metatarsal glands and control beef roasts cooked in separate ovens were noted.

In general, most deer shot in warm weather and chilled outdoors will be tender *without* aging.

In another bulletin (513R) from the same source: "Big game of any species under one year of age requires no aging. Like pork and veal, young game is tender by nature."

In states like Vermont, where in good years as many as two thirds of the deer taken by hunters are only a year and a half old, little aging is needed or desirable to improve meat quality of these deer. By the time they are taken home, they can be cut up for consumption with pretty good assurance the meat will be top quality — if good dressing procedures are followed.

## Skinning

The skinning operation is important, and I'll go into the details of that now. Like the old cliche, "there are many ways to skin a cat," the same may be applied to any animal — including your deer — and the job can be as easy or as difficult as you make it.

I feel that a little extra time and care taken in this operation pays big dividends and saves time in the long run. I work to get the cleanest possible hide without slices or cuts in it. I don't try to set a new record for skinning a deer. Actually a deer is a lot easier to skin than many animals.

Faster methods will be covered for those who want to try them, but usually you can plan on a lot more time and trouble cleaning up the hide. Working on the hide is never as easy as when you have it anchored to the carcass. I try to do a neat skinning job so the hide, when free of the carcass, is just about ready for the salt. Now the details.:

If the head mount is *not* a consideration, you may hang your deer head-up or hocks-up. In either case, tie it securely with stout rope. You will need to pull down hard on the hide while the carcass hangs, and it doesn't help if everything tumbles down in the middle of the operation.


BLOCKS-AND-TACKLE*

Blocks-and-tackle can be put to good use if the deer can be hung from a high rafter, cross-pole or strong tree limb. You will need to be able to reach either the hocks or the head easily (depending on which end you have up), when standing on the floor. Don't make the work harder or dangerous by standing on a chair or ladder. Don't laugh — I have seen it done from both.

Start the actual skinning operation with the deer hung low enough to easily reach its uppermost parts. Chances are some of the deer will be resting on the floor or the ground, and later the moist green hide will fall to the floor. Spread papers or an old sheet or blanket under the deer to keep things clean and save time.

The blocks-and-tackle make possible the easy raising of the carcass as the work proceeds. No matter how the deer is hung, you work down as you proceed.

Whether the head is to be mounted or not, I prefer to hang the deer hocks up;* then I do not have to shift the deer after the skinning operation. I can proceed to the splitting of the carcass and the meat cutting without losing time. But since some prefer to skin the carcass with the deer hung by its head, we'll proceed that way first.


THE DEER HANGING BY ITS HEAD*

(This deer won't have its head mounted.) Begin the skinning operation by making a cut through the hide with a sharp blade completely around the neck. Part or lift the hair ahead of the knife, and cut behind the ears close to the skull. If the throat was not opened earlier, cut a straight line down the center of the throat joining the neck cut with the open belly cut. Make all these cuts shallow — just through the hide to the white tissue layer right under it.

Return to the neck cut. Where it forms a corner with the vertical cut down the throat, pinch that corner of hide between a thumb nail and index finger, working your blade under it to separate it from the neck.

Getting the skinning operation started *right* is most important. You want a clean, fat-free, meat-free hide when you are done without cuts or sliced thin spots in it. Be sure you are in the correct layer. When the free corner of hide is pulled, you should see thin white tissue stretching between the carcass and the hide. The tissue stretches and pulls apart quite easily. This is the layer you want to stay in throughout the skinning operation.

Skinning is mostly pulling or pushing the hide from the carcass. The knife is used only where the tissue holds tight. A light drag with a rather dull, serrated blade across the stretched tissue breaks it down and frees the hide. If fat or red muscle in a thin sheet begins to pick up on the hide as it is worked, use a sharp blade carefully to pare or shave the fat or meat from the hide where it starts to adhere. Pull the fat or meat away until the white tissue shows again. Then, by working the blade under the flap you've made, you can continue in the tissue layer.

Work the hide free all around the neck below the neck-cut. When a couple inches of loose hide can be rolled down, grab a handful, skin-side inside your hand, and pull down. Use both hands, but keep watching for a pick-up of fat or muscle sheet. Work the finger tips or the thick part of the palm into the tissue line as each new handful of hide is grasped. Concentrated pressure

— the pad of a thumb against the hide immediately adjacent to the tissue line joining hide and carcass — often is sufficient to free a stubborn area. Continue down the neck until the shoulders are reached.

Now make a cut completely around the "wrist joint" above the foot on each foreleg. These cuts can be made just through the hide, or the legs can be severed through the joints at this time. If you want to save the lower legs for making a gun rack later, cut higher on the foreleg and saw through the bone. (See p. 50 for details.)

Next, cut through the hide on a straight line, down the inside of each leg, to the belly cut. Again start at a corner, this time at the wrist, and work the hide free of both forelegs. Proceed down the carcass.

You may want to raise the carcass when the body is half skinned to make the last of the work go easier. Cut around each hind leg on the rump side just up from the "paint brush" in the hock joint. Join the hock cut to the belly cut with a straight-line cut made down the *back* and inside of each hind leg. Keep these cuts angled toward the anus, staying in the area of the shorter, smooth white hair on the inside of the thighs. A somewhat better square-out of the hide results than when the line is made down the *middle* of the inside of the leg.

Skin out the legs and around the back, freeing the hide all around the tail bone when you come to it. Push back enough of the hide at the base of the tail to enable you to grasp the bone firmly in one hand. With the other hand, grasp the sizeable knob created by the hide rolled back over the tail bone and force it outward against an inward pull on the tail bone.* The tail bone will pull out, leaving a long thin void within the tail. Cut off the tail skin neatly. Fill its narrow pocket with table salt and hang it butt-up to dry. Anyone who ties flies for fishing will appreciate having it for making "bucktails," bass bugs or "muddler" flies.

A brief pull or two and the hide is completely free of the carcass.

To proceed to the meat-cutting operation, you have to take the carcass down and turn it end for end, hanging it by the hocks. It is an extra operation and that is why I prefer hocks-up from the start.

## THE DEER HUNG HOCKS-UP*

Simply reverse the procedure starting with the hock-cuts, skin the hind legs, work around the back and treat the tail the same way. Soon the hide at both sides of the belly cut will be hanging down. Continue down the carcass to the shoulders. Raise the carcass. Make the wrist cuts. Skin the forelegs and finish at the head.

## WHEN THE HEAD IS TO BE MOUNTED*

The deer *should be hung hocks-up* with the spreader in place, as covered earlier. Hang the deer high enough so the head will be a foot or two off the floor. Place the front feet in more or less natural positions spread apart on the floor with the head hanging over them, midway between them. This positioning is important to keep the deer aligned properly, as well as to steady it as it hangs.

There should be no opening at the throat until *after* the skinning operation is completed. The hide should be intact from the underside of the lower jaw to the back of the brisket.*

You now are ready to proceed with the first step when a head mount is desired, establishing the *cape-line*.* This line determines where the cut (just through the hide), will be made to provide the taxidermist enough hide for the neck or shoulder mount you want. Be sure you have *enough* hide for the cape. Plan for a little extra. The front of the neck on a finished mount usually will be longer than the back — an exception: a low head mount, as when a deer is sneaking along.* When a *shoulder mount* is the end goal, the cape-line should be even fuller.* Check the diagrams (p. 88) and you will see why.

A trick that works well to get an even cape-line is to push common pins through a string and into the hide at fairly close intervals to hold the string on a predetermined line.* Leave extra string where you start at the center of the back for tying with the other end later. Circle the neck or body where you think the line should go, lifting the hair and pushing the string into the valley between the raised hair and the smooth-lying body hair above the line. Stand back and check it. Keep the line even on both sides. Make adjustments as needed until you are satisfied.

Pin the string in place about every three inches. Tie the ends of the string together at the back of the neck. Now lift the string a little at a time, maintaining the part of the hair and cutting through the hide as you go. Remove a pin and extend the cut to the next pin until the ends of the cut meet at the back.

With the cape-line cut completed, abandon the head and neck portion for the time being. Spread papers or an old sheet or blanket under the deer to keep things clean. Then lower the deer so you easily can reach the hocks while standing on the floor or ground. Proceed with the skinning as outlined earlier, beginning at the hocks and working down. Free the hide at the cape-line and put it aside. We'll get back to it before long.

Now, you probably will want to raise the deer up high again. You may, however, want to cover a table or work bench instead of the floor and finish the job with the carcass lying waist high. The important thing is to be sure the head and neck are aligned properly in a straight line before making these "one-shot" recommended cuts.

If the carcass is partially frozen or muscles are set and holding the neck askew or the head cocked, twist and massage the carcass until the head and neck do line up.

Use the well-honed, down-pointed blade of your Stockman's Knife, if you have one, to make these cuts. Check the diagrams* to get the procedure clearly in your mind. Begin at a point 45 degrees inward and to the rear of an antler. Work the knife blade flat and carefully under the burr of the antler and, with a twist, lightly cut into the bony "peduncle,"* the base under the burr. Continue the cut straight down to the skull cutting through the hide. Once the skull is reached, repeat the operation on the other antler.

It is now good to establish the mid-point on the back of the head where you want the two cuts from the antlers to meet. Use two rulers or other form of straight edges,* placing one end of each at the antler cuts just made, and swing the other ends to form a 90 degree intersection on the median line on the back of the neck. Push a glass-headed pin or thumbtack into the hide at the point of intersection.

Then carefully part the hair in straight lines from each antler cut to this point. If you brush the hair to each side of the established line, using a hair brush and a little water, the hair will stay in place long enough to make the cut through the hide between the parted hair at each side. A little hair spray will do an even better job without causing problems.

Next, establish the midpoint on the back of the neck *at the cape-line*. Part the hair in an even line up the back of the neck to join the intersection of the angled cuts from the antlers. Once this has been accomplished, carefully cut through the line of exposed hide along the *back* of the neck to the cape line.

You now have made three cuts on the back of the head and neck: a cut angling from each antler join behind the skull on the median line of the back of the neck, the third extending down that median line from the intersection of the first two cuts to the cape-line. These combined cuts create a long-stemmed "Y" with its base at the cape-line and an upper branch terminating at each antler.* (Does only need the neck cut.*)

Return to the antlers now, and slowly push and twist the blade of your knife tightly up under the burrs of the antlers, carefully working the hide loose around the base of the antlers without cutting the hair. *A medium-sized dull screwdriver does a good job.* Push the blade flat, tight up under the burr and then use the burr itself as a pivot point, prying up on the handle.* Keep pushing in on the screwdriver all the time. Free the hide down each peduncle to the skull.

Now start a corner of hide at each side of the cut on the neck or back at the cape-line. Skin the neck down to the ears, letting the hide invert and roll down around the head. When the bulbous cartilage bases of the ears clearly show, work a sharp blade deeply *under* the bulbous portion until the skull is felt. Cut the ears off close to the skull.

Pinch the point of the scalp in front of the intersection of the cuts from the antlers. Work a blade under the point of hide, and pull it out, skinning under the scalp. Soon the hide can be rolled ahead of the antlers over the skull in a continuous roll about the head. It will appear that the roll has gone beyond the eyes and still they are covered by stretched membranes. This rather transparent covering will have to be pierced. Once that is done, the eyes can be viewed through the openings. Very slowly and *carefully*, cut the eyelids free from the inside, being careful not to slice or otherwise damage the lids. *Be aware that the skin in these areas sometimes will be doubled over.*

The next point for concern will be the angle of the mouth at each side. Study the situation before cutting. Cut the hide inside the lips close to the teeth along the gum-line. *Again be careful of thin, doubled-over hide.*

The final problem area is the nose. Leave the skinning of the nose for the taxidermist. When you reach the soft cartilage of the nostrils cut through it well back on the skull, and leave it attached to the nose pad. Slide the blade along the top of the upper jaw freeing the hide at the lip-line below the nose pad. The skinning for your trophy mount is done. Don't try to trim away excess meat or cartilage at the ears, eyes, lips or nose. And *don't spare the salt* in those areas.

Check the neck skin to be sure all fat and meat have been cleaned from it. Inspect the edges carefully. Rub plenty of fine, dry table salt over all of the hide while it is green and moist. Spread it out smoothly and pour a continuous band of salt around the edge. Work toward the center. You cannot use too much salt; be generous. Roll or fold it loosely, edges flopped over with the bare skin inside. Put the head and cape section of the hide into a large, heavy paper bag with the open end folded over and rolled down to seal it. Put that bag into a cloth bag and get it to the taxidermist as soon as you can. If you have to postpone the trip, store it folded flat in a cool, dry place. After a week or so, hang it over a pole to drain and re-salt it to be sure.

You should cut the head off the carcass at the first joint of the backbone. Wrap and freeze it, or keep it cold. Don't clean it. *Leave it as is.* When you take the hide to the taxidermist, take the head with you, whether your dear is a buck or a doe. Some taxidermists still make their own manikins, building on the actual skull. And most of them like to make some notes and take measurements from the skull with the flesh on it.

Be sure to salt well around the head, if it is to be left in the hide, and carefully rub the table salt into the neck skin, giving special attention to the edges of the hide. Take it all to the taxidermist as soon as you can.

SALTING THE HIDE

The main portion of the hide should be spread out flat and checked for pieces of fat or meat attached to it. Scrape or pare these off, being careful not to slice the hide. This is a good place to try the large "spoon-knife" if you haven't already done so. Push it under offending meat or fat. Pay particular attention to the edges of the hide.

Rub salt all over the "green hide" as soon as possible. Fine table salt should be used, since coarser commercial salt or rock salt crystals do not begin to have the surface area that the same amount of fine table salt has. Being small-grained, the table salt adheres much better, too. Salt draws out moisture to prevent rotting, and it must work completely through the hide. As it cures, the hair follicles tighten to better hold the hair.*

If some areas have dried out partially and the salt does not stick well to the hide, wet them with a cloth. Scrape the area back and forth with the blade of a knife straight up on edge and work it between your hands to soften it. Then pour on the salt and rub it in well. Don't be afraid of using too much salt or rubbing it too hard. A stiff-bristled floor-scrubbing brush can be used to advantage for the first salting. It is a good idea to salt and work the edges first, continuing inward until all is covered. Then salt again and rub it all over with the heel of your palm. Use special care in areas where wrinkles occur naturally. Spread it out flat and rub the salt in well.

The table below gives rule-of-thumb amounts of salt to be used for various sizes of animals. These amounts should be adequate but plan to keep extra (dry) salt sealed and stored in a dry place.

> Bear averaging 200 lbs. — up to 15 lbs.
> Moose — up to 25 lbs.
> Elk and caribou — up to 20 lbs.
> Deer, antelope, goat and sheep — up to 10 lbs.
> Fox, coyote and bobcat — up to 5 lbs.
> Capes and headskin only — about one half of the amounts
>     given
>                         (Check asterisk note on pg. 60).

Basic: Salt must be *dry*. Spread the salt and *rub it into* the *green hide;* don't wait. If in doubt, use more than needed, especially on head mounts around eyes, ears, lips, nose, edges and all openings in hide, natural or artificial (gunshot).

With the salting completed, fold in the edges to hold the brine that will form, and then loosely roll or fold the rest of the hide with the *hair outside.* Put it into a carton or tie it together loosely in a bundle. If the hide must be held more than a week, drape it over a pole and let it drain. Re-salt and fold again. If leather is to be the end result (hair off), store the salted hide in a cool, dry place until you can take it to a taxidermist, or until you are ready to tan the hide yourself. **Caution:** Don't leave curing hide in the sun or where porcupines can get to it — other wild opportunists like salt too!


## SKINNING INNOVATIONS

Traditional skinning practices now have been covered, but there are few things that can't stand some improvement. On the other hand, doing things *differently* doesn't always prove to be doing things *better.* Here are a couple innovations you might try anyway, neither original with the author:

Since skinning a deer is largely pushing or pulling the hide to separate the tissue between hide and carcass, a *skinning paddle\** may be of help. Basically, it is a lever used to pry the hide from the carcass.

Generally the paddles were handmade from ash wood. Various sizes could be used for skinning different animals, but I doubt their value for anything other than deer. The handle provides the leverage, working in conjunction with a smooth, broad base on which the tool pivots against the carcass. The opposite end, close to the pivot, is a smooth, rounded blade that makes contact with the hide. By pushing the flat blade into the tissue line, holding the hide pressed against the working blade and pumping up and down on the handle (much like the working of a manually operated can opener), the hide is continually lifted and the paddle advanced for new purchases on the hide.

A more recent way to accomplish the same feat is by the use of a small hard ball — a wooden one, a hard rubber hand-ball or a golf ball. Start the hide from the carcass in the tissue layer, and make a pocket into which the ball is forced. By grabbing the ball* firmly from the hair side of the hide, it can be shoved, manipulated and rolled over the carcass. Each movement or new grasp of the ball tends to stretch and break down the tissue ahead of the ball, as it is forcibly advanced, separating the hide from the carcass. Give it a try!

# Be Your Own Butcher

Now that we have covered the handling of a deer from the woods to the tanner or taxidermist, the only thing left is the butchering of the meat. Many hunters have a commercial butcher do the work, and when they get their deer back it is all neatly wrapped, nicely marked and frozen. But a lot of hunters do their own butchering, which can be learned quite well, for all practical purposes, from a book.

Check the layouts of the major beef and lamb cuts and my interpolation for butchering deer.* Between all of those you should be able to home-butcher any deer, moose or sheep you might take. If you should have an odd cut or two that do not quite match the pictures, what difference does it really make? You can write a note to yourself on that package, and everything will work out fine. When I first started, I used to have occasional wedge-shaped packages with such notes as "Enough for Penny and a couple kids when I'm away" or "A shoulder that didn't go so well." In time, with a little practice, my work improved.

The first pig I butchered provided the thickest pork chops we will ever see. I cut *between* the ribs instead of cutting in a line through them. They were great eating, but we didn't get very many.

## SPLITTING THE CARCASS

The logical first step in butchering is to split the carcass vertically (making "sides" of the meat—. Take a 10-point (ten teeth to the inch— crosscut carpenter's handsaw and scour it in hot soapy water. Rinse it well and dry it. You will find it will make a fine meat saw. A 16-point cross-cut works even better.

The carcass is hanging hocks up and the tail has been cut off close to the body. Stand in front of your hanging deer facing the open body cavity. Cut with your knife through the center of the muscle overlying the pelvic arch to expose the center of the bone.

Use the ten-point crosscut saw to cut through the middle of the arch. Now line up the tip of the saw with the center line of the exposed backbone where the tail was cut off. Start the saw cut down through the backbone using the sawn pelvic arch as a guide at each side from the front. Once through the pelvis, eyeball your saw cut straight down the middle of the inside exposed backbone. Cut all the way down through the neck. Now you have your deer halved vertically with each half still hanging by a hind leg.

At this point I take down one of the halves and lay it on a covered table, counter or bench to complete the finish cuts of meat. Arrange your side of meat according to the diagrams that follow. Then make the major cuts* with knife and saw. Continue by making the desired individual cuts* for freezing by working each of the major chunks to completion.

BONING

Some home-grown butchers bone all their meat, and you may want to give that a try for it certainly takes less space in the freezer. Boning only demands common sense, but you will find that the work goes easier if you keep the knife more or less parallel with the bone being removed. I don't particularly care for a lot of boned and rolled roasts, however, so I usually vary it. I bone and roll a few cuts, leave at least one half rib section or "rack" for chops (which I saw out as we want them while they are frozen), slice off a fair number of steaks, cut a few rump roasts—and we like hamburg. I blend the fat-free meat for hamburg with a good grade of ground beef suet. Salt pork is also used, but it will not hold its quality very long when it is frozen. Amounts of fat added vary with individual preference, but one unit of beef suet or pork fat to five of lean venison is a good average for a start. Double the pork fat for fresh venison sausage.

In one way venison is like lamb, or worse. All meat from the deer family has to be eaten while it is quite warm or fat congeals on your teeth — not so great! I love venison, but I trim off *all of the fat* and substitute some other kind.

It is generally agreed that the neck of a deer makes the finest mincemeat possible, but it makes a lot of it, so I use a good deal of the neck in hamburg.

Another thing I do, especially since the advent of the crockpot, is to cut up stew meat from what could be a good boned shoulder roast. We rate a good old-fashioned stew right up with the steaks and chops. Each one-half to three-quarter-inch cube of stew meat is carefully trimmed. Caution: Carrots and cabbage can come on too strong in a venison stew. I put them in, but not too much of either.

Of all the cuts, the shoulder perhaps gives the most trouble; there is no graceful way to carve a shoulder roast (bone in) at the table. Either bone it and roll it into a roast, make a cushion roast of it (boned), or cut it into cubes for stew. When *you* butcher your own meat, you can afford to take time to trim out all coarse membrane, cartilage and fat as well as the bone. (The butcher cannot take that time.) Thus, the meat you butcher is noticeably better for the extra effort.

## A FEW FINAL SUGGESTIONS

I mentioned earlier cutting chops of even thickness from a rack that is frozen, since it is much easier. After enough for the first meal has been taken, cut up the rest of the rack and wrap meal-sized portions of chops to be put back into the freezer.

Steaks can be cut more easily and evenly if the chunk is thoroughly chilled first, 36-38 degrees Fahrenheit (3-4 degrees Celsius). The cold meat is firmer and handles much better.

If you have a small home freezer, it is a good idea to box most of the wrapped packages and store them in a cold place like an unheated garage. Freeze only small lots, so you will not overload the freezer with unfrozen meat. In other words, fewer packages will freeze much quicker — important for quality meat. When those are frozen, put in some more until all are frozen.

An alternative, which I use, is to take all of the packages to the freeze locker in several small boxes. I have them quick-freeze the lot for a nominal charge. Then I bring everything home at one time and load my freezer with the hard frozen meat.

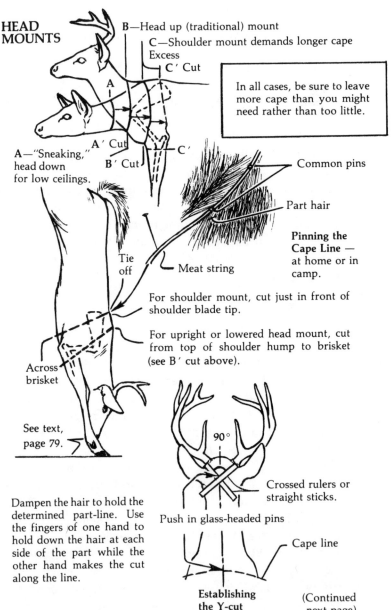

## HEAD MOUNTS

B—Head up (traditional) mount

C—Shoulder mount demands longer cape

Excess

C′ Cut

A

In all cases, be sure to leave more cape than you might need rather than too little.

A′ Cut

A—"Sneaking," head down for low ceilings.

B′ Cut

C′

Common pins

Part hair

**Pinning the Cape Line —** at home or in camp.

Tie off

Meat string

For shoulder mount, cut just in front of shoulder blade tip.

For upright or lowered head mount, cut from top of shoulder hump to brisket (see B′ cut above).

Across brisket

See text, page 79.

90°

Crossed rulers or straight sticks.

Dampen the hair to hold the determined part-line. Use the fingers of one hand to hold down the hair at each side of the part while the other hand makes the cut along the line.

Push in glass-headed pins

Cape line

**Establishing the Y-cut**

(Continued next page)

88

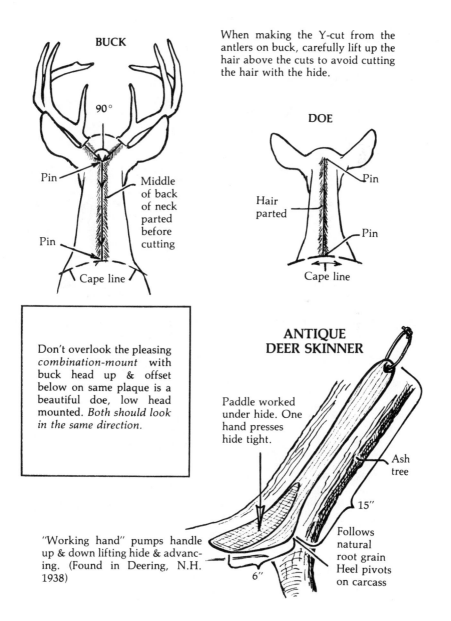

**BUCK**

When making the Y-cut from the antlers on buck, carefully lift up the hair above the cuts to avoid cutting the hair with the hide.

90°

Pin

Middle of back of neck parted before cutting

Pin

Cape line

**DOE**

Hair parted

Pin

Pin

Cape line

Don't overlook the pleasing *combination-mount* with buck head up & offset below on same plaque is a beautiful doe, low head mounted. *Both should look in the same direction.*

**ANTIQUE DEER SKINNER**

Paddle worked under hide. One hand presses hide tight.

Ash tree

15"

"Working hand" pumps handle up & down lifting hide & advancing. (Found in Deering, N.H. 1938)

Follows natural root grain Heel pivots on carcass

6"

89

## SKINNING AROUND THE ANTLERS

Take
Your
Time!

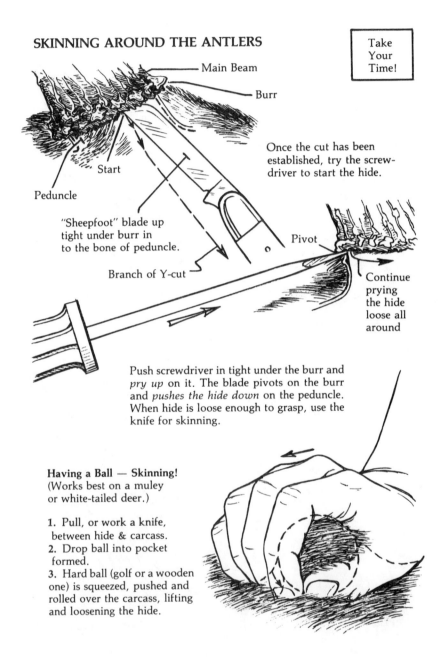

Main Beam

Burr

Start

Peduncle

"Sheepfoot" blade up
tight under burr in
to the bone of peduncle.

Branch of Y-cut

Once the cut has been
established, try the screwdriver to start the hide.

Pivot

Continue
prying
the hide
loose all
around

Push screwdriver in tight under the burr and
*pry up* on it. The blade pivots on the burr
and *pushes the hide down* on the peduncle.
When hide is loose enough to grasp, use the
knife for skinning.

**Having a Ball — Skinning!**
(Works best on a muley
or white-tailed deer.)

1. Pull, or work a knife,
between hide & carcass.
2. Drop ball into pocket
formed.
3. Hard ball (golf or a wooden
one) is squeezed, pushed and
rolled over the carcass, lifting
and loosening the hide.

# CHAPTER 7

# MOOSE AND OTHER
# BIG BRUTES

If you hunt *big* big game alone, be prepared to make some trips back and forth to base camp to get your trophy all in. Regulations for mandatory guiding these days, however, seldom allow such solo hunting. Really big, big game like caribou, wapiti, moose, grizzlies and even large black bears usually demand special planning from the very start.

## Special Considerations

Although basic field dressing is comparable to deer, the moose, for example, can be dressed easier if the legs are pegged out,* or lines are strung from each leg to nearby trees or pegs to steady the huge critter on its back. Take along an extra hank of rope. To move such a monster, the use of a *pole-and-pry** is nearly standard.

### HEAD MOUNTS

The "green" hide of large game is quite a load by itself. When a trophy head or shoulder mount is desired, the cape with the head in should be separated from the rest of the hide (see p. 41), and this will help to distribute the load better on the way out.

In most instances when brown bears, grizzlies, moose and comparable animals with large heads are to be mounted, and there is quite a distance to pack out the load, the head is skinned in the field. *Many* measurements should be taken on the site and noted down for the taxidermist. He can supply you with diagrams and measurement lines to make for different species, before you start out on your trip.

With large antlered animals, the skull is sawed horizontally through the eyes* *after* the measurements* are written down. The resulting skull plate attached to the antlers is packed out, and the rest of the skull is left for the carrion eaters. That saves quite a load.

Bear heads and necks sometimes are left for scavengers, and that saves a lot of weight. If a menacing open-mouth mount is your wish, however, you had better take the head in the hide. Skin it and boil the skull clean back at camp. Again *note down the measurements** as soon as the skin is removed.

**Moose present some special problems.** These deer are *big*, big game. You practically need a horse just to carry the large hide.

When a moose head is going to be mounted, there are a few things to remember: After you have carefully skinned the head, take the measurements from different points on the head as shown. You could do a lot worse than tracing the diagram to take with you, just in case. A retractable, six-foot steel rule, a ballpoint and the diagram to fill in, all sealed inside a plastic sandwich bag in your day pack, will prove very worthwhile and save time.

The thick lips and the overhanging, bulbous nose of a moose need special attention. As soon as you can get at it, lay the hide of the head skin-side up. Slide a smooth board or flat stone inside the inverted skin under the portion of the lip to be worked, to provide an even, firm working surface. Hold that section of the lip you are working stretched tight over your board or stone. Then carefully scrape, cut and trim the big lips, working against the hard surface, outward toward the edge of the lip. Be careful not to slice the hide or nick the soft edges. Remove all the gristle and muscle you can. Then rub in plenty of dry salt immediately.

Another point worth mentioning: Note down the length of the *bell,* that piece of pendulous hide hanging under the neck, though occasionally a moose may not have one.

Check beforehand with your taxidermist whether or not he will need the skull, and perhaps *more important,* ask if you can cut the skull plate* off horizontally through the eyes *and vertically down the median line* between the antlers. If he is willing to set them in epoxy on the manikin, it will make for much easier field packing and subsequent transportation. If you plan to split the antlers,* *first be sure to make several notes* on the measurements across from different tines, and diagram the measurements.

**Caution:** If you wish to have your head scored by Boone and Crockett, or officially listed for other records. DON'T SPLIT THE ANTLERS APART, or they will be disqualified.

**Other big game** such as caribou, white sheep and mountain goats all have hair that's more or less white. The cleaner you keep it during the dressing, the easier the work will be for you or the taxidermist later. If blood does get on it, wash if off with plenty of cold water as soon as possible. Dry it with a rag if you have one, and fluff the hair.

Try to keep fat and grease off it when you roll or fold the hide. Wash and scrub soiled parts well while it is fresh — after you get it into camp. Carefully pare off all fat, then clean it again if necessary. Rub the hair dry and fluff it. Then salt the hide well, as covered earlier.

For caribou, elk and other big game animals that have large racks, check the point under "Moose" about splitting the rack and Boone & Crockett scoring.

BONING THE MEAT

If field conditions and proper planning permit it, you can lighten your load by boning the meat, a quarter at a time. Plan to take enough large muslin bags to accommodate the meat to be packed out. Bone only what is to be packed out immediately. Return to the site, bone out some more, and so on. Big game also means big work!

Really big animals usually are quartered,* no matter who's on hand to help, and if I intend to pack out a big one, my "quartering" will be in *six or seven pieces*, not four. Skinning and quartering also makes possible better cooling of large chunks of meat. Quartering calls for a good saw being carried in the day pack for such adventures. A belt axe can be used as a poor substitute.

**A small meat saw** that will handle any job in the bone department is an important piece of equipment for field use. A pistol-grip hacksaw with a rather coarse blade will do the job, but I find the skeleton handle uncomfortable for heavy work, and solid plastic handles are heavier than need be in a day pack. Some guides tape rough-fitted pine handles on each side of a skeleton handle, but in use the blood and marrow soon befoul them. Why not plan ahead and some winter evening make a handle* to suit yourself and the job to be done?

Lightweight pine or basswood carves easily, stains well and lasts a long time. Draw file the metal pistol grip to flatten both sides. Then fit the rough-contoured wood slabs to each side of the grip. The more carefully the halves are fitted, the better the final job.

When you are satisfied with the fit, score (crosshatch) the fitted and abutting surfaces. Smear both sides of the metal grip and the insides of the fitted wood slabs with epoxy plastic steel. Position the handles on the grip and squeeze them together tightly by hand. Criss-cross a couple of heavy rubber bands over the assembled handle to hold it securely together until dry. Allow twenty-four hours for complete cure.

Remove the rubber bands and shape the handles to suit with a half-round mill file and fine sandpaper. When you are satisfied, try cutting a piece of wood with a blade positioned in the handle. Make any adjustments needed for comfort in use and you are ready for the finishing. You can be fancy, if you wish, and checker or groove the handles.

Depending on how the metal grip holds the blade in place, remove any threaded set screws and coat them lightly with plumber's joint compound or floor wax, but keep it off the wood when you replace the screws. Screw them back so they are flush with the grip. Wipe off any excess compound and lightly sand soiled areas.

Stain the wood with an oil-base, wiping stain to the color desired. Let it dry thoroughly. Then find a clean can that will hold the grip without too much to spare. Mix in it a sufficient amount of spar varnish cut 50-50 with turpentine. Stir it well and then put the grip into the solution, making sure all of it is covered, with some to spare to allow for its soaking into the wood.

After it has soaked for a couple days, wipe off the excess with a clean rag, and let it dry completely. Then give it a light sanding with 00 paper, or steel wool. Wipe all dust from it and give it two even coats of varnish, lightly sanding between coats. Spar varnish works fine, but polyurethane is even better. Push the blade partially into its slot, and hold the partially assembled saw by the blade in a vise to dry. Check in ten minutes to wipe off any excess varnish forming droplets. When it is hard dry, steel wool it lightly, and it won't get so slippery when wet.

If you make this, you will have a good lightweight saw for heavy-duty work the rest of your life — if you don't lose it — and it will be well worth the time spent in the making. If the blade gets dull, just put in a new one. Spiral wrap a narrow buckskin or cloth bandage around the blade, and it will pack easily without damage to other gear in the pack.

## Packing Out a Big Hide

Here is a brief story of a mountain goat hunt, so you can profit from my mistake:

I was hunting one time in Alberta when I got lucky and took a big old mountain goat. While I steadied the goat, my Indian guide, Frank Moberly — one of the finest I've known — caped and skinned the billy. We were in a blizzard, about 7,500 feet up on jumbled rocks. I hate to think what the chill factor was that day.

We skinned the tough old carcass and gave it a push. It rolled and tumbled all the way down to timber where the wolves could make use of it. Frank put the head and cape in a rucksack he had brought along. Lucky Frank, for I was caught without a pack frame.

I grabbed armfuls of "green," slippery hide and stumbled my

way down to shin-tangle until we got into a depression out of the wind. I had extra rope, and we made a horseshoe pack out of the hide. I have always hated a horseshoe pack* and, right or wrong, I have always blamed the British for inventing it.

It was our last day to hunt, and Frank had told me the night before that we would hunt "right" that day. We had *passed the horses* in the dark as we left camp in the morning, and had hiked a thousand miles.

Now, I had a heavy, long-haired hide — nearly a foot in diameter in places — fashioned into a loop with the ends tied together. I knew I had to carry it the same thousand miles back to camp. Every half hour or so, I'd duck my head and change shoulders. It was a great day — one I'll never forget — but I had sore shoulders for a week after. I learned my lesson that day — a pack frame (and I like one with a step on the bottom*) cannot be overrated for big game hunting.


BEARS ARE A LOT OF WORK

The bigger the bear is, the tougher the job. They drag *hard*. Most hunters try to line up a tractor or horse and stone boat beforehand so they will know where to call if they get a bear somewhere near civilization. If the weather is really cold, you would do well to make several trips and live to tell about it.

In the fall bears are fat, very fat, and even after careful skinning there is quite a lot of scraping on the hide to get the fat off.

Because of the fat, heavy hide, the very long dense fur, and thick chunks of meat in a bear, they are hard to cool in mild weather. In warm weather, it is nearly impossible to skin the bear fast enough, pack out the hide, and get it to the taxidermist before the hair starts slipping badly. If you want a good bearskin rug or mounted head, hunt late in the season when the chances are better for cold weather.

If you really want to know the sex of your bear, have a biologist look it over. It isn't as easy as you might think. A good many bear hunters call their bear a male if it is a big one. Or if it's smaller, they call it female.

One time I was with a game biologist examining a bear another hunter had shot. "Got a not-too-big female," the hunter said, a big friendly man. The biologist asked him how he knew it was a female. The hunter replied that he had found some teats. With a straight face, the biologist remarked, "The next time you take a shower, take a good look at yourself." It was a male. After mating season, it's not easy to tell.

If knowing the weight of your bear is important to you, arrange to have it transported in one piece to a set of heavy scales. Few people even come close when estimating the weight of a bear. They usually guess much too high.


## PRIORITIES

Don't kill yourself getting out your trophy. Most hunters past forty probably should *not hunt alone;* if they do, they should not try to get big game back to camp all by themselves, especially in one trip. (I don't always practice what I preach, but I think about it.)

Your big game brute has been field dressed, and there it lies in one big chunk of hide and carcass. What is most important to you? You have to establish your own priorities. Is the head most desired for a trophy mount? If it is, cape the hide and (with the head in or out) take that out on the first trip.

If the meat is all-important and the head is run-of-the-mill or of no particular importance, what meat do you like best — the saddle for chops or the hindquarters for steaks? The neck and fore-quarters are just about everybody's last choice. Whatever you decide, proceed to pack out what you want most. *But,* before you leave, legibly write or print your name, address and complete license numbers and letters from your license and the tag. Secure this duplicated license/tag to what you are leaving. Take the original tag with you, attached, and keep your original license with you, too. Leave a note saying you'll be back. Darned few hunters or wardens will bother a situation like that.

If you plan to use this procedure, what do you do with what is left at the kill site? If the game is big and you "quarter" it in six or seven pieces as suggested earlier, and if you planned right, you can bag each piece. But make sure a duplicate tag and the license infor-mation is left secured to *each,* with a brief note saying you'll be back. By the way, do you *always include a few sheets of paper and a soft pencil or ball point pen* in your field gear?

A lot of four-legged and winged creatures in puckerbrush country are looking for a free meal. Fortunately, they can eat only so much. Some of them have a nasty habit of carrying off what they can't eat, however, and this creates another problem.

**Protect the meat** from scavengers by scattering the separate chunks over a fairly small area, keeping them up high and hanging from a branch if possible. If a scavenger comes along, it probably will be content to work over one bag, if it can get it, and leave the rest if you aren't gone too long. In any case, you took out what you wanted most on the first trip, right?

The only Rocky Mountain sheep I ever shot or ate illustrates what can happen. I shot it late in the afternoon just above timberline in the Canadian Rockies. We had horses, so there was no problem getting it back to camp about dark. The sheep was promptly skinned, and the "rack" or rib section was broken out for "stick meat."

If you've never had stick meat, you can look forward to it. Opposing ribs (usually from meat freshly killed) are sliced off the rack between the rib bones, and the backbone then is sawed down the middle. The "stick" is the rib bone you hold while roasting the thick chop over the coals of a campfire. Dee-lish-shush! I was thoroughly introduced to stick meat that night.

Later on that evening, the big wrangler stood tall on his saddle (mounted on his horse), reached up and spiral-lashed the meat and hide inside burlap bags to a meat pole secured between two big straight pines that were clear of branches for twenty feet. The horizontal pole was well over his head as he stood there on top of his horse. We were camped in grizzly country, but grizzlies can't climb trees like black bears.

The next morning I woke to some loud cursing. From the tent flap I saw the wrangler staring up at the meat pole. Shreds of burlap and rope hung down — and that was all. Grizzlies may not be able to climb trees, but I learned from this episode that they can lift a hind leg and really push off on the rough bark well up a mature pine. With mighty lunges and overhand punches, a grizzly had broken everything loose. We found where most of the meat had landed, but that devil didn't leave a scrap for us. Good thing we had the stick meat the night before, or I might never have known the taste of mountain sheep.

One way to protect a single quarter (or camp food) in a bag when bears are a problem* is to tie the top of the bag together securely with one end of a long rope, and then toss the other end over the outer branches of a heavy limb high off the ground. Pull the bag up tight to the branch, much too high for a bear to reach from the ground. Then pull the free end of the rope to another tree nearby, a pole tree too small for a large bear to climb. Secure the rope around this tree as high as you can reach over your head. The system sort of divorces the bag from the tree trunks, and even black bears and fishers don't like to venture far out on small limbs.

I hate to even think about it, but sometimes a Homo sapiens type hunter may try to steal your game. Ninety-nine percent of the time, the robber is not a hungry or poor person who needs the meat for his family; usually he is a slob hunter without a conscience. He is greedy to begin with, and on such an ego-trip that he cannot face returning home emptyhanded. How he can get satisfaction from such stealing is hard for me to understand.

All you can do to foil him is to effectively hide the game to be left, and brush out your tracks to the area where it is concealed. Don't leave your trophy too near the kill site, and be sure each piece has your name, date of kill and license number on a note attached securely to it.

Today you often have to make a choice in the type of hunting you want. If you hunt in an area with considerable hunter density, chances are some of the other hunters will affect your hunt. You may find they spoil your hunt by blundering into your operation — spooking the game before you ever get near it — or just as easily they may jump game that blunders into you. More people in an area usually means more game moved — to be seen and shot — making for easier hunting. But you also may be damned with more slob hunters and the problems they create.

By choice I prefer the harder, deep woods hunting. The odds may not be so good for seeing as much game, since I have to be lucky enough to be at the right place at the right time on the animals' own terms or jump them myself. But that's all right with me. The greatest satisfaction for me is sport-hunting that works out on a one-on-one basis. Under such conditions, I still may lose all or part of my prize to *wild* robbers. I'll take that chance, for I would rather they outsmart me than a two-legged robber.

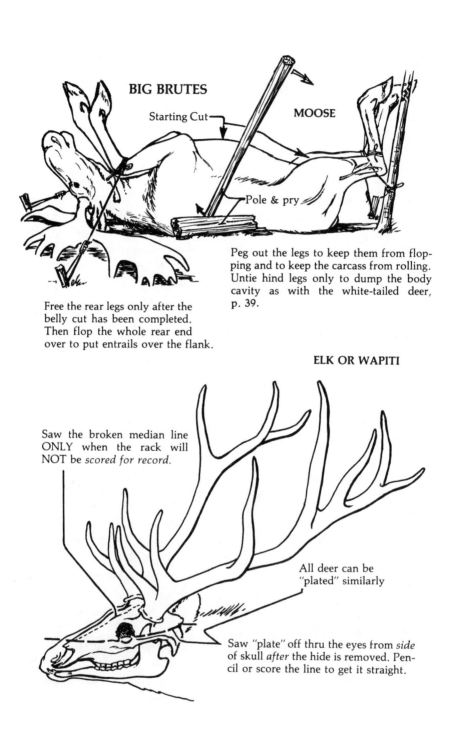

# BIG BRUTES

Starting Cut

**MOOSE**

Pole & pry

Peg out the legs to keep them from flopping and to keep the carcass from rolling. Untie hind legs only to dump the body cavity as with the white-tailed deer, p. 39.

Free the rear legs only after the belly cut has been completed. Then flop the whole rear end over to put entrails over the flank.

**ELK OR WAPITI**

Saw the broken median line ONLY when the rack will NOT be *scored for record*.

All deer can be "plated" similarly

Saw "plate" off thru the eyes from *side* of skull *after* the hide is removed. Pencil or score the line to get it straight.

From *North American Big Game* — a book of the Boone and Crockett Club compiled by the Committee on Records of North American Big Game — Charles Scribner's Sons.

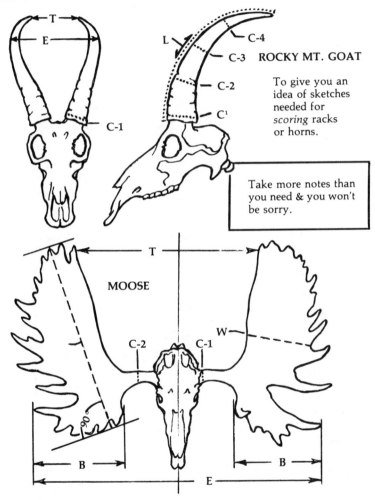

ROCKY MT. GOAT

To give you an idea of sketches needed for *scoring* racks or horns.

Take more notes than you need & you won't be sorry.

MOOSE

Perhaps your taxidermist has sketches of measurements he needs to set up "your" particular trophy, girth measurements, leg lengths for full mounts, and much more. You would do well to discuss all of this with him *before* going on that special hunt.

101

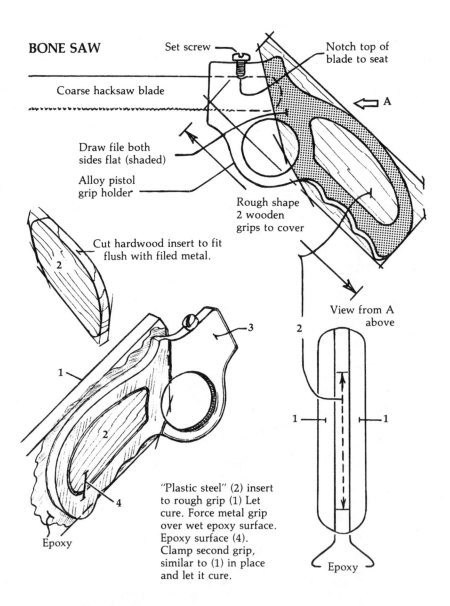

**BONE SAW**

Set screw

Notch top of blade to seat

Coarse hacksaw blade

⇐ A

Draw file both sides flat (shaded)

Alloy pistol grip holder

Rough shape 2 wooden grips to cover

Cut hardwood insert to fit flush with filed metal.

2

View from A above

2

3

1

1 ⟶ ⟵ 1

2

"Plastic steel" (2) insert to rough grip (1) Let cure. Force metal grip over wet epoxy surface. Epoxy surface (4). Clamp second grip, similar to (1) in place and let it cure.

4

Epoxy

Epoxy

Final shaping for comfortable hand-fit is done with knife and finished with ½-round mill file and 00 sandpaper.

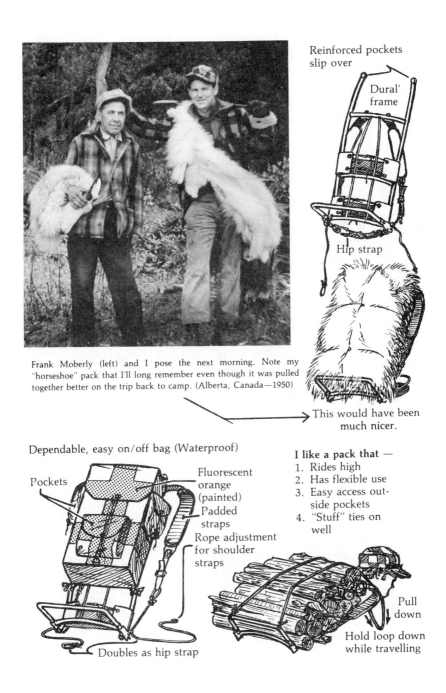

Reinforced pockets slip over

Dural' frame

Hip strap

Frank Moberly (left) and I pose the next morning. Note my "horseshoe" pack that I'll long remember even though it was pulled together better on the trip back to camp. (Alberta, Canada—1950)

This would have been much nicer.

Dependable, easy on/off bag (Waterproof)

Pockets

Fluorescent orange (painted)

Padded straps

Rope adjustment for shoulder straps

Doubles as hip strap

I like a pack that —
1. Rides high
2. Has flexible use
3. Easy access outside pockets
4. "Stuff" ties on well

Pull down

Hold loop down while travelling

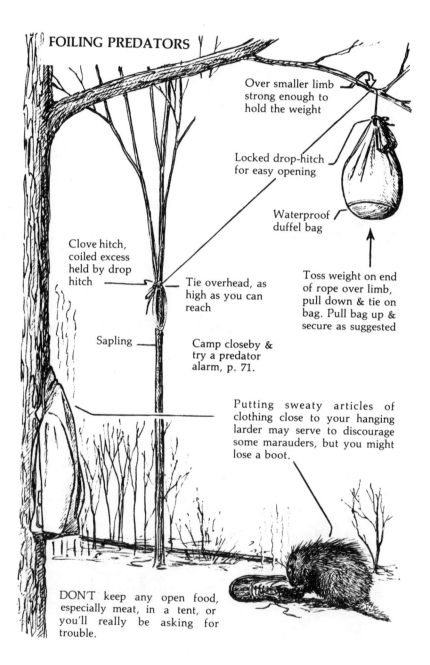

## FOILING PREDATORS

Over smaller limb strong enough to hold the weight

Locked drop-hitch for easy opening

Waterproof duffel bag

Clove hitch, coiled excess held by drop hitch

Tie overhead, as high as you can reach

Toss weight on end of rope over limb, pull down & tie on bag. Pull bag up & secure as suggested

Sapling

Camp closeby & try a predator alarm, p. 71.

Putting sweaty articles of clothing close to your hanging larder may serve to discourage some marauders, but you might lose a boot.

DON'T keep any open food, especially meat, in a tent, or you'll really be asking for trouble.

# SECTION II

# SMALL GAME
# AND FURBEARERS

# CHAPTER 8

# TRAPPING:
# THE ONE-TO-ONE SPORT

The oldtime trapper's gnarled, chapped hands, like the oversized thumbs of the tinsmith, were sure evidence of his trade — of bitter cold on lonely traplines, night work preparing the pelts, the long, tortuous travel to distant fur markets, and the tedious hours spent preparing for the next season.

But today trapping is a seasonal business, and usually only a part-time occupation. White collar workers, policemen, carpenters, firemen, farmers, all sorts of people, are "vacational" as well as vocational trappers. And while providing healthy outdoor recreation for thousands, collectively, trapping is still big business.

Unfortunately, trapping does not provide a dependable income for the work involved. Thus it is not nearly so dependable as hunting in the management of wildlife populations — but it helps. Many things affect the fickle fur market. When raw fur prices go down, they really drop. Then trapping pressure falls off drastically, and it does not do its job. Annual production of the fur-bearers builds populations to problem levels if prices stay down.

To give an idea how much prices fluctuate, a good fox pelt brought fifty cents in the mid-Sixties, and forty dollars in the multi-million dollar fur market of the early Seventies. Even though demand varies greatly, *wild fur* is of consistently better quality than *farmed fur* and consistently brings higher prices.

Years ago, trapping was a major force for exploration, not only in Vermont, going back to Samuel de Champlain, but also through the Midwest, along the Mississippi, on the Pacific coast, and throughout Alaska and Canada. Russia used to send her ships to gather furs of the sea otter off the Alaskan coast and the Aleutian Islands. In those days the sea otter's range extended well down the Pacific coast. Over-exploitation nearly exterminated these quizzical, bewhiskered "old men of the sea." But with protection the otters came back strongly. Off Amchitka in the Aleutians, World War II fliers could watch their playful antics right off the dock. Anchored by strands of kelp around them, they cracked sea urchins against flat rocks that they had brought up from the ocean floor. Their heavy fur kept out the cold as they lay on their backs, rocked by the ocean swell, casually eating from their chests while battle planes took off and landed nearby.

Now the sea otters are established once again along the California coast — so many, in fact, that abalone fishermen continually battle to get their numbers reduced, for the otters like abalone, too.

In the Northeast, the fisher (sometimes called the "American sable" because of its fine fur coat), also has made a remarkable comeback from near extinction. When the great flocks of Merino sheep went west from early New England to better grazing on the Plains, farms and pasture had largely claimed the land of Vermont, and only a quarter of that state remained in forest. Today only a quarter is *not forested.*

Trees had been cut so ruthlessly for the log drivers, making pasture, crop lands and potash that there was no place left for the forest animals. They had disappeared with the forest. But some managed to hold out in remote corners too difficult or uneconomical to harvest with saw and axe. Much of northern Maine remained in timber, and the fisher found some haven there. Gradually the forest encroached on the Vermont farmlands, unworked because of a steady exodus from the farms to higher-paying jobs in southern New England. Now the forest again reigns supreme in the whole northern tier of states, and the fisher has worked its way back with the forest.

Wolves and mountain lions never will return to the East in numbers, probably, but the niche they left is being filled by a newcomer, the eastern coyote — and he is here to stay. He is larger than his western counterpart, and his dense fur coat, like that of the fisher, brings a high price for the trapper. Those tempting dollars provide incentive enough at present to keep both species in balanced coexistence with people. Even so, their presence here is greatly misunderstood, and spawns a good deal of controversy.

## Times Have Changed

When I was a youngster, I gave trapping a try. Money was short, I liked the outdoors, and a reason to be out in the pre-dawn hours when wildlife was still active was very appealing. When it came time for school, I had my animals carefully cooled for after-school skinning and had changed into my school clothes.

Some of the other boys had traplines too, but where we lived already was beginning to change to what later became suburbia. Skunks and muskrats were the usual species with only rare exceptions.

There were very few adult trappers in the area, and they were tight-lipped with their knowledge, for wringing dollars from the economy in the '30s was a very competitive game. Books were expensive, and those giving practical details about trapping were nearly nonexistent. We had to learn by trial and error.

Public concern for wildlife and the environment was still in the future. Frankly, my bungling and lack of know-how *did* bring about needless suffering, and before long I had sold my traps and found other ways to earn my money. Does that mean that today I am a staunch supporter of anti-trapping views? Not by a damn-sight!

The whole picture has changed drastically. I know that in the broad picture of wildlife welfare, trapping is an important — though sometimes imperfect — tool for managing wildlife in this overstocked world of people. I am thoroughly convinced that the relatively few animals that suffer through unskilled trapping, brought about by the likes of me as a youngster, are worth the large benefits gained by wildlife in controlled populations to fit the dwindling habitat. Wildlife suffers plenty under natural conditions, regardless of trapping.

Trappers, if only for their own survival, have organized and have made considerable improvements on the traps themselves, as well as in the techniques for taking animals humanely. Anyone interested in this sport — and it is that, and a lot of work — should find out about local and state trapping organizations. Learn the game and how to play it right. The thrill of being outdoors, in a sport where you meet the one-to-one challenge on the animals' home turf is still there. Furthermore, the service done to wildlife, the honest dollar made, and the pleasure and comfort provided others need not be cause for apologies or any inferiority complex.

Trapper organization publications help the novice today by providing details for proper sets and expanded knowledge of the species trapped. They update the oldtimer, too, by showing and explaining improved traps and methods. Good books on trapping also are listed and reviewed from time to time. In both Canada and the United States, governmental as well as private money is being used to develop new techniques and mechanical devices to make trapping more selective and humane.

As an indicator of the extent of this work, here is what is happening in Vermont: Last year in two widely separated areas, informal seminars were held on trapping properly, sponsored by a trappers' organization. Humane techniques, responsibilities of the trapper, and landowner rights and treatment were emphasized. The organization also has made a point of being involved in state fish and game matters. It supported the setting of a reasonable season for controlled protection of bobcats and foxes. Formerly both species could be taken year-round.

And currently the houndsmen and trappers, concerned about the future of the bobcat, are working with game biologists to adjust other seasons (at a potential loss in dollars and recreation to themselves) to have as many open seasons as practical end earlier and at the same time. In short, they are working together for positive benefits to wildlife, are policing their own ranks and are reducing the number of spoilers.

## Preparing Fur Pelts

You've already skinned your deer, on paper anyway. You'll remember it was opened down the belly, to make an "open" or "split" hide or skin — which is not to be confused with "splitting" a heavy hide to make it thin and more supple. In this real "splitting," a heavy skin such as cowhide is machine-separated *laterally* by a huge knife to make two thin, flexible pieces from the same hide. "Split horsehide" or "split cowhide" often are used in coats and jackets.

Medium-sized animals like the beaver, fox, bobcat, coyote and wolf — as well as small ones like the squirrel and rabbit — can be skinned in much the same way as a deer. The pelt may or may not be salted and is stretched to dry, held flat by toggling* it to a frame or tacking it to a board or piece of plywood.

Tradition and special uses for particular skins, however, dictate certain treatments for each for market. Beaver, for example, customarily have been "split" — the skins opened up the belly and kept flat. Large beaver skins are called *blankets.* Otter and small animals, however, rarely are split. They are "cased" — while foxes, bobcats and coyotes are treated either way. Check with local fur buyers to see how they want pelts handled.

A "case" or "cased" skin is *not* split down the belly. The cut is made across the rear end of the animal,* and the skin is inverted over the carcass until free of it. Thus an inside-out pocket or "case" is formed. Then the case is pulled over a shaped board or *drying frame,* * to keep the skin from shrinking while it dries.

Drying frames traditionally have been called "stretchers," and oldtime trappers really did stretch their skins on them, as tightly as they could, thinking they would get more for larger pelts. But current practice discourages excessive stretching and recommends only slightly stretching the skins. Pelts so treated are more receptive to later working, and the fur is more dense (more hairs to the square inch), making for a more resilient fur and bringing a better price.

Today, many fur buyers suggest that the trapper only skin the animal carefully, clean and shake out the pelt, and then loosely roll or fold it, fur in or out (according to the animal). The pelt then is put into a plastic or heavy paper freezer bag. The air is evacuated from the bag with a vacuum cleaner hose (with radiator wand on the end). The top of the bag is folded under to seal the partial vacuum, is folded over again and taped. It then is kept in a freezer until ready for the local fur buyer or home tanning. (The local buyer would rather get them frozen so *he* can prepare them properly himself for the big fur auctions. One buyer told me, "Some trappers wouldn't know how to treat fur if they trapped for a hundred years." The large commercial market at this time, however, will not deal in frozen furs.)

## Skinning Details

A good deal of the skinning procedure for making cased pelts from furbearing animals is similar to the details for skinning deer. However, deer are among the easiest of all animals to skin. The furbearers' pelts are much thinner and must be handled with greater care. Some, like the otter and coyote, demand much more work with the knife — the same small, folding knife used for the deer.

Medium-sized and small mammals can be skinned on a table or workbench quite satisfactorily, though not as easily as when they are hung by their hind legs. Simple ropes or rawhide thongs can be attached securely overhead to a ceiling crossbeam, and the hanging end of each is roll-lashed and secured around each hind leg of the animal.

A portable *set of chains* often is used,* especially when the animal's feet and lower legs are *not saved*, as with beaver and muskrat. Each of the two chains' ends has a strong, pointed hook which pierces the skin covering the void between the "heel bone," Achilles tendon and the gambrel (ankle) joint of each hind leg.

When the hind legs *are to be included* as part of the pelt, the skinning is started on the floor or on a table, the legs worked out through an abbreviated cut across the rear end of the animal — of sufficient length to allow later inverting of the skin over the carcass and the stretcher. Each hind leg is pulled out of its skin to the foot joint (to the toes on larger animals), and the joints are severed and salted. Then the skinned legs are held by the hooks, which are pushed through the *exposed* gambrels. The rest of the work is accomplished from the hanging position. (A rigid device is also shown for production skinning at home or in a trapline camp.)

A *spreader* dowel* of appropriate diameter and length is inserted between the chains to keep the legs spread apart. An *adjustable spreader-bar* and *parallel chains** are an alternate for a more permanent installation. The latter keeps the carcass steadier, and the adjustable spreader can be used for animals of varying sizes.

## COYOTE

Now we will go through skinning a coyote, making it a 'cased" pelt, with the legs and feet left whole on the skin, in order to cover all points:

First, brush the fur to remove any loose dirt, burrs or other debris. Use cold water to wash off any blood that may be on it. Dry and fluff the fur.

Next lay the coyote on its back on newspapers covering the floor or workbench. Then make a cut, just through the skin, below and close to the anus, between it and the tail. Extend the cut carefully through the skin outward toward the back of each hind leg — for about five inches on each side. Work the skin, using a knife when needed, down to the tail, cutting the anus off close inside. Free the skin all around the tail, and either pull it out (as covered under skinning the deer), or part the hair in a straight line down the center of the underside, and cut through the skin along the part to its tip. The latter way is the safest, to avoid pulling the tip through and perhaps ruining it.

Now skin back the belly. Skin out the genitals as you come to them, cutting connecting tubes off close to the skin. Work the skin loose across the belly and down the back, freeing it from the thighs of the hind legs as far as you can reach.

Compress the near leg strongly against itself until the knee joint is exposed. Keep pushing the skin on that leg, taking full advantage of the stretch in the hide and the loosened skin on the far leg. Soon the knee joint of the near hind leg will be free of the confines of the opening in the skin.* Work the leg skin down over the gambrel joint. Once that is reached and exposed, repeat the same operation on the far leg.

Now that both gambrel joints are exposed, insert the hooks through the gambrels and hang the carcass. The chains should be strong enough to hold the weight of the carcass and a lot more — for you should be able to pull hard against them, to peel down the skin from here on.

With the carcass hung,* work each leg free of the skin covering it until the foot is reached. You will find rather gristly fat over the large pad on the bottom of each foot. Carefully cut across it without slicing the pad. Watch for the skin above it and around it. *Lead* with your thumbnail, pushing strongly ahead before cutting gingerly with the point of the knife, until you have one foot done. Work down each toe in the same manner. Sever the joint of each toe until all have been cut off. Leave the claws *on* the *last joint*, though you really don't have to go that far.

Clean around the toes, trimming off any meat or tendons that you see, and scrape what fat you can from the pads. Before leaving the foot, rub salt forcibly into and around all exposed toe bones and pads. Then rub the leg skin all over with salt, and pull it rightside out. (All salt mentioned is fine table salt. See note, page 60 re. Pickling). Let the leg hang and repeat the operations on the other hind leg, which will go much easier with the experience gained.

Continue rolling the skin down over itself as you proceed down the back, sides and belly. When the forelegs are reached, pull each out, inverting the leg skin over the leg as it is drawn out. Carefully cut across the pad behind the wrist joint, as you did on the pads for the hind feet.

Watch also for the *dewclaw* on the inside of the leg, between the wrist and toes. Slide the knife blade under the tendons attaching that rudimentary toe to the leg, and it will be freed easily. Scrape it clean, cut off any loose tendon, and salt it well later. Work a forefoot the same way you did the hind feet, cutting off the toes, cleaning and trimming away meat and fat, and liberally salting it all — the pads, dewclaw and leg skin. Then pull it right-side out and let it hang. Repeat on the other leg.

Skin the neck to the ears and cut them off close to the skull, as you did with the deer. Handle the eyes, nose and lips with care in the same way, too. Clean up the inside of the head skin when it is free. Snip the cartilage carefully from the nose, taking pains not to cut the nostrils too close to the openings. Scrape the cartilage at the ears, but *do not skin them*. Salt the head skin well, especially the lips, nose, eye areas and ears. Then continue rubbing salt well into all of the pelt if you plan to finish the pelt yourself.

**Other considerations.** For fox, wolf and coyote (and some other long-furred animals) the green pelt is turned right-side out at this point. The legs already have been turned. Now reach in and draw the head skin back through the opening.

Some trappers just let the legs hang as they are, but the skin will shrink and shrivel. Of course the legs can be softened later, stretched and worked after soaking, but here is an idea that will make it all easier:

Mix coarse, *dry* sawdust with table salt. Hardwood sawdust is best (but softwood will do), and the finer the sawdust the more salt should be used. With coarse sawdust from a commercial mill (rough-cut oak for example), a box (1 lb. 10 oz.) of salt to a 10-quart pail of dry sawdust is adequate. If you are not sure the sawdust is dry, spread it out in a large drip pan or broiler and heat it in a moderate oven, stirring it well occasionally. Then store it in sealed, warm containers for later use.

Pour the salt-sawdust mix into each leg, and lightly pack it in. Then let the legs hang in-the-round when the drying frame is inserted. Some taxidermists use crumpled or chopped newspaper for this, but I do not recommend it for the amateur. The professional is available to remove the papers at just the right time, but the amateur may forget and run into serious problems. The salt-sawdust mix works better anyway. When the pelt has dried, tap out the salt-sawdust mix. Dry the mix well, and store it in closed containers to use again, adding a little more salt each time.

Insert the drying frame (skin side in), if this has not been done already. Place the nose skin over the tapered end. After you are satisfied the skin has no wrinkles in it, and has been pulled down as much as it can without excessive strain put on it, tack the bottom edges of the skin at the opening on the drying board. The board should be longer than the stretched hide. On a large cased skin particularly, a sliding wedge frame* works well, and the tail can be held on the extended center wedge.

If the tail was pulled out of the skin, pour salt only down into it. Work the salt into the tip, rolling and rubbing the loose tail between your hands, to get it all well salted on the inside, and then fluff up the hair. Tack the tip of the tail straight on the sliding wedge, or to an additional board attached to the stretcher.*

If the tail was opened full length from underneath, salt it well, especially the edges, and carefully spread it evenly and straight on the wedge or extender board. Tack it along both edges at frequent (2-inch) intervals, working *from the body to the tip,* placing the tacks opposite each other as you go.

The skin of the lower jaw can be pulled up on the drying board and tacked in the hair immediately adjacent to the lips, to keep it more or less a natural shape.

When all is neatly placed on the stretcher, give the fur a final fluffing and brushing. Stand or hang the stretcher *head up* where it is sixty to seventy degrees and dry. Let it cure and dry for at least a week. The procedure just given for the coyote will satisfy the most demanding uses for the pelt for any end product.

**Doing a coyote skin for myself,** I probably would prepare an *open skin,* split the legs, and tack it all to a large piece of plywood. I would plan to use it for a throw rug or a wall decoration, would trim back the legs and eventually would apply layered felt backing and let it extend out from the pelt all around a little, as sort of a frame. Probably I would also split the pelt the same if I were to make a hood or fur collar of it later.

I strongly dislike the use of full mink, weasel or fox pelts with jaws replaced by closures, with glass eyes on a half or full head draped about a lady's shoulders. I much prefer to see furs artistically handled and meticulously sewn as pieces of beautiful fur, without the beady eyes and feet. Anyone with a brain should recognize it for what it is, and appreciate its warmth and beauty.

I also detest toe-breaking, snarling half- or full-headed rugs. Actually the animal spends little time during its whole life in that attitude, and chances are the hunter has never seen it that way either, even when he shot it. The trapper shoots from a distance close enough for a precise shot, but not so close as to threaten the animal. Most of the horror pictures, used to publicize and discourage trapping, are taken after harassment, or in a trap set by a very unknowledgeable trapper.

Before we leave the fur rugs, one point on their practical use — true whether you like them with heads on or off (or squared somewhat as I prefer them): They can be used for taking traditional pictures of baby on them naked as a jay bird, but for the most part fur rugs are only decoration, and are not meant to be walked on. No fur rug will stand up to that and still look like anything you want to have around.

If you trim and stretch a hide or skin to any geometric shape during the original treatment (or when the pelt is soaked and relaxed later), save the pieces trimmed off. They can be used for repairs, or for novelty decorations apart from the main project. Button centers and the backs of mittens (to shed snow and provide warmth and windproofing), can be made from leg skins, for example.

## MUSKRAT AND BEAVER

These two species are the ones most often trapped. Beaver pelts in early times were used like money by the Indians for barter. Today, they are kept under control by trapping, since they occupy nearly a maximum of the habitat that can support them.

Muskrats are by far the most trapped single species — several million each year. It is a good thing they are, too, for without this means of keeping their numbers in line, they soon would become overpopulated, and disease, some of which can spread to people, soon would deplete their numbers to survival levels. The muskrat's beautiful, resilient fur coat is attraction enough in most instances to maintain tolerable populations.

Even though muskrats usually are termed "rats" by the trappers, they should not be confused with our other rats. Do you know that muskrats help to improve waterfowl production on the marshes? Their network of channels through the shallows keeps avenues of travel and escape open to fledgling broods. Their insatiable appetites for marsh grasses help to keep small pothole areas open, and geese often use the tops of the cattail mound houses as bases for their nests. As long as muskrat numbers are kept in reasonable balance, they provide an important link in the chain of marsh environment. Because millions of them are taken each year, and because they make up such a large part of the fur harvest, they deserve special recognition here.

In skinning a muskrat or beaver (and 'possum too), the first step is to cut off the feet at the wrists and gambrel joints — that is, when the carcass is to be *dressed on a table.* When chains are used, however, each rear leg is just ringed with a cut through the skin *across* the gambrel joint. Don't cut the tendon, since the hooks are placed between the gambrel joints and the tendons, as covered earlier.

The bare tails of muskrat, beaver and 'possum are cut off immediately beyond where the fur stops growing. With the muskrat and 'possum, the cut for the opening of the "case" is made along the inside of the legs toward the rear of them, across the rear end of the body, to the underside of the tail cut. Thus, the leg cuts in the skin are joined in almost a straight line to the tail cut underneath.* The *beaver* pelt, you will remember, is *stretched* flat and is cut down the belly.

The hind legs of the 'rat are skinned out when the chains are used, or are pulled through when they are not. The back skin is rolled down over the carcass, keeping about even with the skinning of the sides and belly. Cut the anus off close to the skin and skin out the genitals, cutting the tubes off close to the skin as they are encountered.

When the forelegs are reached, each one is pulled through, as the skin is forced back on the leg. The forelegs attached to the carcass now are free of the pelt. Pull the skin down over the neck to the ears. Carefully cut the ears off close to the skull.

Continue skinning to the eyes, and when they can be clearly seen, pierce the transparent membranes and carefully cut around the eyelids, as you did on the deer. Remember that the thin, loose skin around the eyelids may be doubled over. Do not cut through both layers. Any slices in the skin around the natural openings, while not a disaster, may mean a ripped skin later during the drying process.

Skin to the corners of the mouth. Pull out the loose fold and pierce the hair-free skin, making an opening into the void of the mouth. Now you can see what you are doing. Cut carefully along the *inside* of the lips next to the gumline. Again be very careful not to cut too deeply, for the thin skin will be doubled over at times. The job will be easier if, with your free hand, you pull the skin away from the jaws, stretching it to the base of the gums. The pelt will fall free of the jaws as the lip line is cut, hanging inverted from the nose. Cut through the nostril cartilage close behind the nose pad. Finish skinning across the front of the upper jaw below the nose. The pelt will be free of the carcass when the last of that lip line is cut.

Pull the hide right-side out and be sure the fur is as clean as you can get it. Soak off any congealed blood with cold water. Then rub the area dry with a cloth and fluff up the fur. Shake the hide out and brush it. *Then turn the hide inside-out again.* Carefully remove all fat and meat attached to the pelt now or after it is stretched.

If *you* are going to tan the muskrat skin yourself, put it in a tanning bath. Follow directions if another tanning method is to be used. Otherwise, pull the skin, *fur side in,* over a drying frame or stretcher of a size only to stretch the skin taut. Fit the tapered end of the stretcher into the nose and upper jaw skin. It will pocket over the end to hold the head secure, as the pelt is pulled down on the board. The stretcher should be longer than the pelt when it is pulled down.

The foreleg skin can hang loose, and they will stretch somewhat when the skin is pulled. Toggle or tack the bottom of the taut skin evenly on the stretcher. Then put the pelt and stretcher in a cool dry place.

You may want to try the partial vacuum, sealed bag and freezing technique, explained on page 112, to store the skin until you have enough of them for your own use or sale to local buyers.

## MUSKRAT "CASE SKIN"

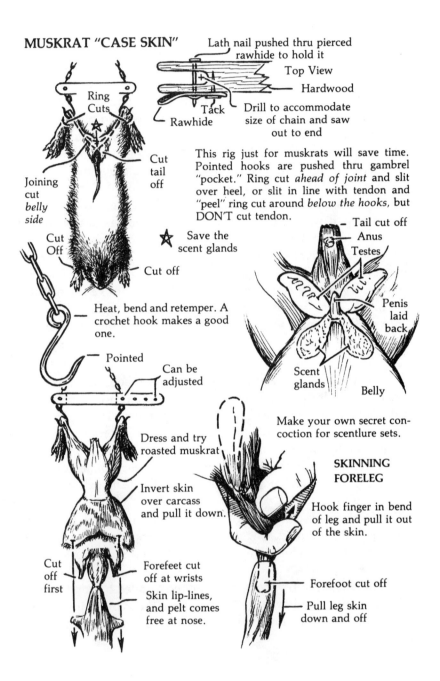

Ring Cuts

Lath nail pushed thru pierced rawhide to hold it

Top View

Hardwood

Tack

Rawhide

Drill to accommodate size of chain and saw out to end

Cut tail off

Joining cut *belly side*

This rig just for muskrats will save time. Pointed hooks are pushed thru gambrel "pocket." Ring cut *ahead of joint* and slit over heel, or slit in line with tendon and "peel" ring cut around *below the hooks*, but DON'T cut tendon.

Cut Off

☆ Save the scent glands

Cut off

Tail cut off

Anus

Testes

Penis laid back

Heat, bend and retemper. A crochet hook makes a good one.

Pointed

Can be adjusted

Scent glands

Belly

Make your own secret concoction for scentlure sets.

Dress and try roasted muskrat

### SKINNING FORELEG

Invert skin over carcass and pull it down.

Hook finger in bend of leg and pull it out of the skin.

Cut off first

Forefeet cut off at wrists

Skin lip-lines, and pelt comes free at nose.

Forefoot cut off

Pull leg skin down and off

120

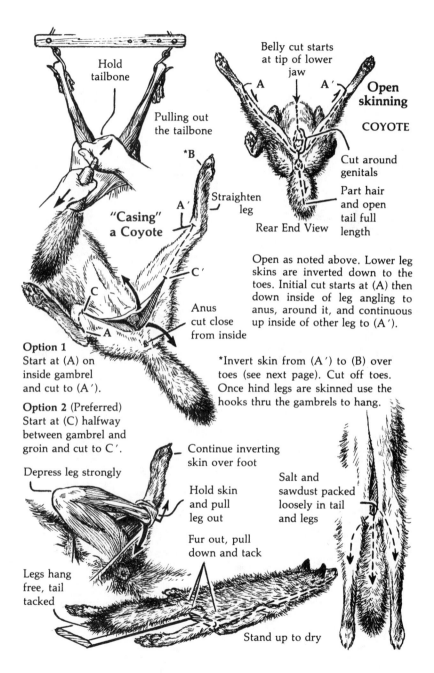

Hold tailbone

Pulling out the tailbone

**"Casing" a Coyote**

*B

A' — Straighten leg

C'

C

Anus cut close from inside

A

**Option 1**
Start at (A) on inside gambrel and cut to (A').

**Option 2** (Preferred)
Start at (C) halfway between gambrel and groin and cut to C'.

Belly cut starts at tip of lower jaw

A        A'

**Open skinning**

**COYOTE**

Cut around genitals

Part hair and open tail full length

Rear End View

Open as noted above. Lower leg skins are inverted down to the toes. Initial cut starts at (A) then down inside of leg angling to anus, around it, and continuous up inside of other leg to (A').

*Invert skin from (A') to (B) over toes (see next page). Cut off toes. Once hind legs are skinned use the hooks thru the gambrels to hang.

Depress leg strongly

Continue inverting skin over foot

Hold skin and pull leg out

Fur out, pull down and tack

Salt and sawdust packed loosely in tail and legs

Legs hang free, tail tacked

Stand up to dry

121

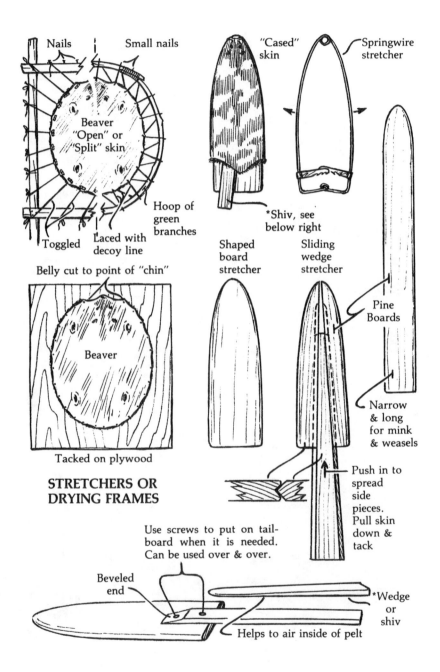

Nails  Small nails

"Cased" skin  Springwire stretcher

Beaver "Open" or "Split" skin

Hoop of green branches

Toggled  Laced with decoy line

*Shiv, see below right

Belly cut to point of "chin"

Shaped board stretcher  Sliding wedge stretcher

Beaver

Pine Boards

Tacked on plywood

Narrow & long for mink & weasels

**STRETCHERS OR DRYING FRAMES**

Push in to spread side pieces. Pull skin down & tack

Use screws to put on tail-board when it is needed. Can be used over & over.

Beveled end

*Wedge or shiv

Helps to air inside of pelt

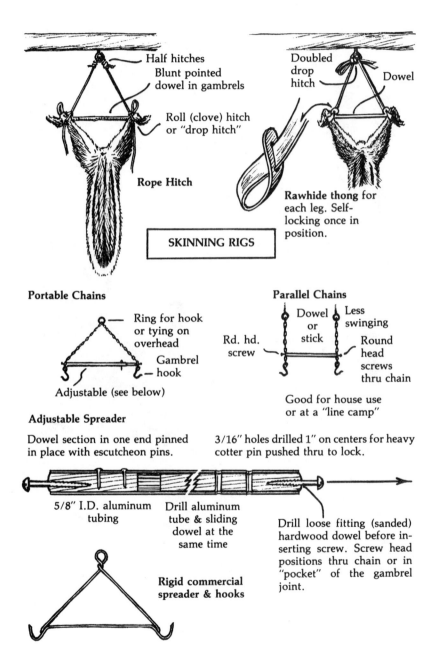

Half hitches
Blunt pointed
dowel in gambrels

Roll (clove) hitch
or "drop hitch"

**Rope Hitch**

Doubled
drop
hitch

Dowel

**Rawhide thong** for
each leg. Self-
locking once in
position.

**SKINNING RIGS**

**Portable Chains**

Ring for hook
or tying on
overhead

Gambrel
hook

Adjustable (see below)

**Parallel Chains**

Dowel
or
stick

Less
swinging

Rd. hd.
screw

Round
head
screws
thru chain

Good for house use
or at a "line camp"

**Adjustable Spreader**

Dowel section in one end pinned
in place with escutcheon pins.

3/16" holes drilled 1" on centers for heavy
cotter pin pushed thru to lock.

5/8" I.D. aluminum
tubing

Drill aluminum
tube & sliding
dowel at the
same time

Drill loose fitting (sanded)
hardwood dowel before in-
serting screw. Screw head
positions thru chain or in
"pocket" of the gambrel
joint.

**Rigid commercial
spreader & hooks**

123

## Coyote Front Foot

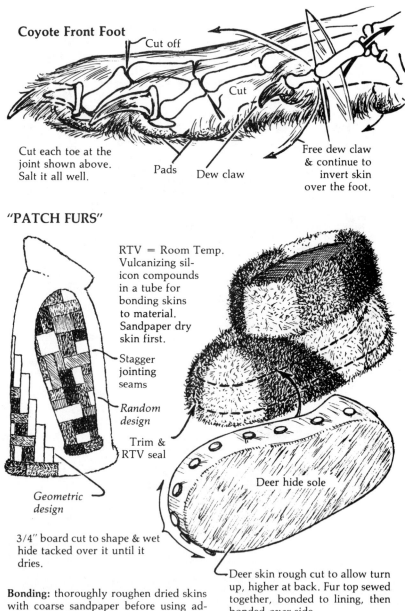

Cut off

Cut

Cut each toe at the
joint shown above.
Salt it all well.

Pads   Dew claw

Free dew claw
& continue to
invert skin
over the foot.

## "PATCH FURS"

RTV = Room Temp.
Vulcanizing sil-
icon compounds
in a tube for
bonding skins
to material.
Sandpaper dry
skin first.

Stagger
jointing
seams

*Random
design*

Trim &
RTV seal

*Geometric
design*

Deer hide sole

3/4" board cut to shape & wet
hide tacked over it until it
dries.

**Bonding:** thoroughly roughen dried skins
with coarse sandpaper before using ad-
hesives to bond skins to other materials.

Deer skin rough cut to allow turn
up, higher at back. Fur top sewed
together, bonded to lining, then
bonded *over* side.

124

# MAKING BELLY CUT ON SMALL GAME
## (open skins)

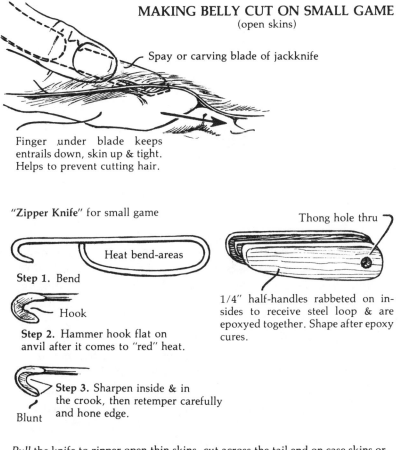

Spay or carving blade of jackknife

Finger under blade keeps entrails down, skin up & tight. Helps to prevent cutting hair.

**"Zipper Knife"** for small game

Heat bend-areas

**Step 1.** Bend

Hook

**Step 2.** Hammer hook flat on anvil after it comes to "red" heat.

**Step 3.** Sharpen inside & in the crook, then retemper carefully and hone edge.

Blunt

Thong hole thru

1/4" half-handles rabbeted on insides to receive steel loop & are epoxyed together. Shape after epoxy cures.

*Pull* the knife to zipper open thin skins, cut across the tail end on case skins or to zipper open the belly on open skins. Great for slitting leg skins (below). It cuts from *under the skin up* — no hair on meat!

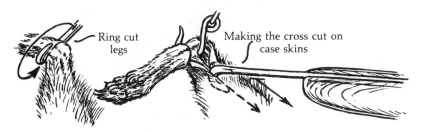

Ring cut legs

Making the cross cut on case skins

CHAPTER 9

# ACCENT ON FUR,
# MEAT — OR BOTH!

It may come as a surprise to many that some of the animals with valuable or just useful pelts also are good to eat. This source of delicious meat often is overlooked, though many trappers do get by-product profit when they sell the carcasses to fur-farmers to feed domestic mink or foxes.

Every fall, when "game suppers" are held in hunting country, raccoon, beaver and muskrat are included on the menu, along with rabbit, squirrel, bear, moose and venison. Some exotic items usually are offered, too. Skinned beaver tails, for instance, are used for a gourmets' soup — served before the pot-pourri.

Some small mammals destined for the table are taken by trapping, but hunting with a gun provides the bulk of them. The bow and arrow takes some, too. The bow, used with blunts and floo-floos, offers a lot of excitement and shooting opportunity, but the many near misses do not provide any better eating than "track stew" does for the frustrated deer hunter.

GRAY SQUIRRELS AND FOX SQUIRRELS

These heavyweights of the bushy-tails are the only squirrels hunted, historically. They have been hunted hard for centuries — in the 1800's they even were bountied in some states — yet they still are abundant where nuts and good habitat go together.

If you want to know more about squirrels and hunting them, I certainly would recommend an Olin Mathieson (Winchester-Western Corporation of East Alton, Illinois) Conservation booklet, "Gray and Fox Squirrels," written in 1964 by John Madson. I know John, and he is a very interesting, knowledgeable writer and an experienced outdoorsman. He has taken and eaten so many squirrels that he looks for loose hairs on the meat when he fixes ducks! The whole series of Olin Mathieson Conservation booklets about individual species and hunting them is well worth your serious study.

There are methods for skinning squirrels as well as rabbits and hares that are easier and quicker if meat is the only concern — but why waste all those pelts? Current vogue, which may eliminate some of the waste, makes use of small, contrasting pieces of fur sewed or stuck together in geometric or mosaic patterns (illus. p. 124) for use in varied items of outdoor winter apparel and in slippers and robes for indoor use. Often these items are strengthened with modern adhesive-bonding of the tanned skins to tough fabrics that subsequently provide the lining. Take only a little more time to "case" the pelts. Save the tails for fly-tyers, the rest of the pelt for the tanning barrel.

**Skinning squirrels.** In the field, a portable* set of chains can be carried in a pocket. Tie the top ring to a stout branch at head height. Put the hooks through the gambrels and "peel cut" a ring around each hind leg below the hocks, being careful *not to cut* the heavy tendon at the back of the legs. Then cut from leg to leg across the rear between the tail and the anus, just through the skin. Pull out the tail, then blow and brush loose hairs off the carcass, *before* you start shucking the skin.

With your set of chains, a good thumbnail and a tough index finger for starting the skin, and a "teaspoon skinner,"* the pelt can be turned down over itself readily. Strong, steady pulling on the skin against the chains does a quick job. Cut off the front feet at the wrists, and pull the forelegs through. Skin the neck and head as with the muskrat. Once you have done a couple of squirrels, they will go quickly. After the chains are set, this system takes only a little more time than the "shirt-and-pants" method — standing on the tail after cutting across the back. These speedy methods often mean more hair on the meat — *a real problem with squirrels.*

Once the carcass is free of the pelt and still hanging, cut around the genitals and make an incision into the body cavity below them, being careful not to puncture the viscera. Hold the spay blade of your knife as illustrated on p. 125. Protect the back of the blade point with the index fingertip pressed outward against the inside of the stomach wall, and zip open the squirrel's belly to the center junction of the rib cage. Or make a "zipper" knife (see p. 125). Gutting follows the usual procedure. The heart and liver can be saved, and the well-developed cheek muscles should be sliced off close to the skull at each side, for they make great appetizers. (Some people eat the whole head, but not this guy. I leave the skull and guts with the hind legs cut off at the gambrels and forelegs cut at the wrists for the scavengers.) Wash or wipe out the whole body cavity.

It is a good idea in the field to keep the meat in a re-usable, washable unbleached muslin bag with drawstring top,* carried separate from the salted skins *in another bag.*

### RABBITS AND HARES

The several species and subspecies of cottontails and jacks that range across North America are of considerable economic importance by providing dollar input through recreation and a large tonnage of table meat.

Try using the chains for dressing rabbits and hare, following the same procedure given for squirrels. Save the skins and make a soft "patch-robe" for little Jennifer and bootees to match, all treated with *non-toxic tanning methods* — in addition to having the normal complement of meat.

### WOODCHUCKS

Every year flat-shooting rifles and broadhead arrows take many woodchucks, those wild vegetarians with useful pelts, which also can provide fine table fare, especially for those who like lamb.

"Chuck" meat looks, smells and tastes like lamb when it is cooked. Some glands, however, *must be removed* before cooking. Pinch out or cut off anything that looks like small pieces of gray-to-brownish fat, glands that are easily found under each foreleg (armpit) and at the top of the shoulder blades.

RACCOONS

When long fur is in style, raccoons are used heavily for fur, and it is a good thing for them and the farmer. While not as prone to some diseases as the fox, the 'coon is particularly susceptible to them when numbers are high.

Most 'coons are hunted with hounds at night. Their nocturnal mischief often is responsible for the chase starting at a cornfield when the corn begins to ripen. Then the pelts are of little value and their meat is first priority. Later, as cold weather approaches, the fur improves, but they have to be taken before they turn in for their winter naps. Raccoons have oily glands like the woodchuck, and these also must be removed before cooking.

## Field Care of Fur and Meat

GENERAL

What do you do with fur and meat in the field after the dressing? Here are some practical ideas to cope with the situation, even in warm temperatures: Allow a half cup of salt for each skin. Is a day's bag of a half-dozen squirrels or rabbits too optimistic? If not, carry three cups of salt — a mere two pounds — in a special muslin bag in a game pocket or day pack. As soon as the skin is removed from the carcass, drop it into the bag of salt. Shake and work the bag from the outside with your fingers. The green hide will pick up what salt it needs. Keep all the pelts together in the salt inside the bag. When you get home, rub the salt into the skins more carefully and stretch the pelts.

And the dressed meat? A light and well-ventilated canvas trout creel* will hold all your squirrels and most of the rabbits — all of them if they are quartered.*

Here's a new twist: Buy a bunch of stiff plastic-looped scouring balls. With nylon string tie six or eight of them together, two wide by three or four long,* to make a mat that fully fits the inside bottom of the creel. Lay the whole skinned squirrels or quartered meat of hares or rabbits between separated layers of the connected scouring pads, which make for easy air circulation in the creel. When wetted in warm weather, the creel keeps the meat cool, the same way it does fish in the summer. It is a mobile refrigerator for temporarily keeping fresh meat in top quality condition. Put meat in a portable refrigerator loaded with ice or "freeze-cans" for the trip home. Once home, the meat is washed and put in the pot, or wrapped and put in the freezer. I think you will notice the difference in the eating. The joined scouring balls can be rinsed in cold water to clean off any blood, then in hot water. Shake them out and they will dry quickly. Store them in a clean bag for use next time. They should last for years.

The extra time needed to dress game as suggested this way will hardly be noticed. You soon will be back hunting, and your prize will be insured — fine soft fur and the finest possible meat for the table.

Note: "finest possible" when hare meat is on the menu is a bit *exaggerated!*

## SMALL GAME FIELD BAGS

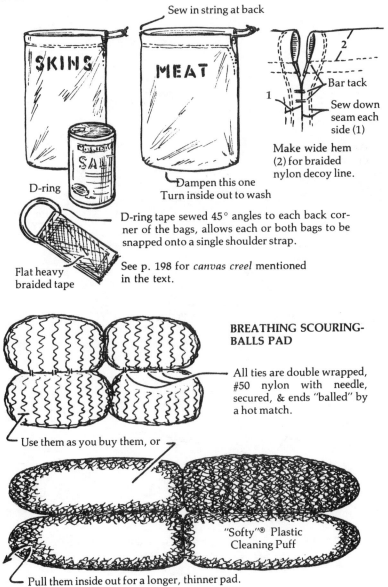

Sew in string at back

SKINS

MEAT

SALT

D-ring

Dampen this one
Turn inside out to wash

2

Bar tack

1

Sew down
seam each
side (1)

Make wide hem
(2) for braided
nylon decoy line.

D-ring tape sewed 45° angles to each back corner of the bags, allows each or both bags to be
snapped onto a single shoulder strap.

Flat heavy
braided tape

See p. 198 for *canvas creel* mentioned
in the text.

### BREATHING SCOURING-
### BALLS PAD

All ties are double wrapped,
#50 nylon with needle,
secured, & ends "balled" by
a hot match.

Use them as you buy them, or

"Softy"® Plastic
Cleaning Puff

Pull them inside out for a longer, thinner pad.

## "QUARTERING" SMALL GAME MAMMALS

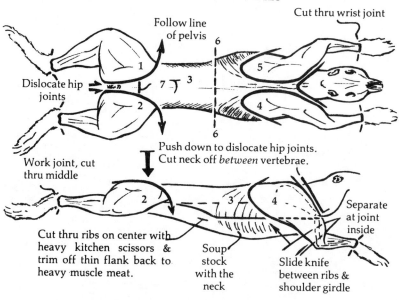

Follow line of pelvis

Cut thru wrist joint

Dislocate hip joints

Work joint, cut thru middle

Push down to dislocate hip joints.
Cut neck off *between* vertebrae.

Cut thru ribs on center with heavy kitchen scissors & trim off thin flank back to heavy muscle meat.

Soup stock with the neck

Slide knife between ribs & shoulder girdle

Separate at joint inside

Larger(domestic) rabbits & hares fit pans better if divided at 6 - 6 between the vertebrae.
Trim up the saddle section (3) by cutting backbone off at (7) & dispose of the aft section.

## BONED SQUIRREL

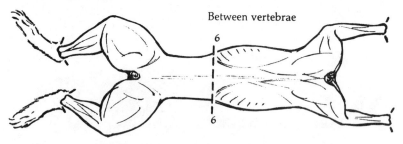

Between vertebrae

Try this "quartering" for tender squirrels. Cut whole, cleaned carcass thru 6–6. Cook in pressure cooker 10 min. Then pull meat from bones. Drain, cook & braise, or make a fricasse of it. (Try the same on rabbits, muskrat, etc.)

# SECTION III

# FOR THE BIRDS

# BIRDS FOR TROPHY DISPLAY

Chocolate, my curly coated American water spaniel lying beside my chair, heaved a sigh, stretched and got to his feet. It was too warm for him by the crackling fire. I scratched his back and he looked up at me. Then he flopped behind the protecting chair. He was only seven months old, but a great and loveable companion already. He showed a lot of promise and next fall we would work the marshes together.

I glanced up at the wood duck, standing as he had for four years, on my gun cabinet. It's not the greatest I've ever taken, the black and white flank feathers just peeking out behind those fine-barred sides. But the bird, still beautiful even though imperfect, is more than a decoration in my living room. He is a reminder of a memorable day on Mud Creek in Alburg.

My hunting buddy, Herb Taylor, had dropped the woodie clean — or so we thought — and my old spaniel, Sam, had only seen it fold in mid-air. The tall cattails blocked the dog's view of the fall, but he took the line and followed it true, swimming across the open water and working the edge of the floating mat across from where we had grounded the canoe.

Herb and I waited while Sam worked the punishing button-bush. He was right where the duck fell, but he couldn't find it, and after quite a search, he climbed onto a floating cattail island and looked back at me. Damn it, the woodie must have dived.

I put the canoe in and paddled over to help. Sam went back to work. I pulled the canoe up on the mat and stepped out gingerly. The mat sank a foot or two under every step. It was nervous going, but I hate to cripple or lose a bird. I flailed the cattails with the paddle, pushing, poking and looking. Sam kept sniffing, searching on his own. He made his way out onto a narrow peninsula of cattails in the maze of tangled roots and dead branches of the flooded buttonbush. Then he began making game, his tail wagging faster and faster.

I tried to go over to him and nearly went through the mat. I couldn't get to him on foot or by canoe, so I stood by and watched. He was well off the line, and I didn't think he was really working the duck. He growled and started digging. Six-foot cattails began falling like timber as he cut them off at their bases with his bolt-cutting jaws. (It never ceased to amaze me how gentle those powerful jaws were when he handled a bird.) I was sure he was playing with mice or a muskrat and I let him have his fun, for I had given up.

Sam stuffed his nose into the hole he had made in the mat. Then he began digging in earnest, chewing and clawing through the roots, all the time growling softly. Once he looked over at me, and I asked, "What cha got?" Back he went to work, tail wagging madly. Soon he had his whole head in the hole, well over his ears. His neck arched and he went down on his belly. Slowly and proudly he pulled Herb's dead woodie up through the hole by its tail end.

Now both of my companions are gone. And that woodie on the gun cabinet means a lot to me.

## Bird Mounts

The mounted bird is about the only way hunters use wild bird skins today, and the life-like replica of any beautiful game bird recaptures many treasured memories of days afield. And it is a thing of beauty to look upon, if the taxidermist is an artist. Some skins are also saved for fly-tying when they are allowed by law, but selling wild feathers can lead to big problems nowadays.

There are a few things you should know or review about proper field care so beautiful specimens can be mounted.

**Feathers,** though amazingly strong, are quite fragile when forced into unnatural attitudes, and feather repair on a mounted bird is almost impossible and very costly. Feathers also stain rather easily, and removing the stains is difficult. If blood or grease gets on them, clean it off immediately — cold water for blood, mild soap and warm water for other stains that cooperate, but do not wet or disturb more feathers than you need to. Carefully dry the feathers, picking them up and pinching them lightly between clean cloths or paper towels. Stroke the individual feather only with the grain, in line with the shaft of the feather being worked.

When the exceptional specimen is being gently delivered to hand by your proud, tail-wagging companion, take these steps immediately. Wash off all blood, giving special attention to any found on white or light-colored feathers. If water is not handy (in the case of upland birds), wipe off the blood the best you can, and in *all cases* stop or plug any source of bleeding or fouling. Plug the anus and mouth with soft dry grasses, cleaning tissues or cloth. Lay the bird down carefully* with its head and neck outstretched and its wings and tail folded naturally. Stroke the leg feathers to hold their natural overlay, as the legs are extended behind. Shade the bird, and get it back to civilization fast. Buy a newspaper or take some along in your car. The bird can be rolled inside an insulated newspaper cone held together by pins or tape, or eased into it, head first.

Position duffle about the cone on its side to keep it from rolling around. Cover the large top opening of the cone with more newspaper if the whole bird, including its tail, rests inside it. With a long-tailed bird like a pheasant, you can roll the cone up in additional papers to form a protecting cylinder about the tail. Lay the roll so formed against a seat back, or side wall in a trunk or wagon for added protection. Some taxidermists recommend lightly wrapping the bird completely in gauze bandage or strips of an old bed sheet. Arrange it in the same position. In any event, keep the bird cool, keep the flies away from it, and take the bird directly to the taxidermist if possible. If not, seal the cone or roll, and freeze it until you can deliver it to him.

**The fanned tail** of certain birds can be preserved for display and decoration — wild turkey and members of the grouse family being prime species for such wall fans. You can preserve wall fans on your own if you want to work on the big problem for homegrown taxidermists — insect damage. But before that worry comes, the dermestid beetles and other such nifty little monsters have to have something to attract them.

Here's how to make a beautiful wall decoration from your trophy. First tape two or more pieces of smooth-surfaced, corrugated cardboard together* to form a thick, portable working surface much like a drawing board. It should be somewhat larger all around than the tail is when it is spread. Get a handful of common pins, glass-headed corsage pin or darning needle, a small bottle of formaldehyde or embalming fluid (non-poisonous borax mixed four to one with powdered alum can be substituted), a mill file, a six-penny box nail, a hammer and paper towels or rags. You are ready to proceed when you have these things assembled.

Cut the whole meaty knob of the tail off the carcass close to the body. Whenever you work with skin holding feathers, be careful not to cut the bottom part of the feather that protrudes inward. Scrape, instead of cut, when fat and membrane are being removed from between them. The bulb of the tail has a preening gland on top. From this erected paint brush, the bird oils its feathers by wiping its beak and the sides of its head against the oil-soaked brush, relaying the oil to its feathers. Most of this gland can be removed from below the paint brush by carefully opening the length of the underside of the meaty tail. Work paper towels into the opening to absorb the oil as much as possible. Do the best you can to clean out the tail, but *do not take unnecessary chances* with disrupting the structure. Soak up all the oil you can and then rub borax into every nook and cranny. Use plenty.

Turn the tail over so the *top of the tail is up,* and the underside down on the corrugated cardboard pad. Spread the tail naturally.* Line the middle feather up with a centerline drawn on the cardboard. Push common pins carefully between the filaments of the feather into the cardboard at opposite sides of the quill, about one fifth the length of the feather outward from its base. Push in two more pins about an inch further out to keep the center feather lined up properly. Now file the point of the six-penny nail to a finer point. Push the nail through the middle of the top of the base of the tail. Hammer it well into the cardboard or all the way through, being careful to keep the rump feathers away from the action. The head of the nail should be covered by the rump feathers when they are lifted up and allowed to drop naturally.

Now work a feather at a time, first on one side of the center feather, then on the other side, pinning with common pins the quills of each in proper position, slightly underlying the feather next to it, outward, until the outermost feathers at each side are positioned.

Take the long glass-headed corsage pin or darning needle and preen the feathers so all the filaments of each feather lock together naturally, and each feather lies properly in relation to the next feather. Lift the shorter, covering feathers and let them fall into place. When all is organized, and everything looks neat and natural, place the cardboard, with the tail mounted on it, in a warm, dry place (about seventy degrees Fahrenheit), and leave it for four or five days. Then the pins can be removed and the fan will hold its shape. Tap out the excess borax and inspect the open side of the base.

Take the tail outdoors and do the next operation with caution. *It is recommended only for adults.* Lightly spray the underside of the feathers with a household roach or ant-killer. It is POISON so be careful. Then, with the aid of a cotton swab, work plenty of embalming fluid or formaldehyde *(poisonous)* into every crevice inside the opened base of the tail. Stuff cotton soaked with poison into the pocket. After two days remove the cotton and bury it. Put the tail in a safe place to air — away from pets and children — and let it dry for a week or two. Pure borax (or cut four to one with dry alum) will do a satisfactory job, the other poisons are added only for insurance.

Once the tail has dried, remove the cotton. Mix plastic steel epoxy and fine sawdust (for additional filler) in sufficient quantity to fill the voids in the base of the tail. Mix it well so its color is consistent. Use a small flat stick as a spatula to tamp and fill the void evenly to the edges. While the fill is still soft, work the bent ends of a hanger* into the mix. Then vibrate-tamp the epoxy around it, but be careful not to get any of it on the feathers. If you should, wipe it off quickly with a paper towel.

Let the epoxy cure overnight. If any feathers hang down to off-balance the geometric design of the spread tail, pull them out to satisfy your artistic taste.

All you have to do now is dust the tail occasionally. A feather duster works well. Renew the "bug spray" once in a while on the underside of the feathers, and you should have no problems.

Wings can be used separately or in combination with various tails for added decoration, for wing study in duck identification or for wildlife exhibits. Open the underside of its wings and clean out the meaty areas along the bones from underneath, treating these open areas as outlined earlier for the base of the tail. Arrange the wing* in the desired position and pin it securely and with care to a cardboard pad, preening the feathers carefully and naturally as with the tail. See also page 171 under "Injecta-dermy."

# FIELD CARE OF BIRDS
# FOR THEIR MEAT

There is more to field care of birds taken by hunters for eating than the special demands for birds to be mounted. Because upland bird hunting usually is pursued in that greatest of all times of year — early fall — temperatures often are comfortable if not quite warm. This is great for the hunter, but not so great for the birds taken, if quality food is desired.

Most hunters realize that meat deteriorates fast around areas of bullet penetration, and this blasted or discolored flesh is trimmed off later when the meat is prepared for use. Some of the problem can be lessened, however, if game is washed out as soon as possible after the kill. Gut or "paunch shots" on big game means the meat will be exposed to sour mash or distasteful body fluids from ruptured organs. Most big game hunters know this, and if they do not wash out the body cavity, they wipe it out thoroughly, *as soon as* the animal is field dressed. And with big game, field dressing occurs *immediately* after death.

It is so different with the bird hunter — and many small game hunters taking squirrels, rabbits and hares — that I wonder how current bad practices in field care of small game got established. These warm blooded creatures, like the big game animals, have the same problems of bacterial deterioration. Furthermore, the potential for destroying meat flavor is much greater since the scattergun is used almost exclusively rather than the more selective, single slug firearm. More often than not, several pellets tear into the entrails, and too often the blood trapped with the viscera heats up to a fetid mess inside the small game, where it stays until it is dressed later at home. I think this situation is more prevalent in northern climates, where hunters take too much for granted because of cooler weather.


THE BUTTONHOOK

Supposedly the Indian "buttonhooked" his small game upon taking it, but you cannot prove it by me. If he did, he deserves a lot more credit than is due the majority of modern small game hunters. You can get fancy and make your own buttonhook straight or folding model (or buy one in combination with cutting blades of a special pocketknife*), but there are millions of them growing almost everywhere, so why bother? If you are like most hunters, you already have more than enough valuable junk in your pockets without including a buttonhook. And you do have a good sharp jackknife, right? Well, here is another reason for carrying it.

Whether you have a good big goose or turkey to contend with or a small timberdoodle or green-wing teal, it makes little difference. Choose a forked branch of a bush or tree about an eighth inch in diameter at the fork and extending beyond it six to eight inches. A legitimate side branch angling off the main stem, that is straight or nearly so, is better than an even fork.

Cut the main stem off just *below* the fork or side branch.* Then cut off the "hook." Scrape smooth edges of the cuts.

Push the hook into the anus of the dead bird or mammal, point first. Ease it in a good distance and give it about a ninety-degree turn. Now carefully pull it back out. If you did not make the hook part too long, the intestines will loop over the hook, filling the gap of it for easy withdrawal. Out comes a loop or two with the buttonhook. Just gently pull and keep pulling, until all of the intestines come tumbling out. Break off both ends and wipe any fouling of feathers on nearby grass or leaves. Unless the day is really warm, you have done enough.

When temperatures are really warm, clean out the whole body cavity, *wipe it out* (keeping feathers dry) and protect it from flies. See pgs. 154 and 155 for graphics including the cut.

Wiping out the cavity is the safest way, unless you are *sure* of the purity of the water at hand, or brought some with you from home. Check pg. 34, DANGER — WATER UNSAFE!

## THE INCISION FOR EVISCERATING

Some hunters make an incision straight down the middle of a bird from the aft end of the breast bone to the anus in order to remove the viscera. It works well on large birds, and these nimrods are to be commended for the practice, but I prefer a more lateral incision for all birds.

My duck hunting usually is a two–day–at–a–time affair, and I keep my first day's bag outdoors, each duck hanging by a leg until it is time to go home. I field dress them this way, and use the same procedure for quail, dove and all the others. The technique comes into its own on small birds, when the center cut doesn't leave much room to manipulate big fingers inside. It is a fast method and works well for me*.

Pinch the feathers off one side in a line from under a leg to the center of the pelvic arch ahead of the anus. Roll the bird on its side so entrails will fall away inside, and make an incision into the body cavity with the point of a sharp blade at the anus, being careful not to pierce the intestines. Then extend the cut *forward* from inside the body cavity, following just under the line of the breastbone on that side.* (You may cut through some of the fragile ribs on small birds to make the incision large enough.) Reach inside and pull out the gizzard and intestine. Lightly pinch and stroke back the forward end of the gullet to push any remaining food into the intestine. Break off the tube as far into the throat as possible. Void the end of the intestine in like manner and break it off close to the anus.

A return trip inside will get out the heart, liver and lungs. It is relatively easy to wipe clean the inside of the body through this incision when a small clean rag is used. Remember: *no water on feathers during warm weather.* The feathers tend to pack tight and heat up. *Wipe out* the cavity. Use a damp cloth, dry cloth or even paper towels. Once home or back to camp, then will be the time to finish what you started in the field. Pluck, rinse out, wipe again . . . and refrigerate. *Do it NOW!*

If your hand is large and the bird is small — dove and quail for example — you can use a hooked finger to get out the innards. In the South, keep feathers as unsoiled and dry as possible, for wet feathers pack down tight and have little insulating value. Until the body heat dissipates, leave the bird hanging by a leg in the air so the cut will stay open. Keep flies off with netting if necessary. And pop an ice cube into the body cavity when you return to the car. Then place the bird in the portable refrigerator on a rack with the breast and incision *down*, to drain as the ice cube melts.

Include a portable refrigerator and a plastic bag of ice cubes with your hunting gear in the vehicle. When dressed birds or small game are put into the refrigerator, make the above procedure standard practice. A rack from a broiling pan or cake cooling rack should fit all right. Keep the bag of cubes upright at one end, and drain the melt water off periodically.

See p. 131 in the small game section for a good idea, and p. 198 showing the canvas creel.

# CHAPTER 12

# FINAL PREPARATION OF THE BIRDS FOR COOKING

You have several options when it comes to taking feathers off a bird, and much depends on your follow-up method of cooking or problems encountered with particular species.

For example, if the grouse in hand is an old bird (or you think it is — no pin feathers showing), you have two choices: pluck it or skin it. You can leave it whole, remove the feathers and wash it all thoroughly. Parboil the bird in a covered pan for a short time and drain it. Then it can be roasted or broiled like a chicken.

The alternative is to rip the skin off, taking the feathers with it, disjoint the bird* and make a "partridge stew" of it.

## Plucking Methods

DRY PLUCKING

This method is just what the name implies. Young birds probably will be nicer looking if carefully plucked dry — and eye appeal for food is important to many, including the author.

Flight feathers and tail feathers are usually pulled out first. Pliers make the job easier on the large birds. One trick with large feathers is to pull them back slightly "against the grain," rather than straight out in line with the quill. Smaller feathers are just pinched between the thumb and a crooked index finger. They too are pulled against the lay of the feather or at an angle to the grain.

Many birds will have some "down" on them after the regular feathers have been removed. Ducks have a lot, and some have complete sets of winter underwear on. With patience, the same pinching and plucking works all right with the down, but a light cotton glove (like the white ones used for ceremonial wear) work much better, especially if they are dampened. You can almost rub off the down with them. Even a damp cotton rag helps, and plastic or rubber gloves work well, too, particularly those with tiny raised pimples on the finger tips, intended to help in gripping wet dishes and the like.

*Pin feathers* are picked out by putting the point of a knife into the base of the "blue tube" and pressing it against the blade with the thumb of the knife hand, while you pull back on the blade.

Even after all the regular feathers and the down have been removed, you still will find rudimentary feathers *(filoplume)* that look like fine hairs on parts of the carcass. Singe these off with an open flame — cigarette lighter, a rolled newspaper or a gas burner on the stove. Don't try to short-cut the removal of down, however, by using the burning process, or you will end  with a dirty looking bird and smell up the whole house.

Broil or roast the dry-plucked bird perhaps with an apple or cranberry stuffing to keep the meat moist.


## WET PLUCKING

This method used to be standard with commercial poultry-men preparing chickens for market. They called it "scalding," but the name is misleading, for scalding the bird is to be avoided. The water should not be boiling — just under a boil, about 180 to 190 degrees Fahrenheit.

The water temperature always varied as the heat was absorbed by the birds, and when feathers began to hold tight, the water was heated up again. Then a bird or two *would* be scalded, and large patches of the thin outer skin would rub off with the feathers. When finished and dry, those birds looked like they had a bad skin condition — or worse.

Birds do pluck fast with this method, but the secret is keeping a pretty even temperature, hot enough but not too hot. As soon as the birds were done, they were put into a tub of ice water to cool them quickly.

As a kid, I used to hire out for this work. I got three cents for a hen and a nickel for a broiler loaded with pin feathers — not very lucrative summer work!

## WAX PLUCKING

This technique will work for any bird, but is used most often for ducks. The wax can vary from pure paraffin to mostly beeswax. My own preference is about a half-cup of melted beeswax to each pound of paraffin.

Melt the wax in a bucket kept for this purpose only, and which is large enough to receive a whole mallard-sized duck or half a goose at a dip. While you can heat the wax container directly on the stove, I do not advise it. Such practice is dangerous (from a flash fire standpoint), and messy at best. I partially fill with water a large preserving kettle or other pan big enough to take the wax bucket with room to spare. This method saves clean-up time and is much safer. In effect you melt your wax in a big double-boiler. Only use enough heat to melt the wax to fluid consistency, and then only as much as needed to keep the wax fluid.

Rough-pluck your duck before waxing it, cutting off wings as desired, and the feet. (I leave one on for a handle until later.) Dunk the duck into the wax, and push it down as needed with a wooden paddle or by the leg. Scoop-splash wax onto the bird. Lift it out, and the wax will harden rapidly. You can put that bird on newspaper and do a second one. When the first one has a hard film all over it, dip it again and then a third time, to build up the wax layer. When all the ducks are covered adequately, put them out in the cold.

Bring them in when they are well-chilled. Work over a large plastic waste basket or use the dried, empty preserving kettle to catch the wax. The wax will split and crack off the bird easily, taking the feathers with it. (The beeswax helps to keep the wax in large pieces with few small chips.) Pull all the wax off and dump out any balls that may have formed in the body cavity. Your bird should be beautifully plucked, without a trace of down. If down still is a problem, another dip will take care of it.

When all the ducks are done, take the excess wax off the news-paper — and if a little paper is included that's all right. Just toss it, with the wax and feathers into the waste basket, then empty the mess into another bucket, and melt it down in the double boiler rig you used first. When the wax has liquified, strain it through quarter-inch hardware cloth into your dipping bucket. Throw out the old feathers and paper. Let the dip-bucket wax cool in place, and you will be ready to use it for your next bag of ducks.

## COMMERCIAL PLUCKERS

Rubber-fingered, commercial pluckers that whirl around above a feather-catcher, can be purchased these days. If the expense can be justified, you'll find they work well.

## PLUCKING THE LAZY WAY*

I have plucked a lot of birds every way mentioned, except the last. Maybe I am getting lazier as I get older, since most of the time I fix my ducks the lazy way. About 90 percent of the meat of a wild duck is in the long, deep breast, and I try to retrieve another 5 percent. Sometimes I weaken and toss in the legs too, but they are chewy to say the least. In fact, duck legs are tough!

Here we go the lazy way: I start from the incision on the side (covered under field dressing), and rip the skin off the duck's breast. A little knife work may be needed along the keel of the breast if the skin holds tight there. Pull the skin off the front of the breast. Once the whole breast is exposed, I shove the skin down each side of the neck at its juncture with the body. Then slice one side of the neck in close and twist it off. Next I push the skin down on one wing, inserting a thumb in close behind it, next to the body, until the wing is exposed to the first external joint — like pulling an arm out of a sleeve of a sweater. Cut off the white, exposed tendon at the front, close to the body. Now I cut through the wing joint, leaving the meaty first section of wing attached to the breast.

Shove or rip off the skin across the top of the back between the wings.* You will see the exposed tops of the scapulas (the shoulder blades), which have enough meat on them to save. Furthermore, they are tied in with the first wing bone, the "big rib" and the wishbone. All together there is quite a lot of meat there on each side, in a neat package. Why mess up nature's design before the cooking?

Slide the pointed blade of a knife flat *under* the scapula, from the backbone, outward behind the joint where all these parts come together — at the front of the breast on the dorsal (top of the back) surface. Push the blade through, slicing under the scapula to the rear until the scapula is freed to the rear. Repeat the operation on the other side.

Now all you have to do is get rid of the backbone. Turn the duck over on its back and push down with the palm of one hand on the underside of the back (breast up). Then with the other hand pull up and forward on the rear end of the breast bone by hooking your fingers under it.* The "breast unit" is free of the carcass.

The remains of the fragile ribs on each side inside the breast bone can be easily pushed loose from the breast bone with a little thumb pressure, but the first *oversized* rib on each side is left, being a part of the shoulder girdle at the front of the breast.

The big breast muscles, meat-covered wishbone, first wing bones (neatly cut off through the joints) and the meat-covered scapulas make a compact bundle.* The wings and scapulas fold neatly below and to the sides of the breast when it is cooked (meat side up).*

Some hunters only remove the *hand* — the outermost part of the wing holding the flight feathers — but there is only minimal meat on the double-bone section of the wings of most wild birds. I usually only save the first wing section that is attached to the body.

There is no skin left on the meat with this method. "Puddle ducks" have very little fat, and the lazy way leaves the fat of "diving ducks" and "sea ducks" fully exposed or it has been disposed of with the skin. Every speck of that stubborn orange fat on diving and sea ducks should be removed.

One fact you will soon learn if you are just getting exposed to bird hunting: wild birds really use their wings. They don't just flutter around a barnyard, and as a result, the wings tend to be tough. The same is true for their legs, varying with the species. Because ducks are rather badly balanced for land travel, their leg muscles must get extraordinary exercise. Eating them appears to bear this out.

When any bird is to be cooked whole, the paint brush on the tail and the oil gland under it, mentioned earlier, must be removed. Make a broad V*, with one cut in front of the paint brush from the top and the other cut behind it, joining under the paint brush. Lift the "V-ed" section out as a unit.

**The wild turkey** is a story in itself. Their range is expanding all over the United States where tolerable habitat is found. Forest areas, too small for economical commercial cutting, often mature to the point where the ground cover needed by many wildlife species is lacking, and they gradually disappear. But the turkey thrives on the mature forest, especially where mast or nut trees are abundant, and the winters are not too severe.

The type of life a turkey leads is reflected in the eating of this fine wild game bird. Turkeys are strong flyers, even though they have a lot of weight to get off the ground and support in the air. They fly well, but usually only for comparatively short distances. They use their long, strong legs and run as a matter of preference, unless their wings really have to be used. They scratch for their food a good deal too. Thus, wings and legs of the mature wild turkey, especially the old "toms," are apt to be *tough*, with many strong tendons.

Check the illustrations at the end of Section V and you should be able to tell the old birds from the juveniles, which can be treated like domestic turkeys when it comes to cooking, Mature wild turkeys should be given special attention.

# CARE OF BIRDS TO BE MOUNTED

**Layout for transporting**

**Step 1.** Feet & legs pulled straight to rear.

**Step 2.** Tail flat, feathers natural & together.

**Step 3.** Wings folded close to body, feathers smooth.

**Step 4.** Neck straight.

**Step 5.** Head straight with neck, feathers smooth.

**Step 6.** Anus plugged with cotton or cloth strips.

**Step 7.** Mouth plugged with cotton or cloth & wrapped bill keeps it closed.

**Step 8.** Shot holes plugged ("Q-tips," broken off short, do a fine job).

**Step 9.** After layout, check again to see that all soiling, especially blood, is removed from feathers.

**Step 10.** Shade bird, drape wet handkerchief over it & get it to cooler conditions as soon as possible.

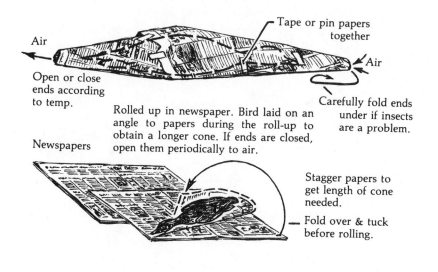

Tape or pin papers together

Air

Open or close ends according to temp.

Air

Carefully fold ends under if insects are a problem.

Rolled up in newspaper. Bird laid on an angle to papers during the roll-up to obtain a longer cone. If ends are closed, open them periodically to air.

Newspapers

Stagger papers to get length of cone needed.

Fold over & tuck before rolling.

# TAILS AND WINGS FOR DECORATION

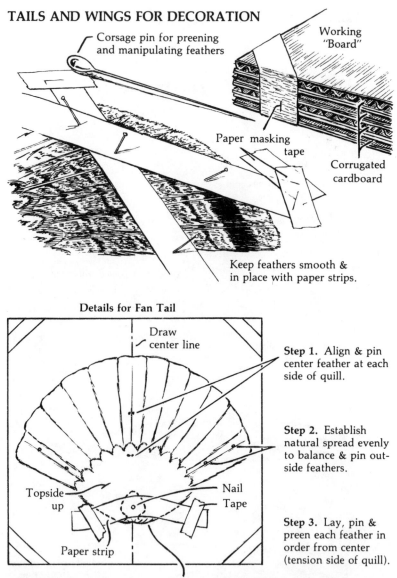

Corsage pin for preening and manipulating feathers

Working "Board"

Paper masking tape

Corrugated cardboard

Keep feathers smooth & in place with paper strips.

**Details for Fan Tail**

Draw center line

Topside up

Nail

Tape

Paper strip

**Step 1.** Align & pin center feather at each side of quill.

**Step 2.** Establish natural spread evenly to balance & pin outside feathers.

**Step 3.** Lay, pin & preen each feather in order from center (tension side of quill).

Cleaned out & treated knob is placed *down* on cardboard.

Smooth all feathers *up over tail* & hold in place with strip of paper pinned or taped to board.

# FINISHING THE FAN

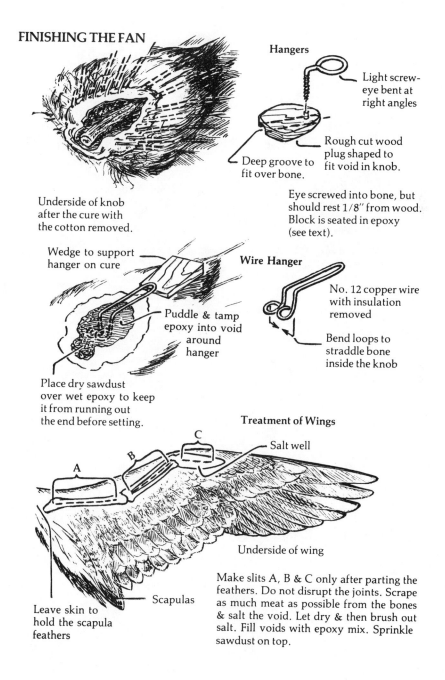

**Hangers**

Light screw-eye bent at right angles

Rough cut wood plug shaped to fit void in knob.

Deep groove to fit over bone.

Underside of knob after the cure with the cotton removed.

Eye screwed into bone, but should rest 1/8" from wood. Block is seated in epoxy (see text).

Wedge to support hanger on cure

Puddle & tamp epoxy into void around hanger

**Wire Hanger**

No. 12 copper wire with insulation removed

Bend loops to straddle bone inside the knob

Place dry sawdust over wet epoxy to keep it from running out the end before setting.

**Treatment of Wings**

Salt well

A    B    C

Underside of wing

Leave skin to hold the scapula feathers

Scapulas

Make slits A, B & C only after parting the feathers. Do not disrupt the joints. Scrape as much meat as possible from the bones & salt the void. Let dry & then brush out salt. Fill voids with epoxy mix. Sprinkle sawdust on top.

153

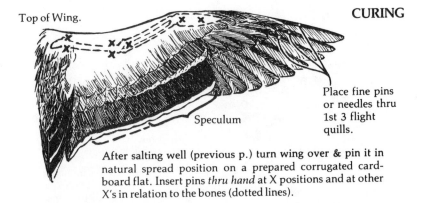

Top of Wing.

Speculum

Place fine pins or needles thru 1st 3 flight quills.

After salting well (previous p.) turn wing over & pin it in natural spread position on a prepared corrugated cardboard flat. Insert pins *thru hand* at X positions and at other X's in relation to the bones (dotted lines).

Give the wing a final, careful preening & let it dry in a cool, insect-free place. Finish later according to instructions at bottom of previous page. See p. 171 under Injectadermy regarding both wings & tails.

## BUTTONHOOK EVISCERATORS

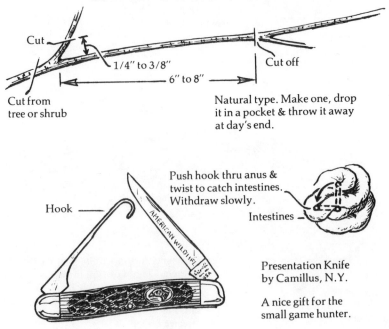

Cut

1/4" to 3/8"

6" to 8"

Cut off

Cut from tree or shrub

Natural type. Make one, drop it in a pocket & throw it away at day's end.

Push hook thru anus & twist to catch intestines. Withdraw slowly.

Hook

AMERICAN WILDLIFE

Intestines

Presentation Knife by Camillus, N.Y.

A nice gift for the small game hunter.

## FIELD DRESSING BIRDS

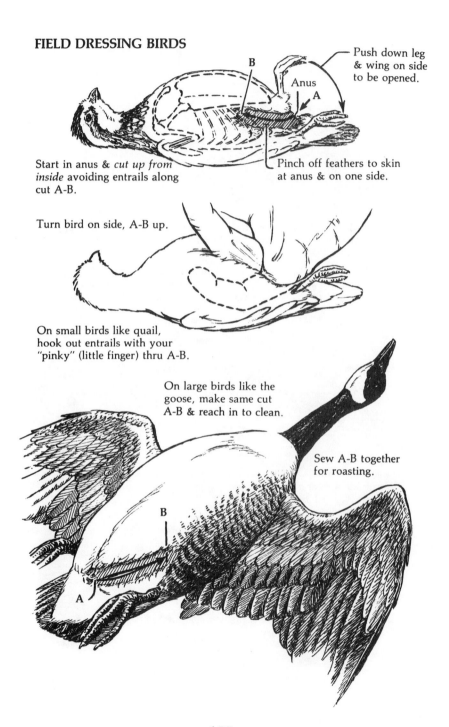

Push down leg & wing on side to be opened.

Anus

A

B

Start in anus & *cut up from inside* avoiding entrails along cut A-B.

Pinch off feathers to skin at anus & on one side.

Turn bird on side, A-B up.

On small birds like quail, hook out entrails with your "pinky" (little finger) thru A-B.

On large birds like the goose, make same cut A-B & reach in to clean.

Sew A-B together for roasting.

B

A

155

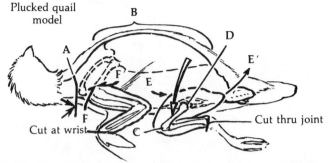

Plucked quail model

Cut at wrist

Cut thru joint

**Step 1.** Cut off neck between the vertebrae at A. Pull out windpipe & any remaining gullet.

**Step 2.** Hold bird on its back with hand on breast (B) & use other hand to push down & out to dislocate hip joint (D).

**Step 3.** Make cut E-E′ thru popped out hip joint. Leg & hip are off in one piece. Repeat other side.

**Step 4.** Pull wing forward & cut F-F′ angling into joint (wiggle it to locate exactly) from in front & behind. Twist wing & cut thru joint. Repeat on other wing.

**Step 5.** Pull up & forward.

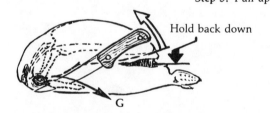

Hold back down

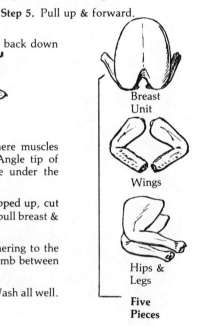

Breast Unit

Wings

Hips & Legs

**Five Pieces**

Slide knife under shoulder blade where muscles from back appear to cross breast. Angle tip of blade in toward backbone and slice under the shoulder blade, coming out at G.

**Step 6.** See p. 157 (4). With breast tipped up, cut each side of backbone up into neck & pull breast & shoulder meat off backbone.

**Step 7.** Break off fragile ribs still adhering to the inside of breastbone by running a thumb between them & the breastbone.

**Step 8.** Dispose of backbone & tail. Wash all well. Trim shot holes if necessary.

# DUCKS — THE LAZIEST WAY

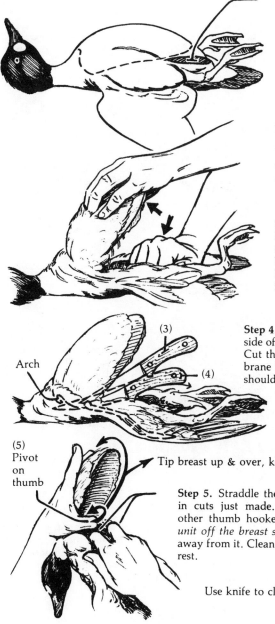

**Step 1.** Insert thumb of one hand under breast-bone in field dressed cut.

Insert other hand palm down in the cut & press down hard on the back.

**Step 2.** Forcibly push the breast away from back. After a loud crunch, the breast will remain cocked.

**Step 3.** Work point of knife into wing joint & separate wing from breast at each side. Don't cut into the breast itself.

Arch

(3)

(4)

**Step 4.** Slice down along each side of backbone up into neck. Cut thru the tendons & membrane holding backbone to shoulder girdle.

(5) Pivot on thumb

Tip breast up & over, keep pulling.

**Step 5.** Straddle the backbone with fingers in cuts just made. *Tip breast over* with other thumb hooked in arch & *rip breast unit off the breast skin* as it is pulled up & away from it. Clean breast unit & dispose of rest.

Use knife to clean around shot holes.

157

## BIRDS MISCELLANEOUS

If ducks are to be kept overnight before final dressing, it is best to hang them head up so any fluids will drain from the best & biggest chunk of meat — the breast.

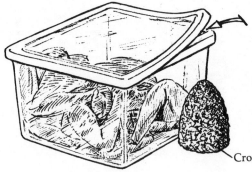

Paint brush — Quill of tailfeather

Side view

When the tail knob is left on a bird to cook, as in roasting plucked birds, cut each side of paint brush to form broad V & lift it out.

## MAKE A POTPOURRI OF LEGS & WINGS

Legs & wings of game birds usually are pretty tough. Keep a Tupperware® container in the freezer & add to it each time you dress a bird.

Croquette

When you have a good supply for a meal treat them specially. Strip the meat from the bones after pressure cooking (tenderizes) & sauté the pieces for appetizers or fine chop the pieces for croquettes. Or braise the lot, bones & all, for some sweet "pickins." In other words cook the breast unit as you wish & handle the legs & wings separately. That way you can enjoy both.

# SECTION IV

# INJECTADERMY

# CHAPTER 13

# A NEW SCIENCE

The use of formaldehyde to preserve animals and soft-bodied insects for later biological study is not new. For decades biologists have been filing all kinds of wildlife or parts thereof in bottles of Formalin solution (formaldehyde and water). More recently attempts have been made to mummify specimens in a dry state for less bulk storage and greater ease of handling. Both freeze drying and Formalin injection techniques are being constantly improved. Freeze-drying at present demands substantial expense for highly specialized equipment. Specimens treated with injections of Formalin result in little expense and a lot of promise. They are toughened by formaldehyde and shrinkage is no great problem. Weak aqueous solutions of about 10 percent formaldehyde were adequate for keeping specimens when they were continuously soaked in it, but more potent solutions were needed when specimens were removed from the solution and left to air dry. Preserving aspects were then satisfactory, but coats of fur and feathers rarely recovered their natural appearance. It was inevitable that the mortician's approach would evolve, and it has.

Wildlife specimens as large as woodchucks and ducks have been successfully preserved by Formalin injections for at least a few years, and they may last indefinitely. Time will tell. I call the process "injectadermy" because the mounted specimen is thoroughly injected with hypodermic needles loaded with strong Formaline solutions. The animal is thoroughly saturated internally.

*Injectadermy eliminates all need for cutting open the specimen.* Thus, sewing of the skin also is eliminated except for pulling together shot holes or other damaged skin.

Be forewarned, however. Injectadermy is a *recent development* using materials long known, but unrecognized for their adaptability. I have only begun to experiment with this fascinating art. Earlier study and accomplishment in normal taxidermy plus good biological exposure for more years than I like to recall should help me in this pursuit. I'll share my present knowledge with you for what it's worth. And perhaps you can come up with some ideas of your own.

I am presently using 40 percent Formalin, the slightest concentration generally available. You have to be careful in handling it. It is poison; the stronger the solution, the more dangerous, but normal care and common sense is all that is required for safe handling, in addition to good ventilation and rubber or plastic gloves. *This treatment, however, is not something for youngsters to fool with.* They will learn a lot pursuing normal taxidermy with borax, alum, naphtha soap and safer non-toxic compounds for the time being. When they have mastered that, maybe the current crop of interested adults will have mastered injectadermy so the perfected techniques can be passed on to them with complete confidence.

When an animal dies, its normal body functions cease and production of fluids stop, blood coagulates internally soon after. If your specimen feels cold to touch, it is ready to have wires or rods inserted* into wings, feet and legs to give support to display specimens, much the same procedure as in taxidermy. Study specimens do not need them. Let's work with a wood duck we want for exhibit in the den.

Its mouth and anus were lightly stuffed with absorbent cotton out on the marsh. We took the cotton along in a pocket — just in case. But that was four hours ago. Now we are home, and it's time to go to work. We followed all the earlier advice for field care, and this woody is spotless and stretched out.

First cut four pieces of annealed, rustproof steel wire, the same that taxidermists use for the same purpose, about 15 inches long. Point one end of each with a mill file. The rear of the ball pad on the foot is pierced by the point on one wire and it is worked up the leg on the inside between the bones and the heavy tendon.*

All goes well until the joint just below the feathers is reached. Work the joint back and forth some and ease the wire ahead under the  tough skin at the *inside* of the joint. Be careful not to pierce the skin. Continue pushing the wire up the leg, now well into the meat, still keeping to the inside. The legs, though somewhat stiff were held straight in the cone protector on the trip home, so the task goes quite easily. The wire soon makes its way into the body cavity, where there is little resistance. Keep pushing until you strike bone inside — but don't push through it or the skin on the back. Try to penetrate the backbone with only the point. To do so, you may have to bend the leg to bend the wire inside. When good resistance is felt, a little final thrust sinks the point into the bone. Then repeat the process on the other leg.

Now the wings. Take the "hand" that holds the long flight feathers at the wing tip*, and firmly pull it out straight or nearly so. Start the point of another wire in between the two separated bones immediately below the hand and wrist joint, pass through or under the next joint, then follow the single bone in the meat and through the shoulder into the body a few inches *but don't* penetrate the opposite side. Leave the wing outspread even if it is in a rather awkward position and bend a large eye in the exposed outside end to rest flat under the "hand." Cut off the excess wire from the loop formed.

Put the foot wires into a vise to hold the duck upright. You will readily see what your next job will be — the neck.

Cut another wire, 18 inches long. (You won't have to point this one.) The head is already outstretched, so force open the bill and push the wire down the throat following the path of least resistance. You can force it around or through any barrier encountered, but again, *be careful not to pierce the skin*. Bend the wire up inside to avoid this problem if you feel the wire from the outside. Follow its progress along. Extend it all the way through the body cavity. Again force the end up into the back, bending the wire from the soft underparts at the rear underneath, and stop.*

There should be some wire extending out of the mouth. Pull it to one side of the open bill, make a small loop in the end, and cut the excess off with sidecutters. Bury the end in the thin bone on the underside of the upper mandible (bill). Repack the mouth with cotton and hold closed with a rubber band. Now grasp the body firmly*, but do not disarrange the feathers across the back. Gently but firmly raise up the neck to bend the wire inside it, and again at the head. Grasp the neck firmly below the head and force the head down making the wire bend a little in front of the back of the skull and just below it. These bends are only to stiffen the bird. Final arrangements will come later.

The cotton in the mouth and anus should be replaced, if any of the manipulation forced blood or fluids out onto the feathers. Clean them now, and you are ready for the injections.

There are two methods. Give each a try and decide which you think is best. I prefer the first. In either, a fairly long needle is needed. You can buy one from a surgical supply house. It will fit your syringe or jury rig it to fit and stay in place with plastic steel. One needle used for radiology is a foot long and lists between seven and ten dollars at present prices. Get one if at all possible. Use it that length for larger specimens, or you can make one four inches and another eight inches long from it.

*Method 1*, the grid system*: In this technique you use an imaginary grid with squares of an inch or two on a side. The bird is held *upright* by the foot wires locked in a vise. Only inject *downward* (straight or angled) from the top (the back or dorsal surface). Part the feathers (or fur on a mammal) at each imaginary crossing of the grid lines. You use gravity to best advantage this way, the solution being drawn down into the bird rather than possibly weeping from the puncture holes after the needle is withdrawn. Be sure to give shots into fatty areas of the feet from the side or between the toe bones from above.

Start at one end of the bird and work methodically to the other, thoroughly saturating all of the meat and viscera. Concerning the latter, don't be stingy with the solution. Penetrate nearly to the skin of the belly and start releasing the Formaline and continue doing so as the needle is withdrawn, stopping *just below the skin on the top*. If you have a smaller needle, inject the tail at much closer intervals. Be sure also to get a good quantity in the crop (from the back of the neck, avoiding bones whenever you can). The skull on this wood duck should present no problem. If penetration through it is too much to ask of your needle, use any sharp solid steel point to make a small neat hole through the thin bone to put your needle through. Be sure to get

the solution into the brain cavity. Be thorough with the head —
jaw and cheek muscles, from the top down, and the tongue, lips,
et al from *inside the mouth.*

Carefully put the bird into the desired natural position, bene-
fitting from the natural muscles, bones and joints, all in correct
relationship. They will demand some forcing, but if you use
care, feathers won't be disrupted. (Furry animals are easy.)

Once you're satisfied the position is life-like, lift, pat and pick
the feathers to lie naturally (brush the fur). Work filaments* of
the feathers with a large corsage pin for near perfection. The
time you spend on this task determines the beauty of the finished
product.

Natural eyes should be removed by hooked wire and the
cavity swabbed with Formaline. Then mix a teaspoon of fairly
stiff plaster and force a small pill of it into the socket, followed
by the *proper size* and color of glass eye. If you have to buy the
artificial eyes, leave plain cotton balled up in the eye temporarily.
When you do get the eyes, wet the cotton with water and let it
stand. The lids will soften (relax). *Then* you can set the eyes as
described, bringing the lids up around the eye naturally. The
eyes are then given a little wax with a heated needle or paper clip
to seal the lids and smooth the juncture of skin to glass naturally.
A little oil paint of the right color (take notes from the fresh-
killed specimen for such use later) gives the artistic touch needed
for a fine job.

Before leaving the bird to dry, push a cotton ball soaked in the
Formalin into the anus and mouth. (Pad the crop a little, too —
simply push Formalin-dampened cotton down the throat.)
Massage them in place to eliminate unnatural bumps. Wrap bill
(or muzzle of a mammal) to keep it closed. A stitch or two across
the anus makes it unnoticeable. Tape pieces of cardboard under
the feet and spread the toes naturally to fit the mount you will
put the finished, cured bird on. You can drill small holes through
driftwood or other mount to receive the foot wires now (best
procedure) and put the feet in correct position to dry on it.
Clinch over the ends of the wires and bury them in the mount.

Check the duck periodically, but plan to leave it in a safe, airy
and dry place, at normal room temperature for a few weeks or
more. The chemical odor will leave it upon curing.

Feet, legs, bill and around the eye look better when painted with oils or acrylics lightly and smoothly to match natural colors from your notes.

*Method 2\**: This is largely the same throughout except for the manner of injection for the body. The long needle is used almost exclusively. Many trips are made through the mouth and anus at varied angles and depths without piercing the skin with the needle point. A good eye and sense of distance at short range are necessary for success with this approach. Method 1 is recommended for most.


## GENERAL TIPS ON INJECTADERMY

Avoid splashing or wiping Formalin on your eyes. Take steps *immediately* to resolve any such problems by following instructions on the label of the bottle. With reasonable care, common-sense use and no allergy problems, there should be no difficulty in handling the chemical.

The meat areas of wings and tails for decoration described earlier can be injected simply with 40 percent Formalin, spread and pinned to dry.

If you wish to experiment with this relatively new technique, you should obtain a few hypodermic needles of varying sizes and lengths. A long, coarse one will be needed for injecting the viscera and deep muscle areas. If things continue to work out well, and enough hunters practice injectadermy, future generations will not only have wildlife preserved, but the foods the animals eat also will be preserved for time-lock studies.

A word of caution: the importation, exportation, and the collection laws for plants, fish, birds and mammals have been substantially strengthened and enforced in recent years. Collection permits must be obtained to even make use of game animals found dead between open hunting seasons. Special permits are needed to work with any protected species no matter what the cause of death. Even with the proper permit, triplicate disposition papers — personal, state and federal — must be filed if protected species are preserved. Thus, unprotected species or those taken during a legal hunting season are the only ones to experiment with if you try injectadermy.

There is some shrinkage inherent with injectadermy in its present state of development, but it is negligible in feathered or furred specimens. Before this method can be used successfully for fish, amphibians or reptiles, improvements in the process will have to be made in order to replace the volume of evacuated water in the tissue with some liquified solid. Low viscosity silicone compounds may provide the answer.

Furbearers are done the same way, but with wires in all four feet* and legs. The muscles harden as they cure, and they hold the wires firmly in place. Joints cure and lock too. The end result is no flimsy re-creation. Larger wire or rod stock is needed in larger specimens.

Curing in an attic, shed or spare room is recommended if normal room temperatures can be maintained. There should be good ventilation when you work on the animal. An exhaust fan is very helpful. And the curing room should be ventilated too. If you follow these directions, you should experience odor only from the formaldehyde which will dissipate in the time allotted. Spray the feathers (or fur) to discourage insects on the outside.

Good luck!

## INJECTADERMY EQUIPMENT

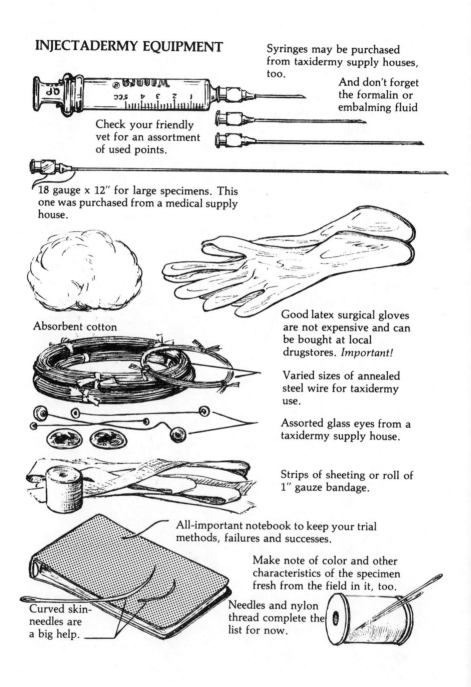

Syringes may be purchased from taxidermy supply houses, too.

And don't forget the formalin or embalming fluid

Check your friendly vet for an assortment of used points.

18 gauge x 12" for large specimens. This one was purchased from a medical supply house.

Absorbent cotton

Good latex surgical gloves are not expensive and can be bought at local drugstores. *Important!*

Varied sizes of annealed steel wire for taxidermy use.

Assorted glass eyes from a taxidermy supply house.

Strips of sheeting or roll of 1" gauze bandage.

All-important notebook to keep your trial methods, failures and successes.

Make note of color and other characteristics of the specimen fresh from the field in it, too.

Curved skin-needles are a big help.

Needles and nylon thread complete the list for now.

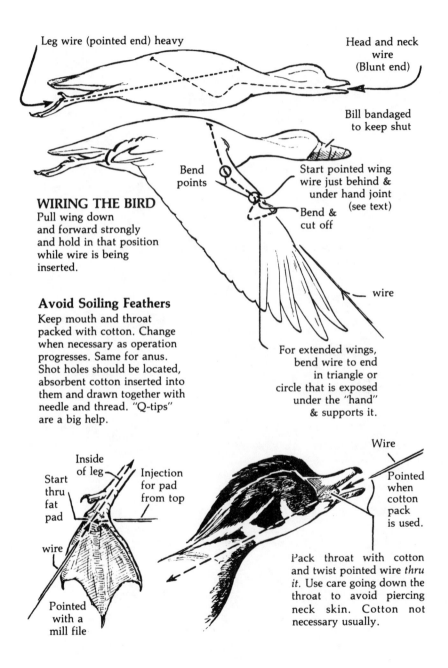

Leg wire (pointed end) heavy

Head and neck
wire
(Blunt end)

Bill bandaged
to keep shut

Bend
points

Start pointed wing
wire just behind &
under hand joint
(see text)

Bend &
cut off

## WIRING THE BIRD

Pull wing down
and forward strongly
and hold in that position
while wire is being
inserted.

wire

### Avoid Soiling Feathers

Keep mouth and throat
packed with cotton. Change
when necessary as operation
progresses. Same for anus.
Shot holes should be located,
absorbent cotton inserted into
them and drawn together with
needle and thread. "Q-tips"
are a big help.

For extended wings,
bend wire to end
in triangle or
circle that is exposed
under the "hand"
& supports it.

Inside
of leg

Start
thru
fat
pad

Injection
for pad
from top

wire

Pointed
with a
mill file

Wire

Pointed
when
cotton
pack
is used.

Pack throat with cotton
and twist pointed wire *thru*
*it*. Use care going down the
throat to avoid piercing
neck skin. Cotton not
necessary usually.

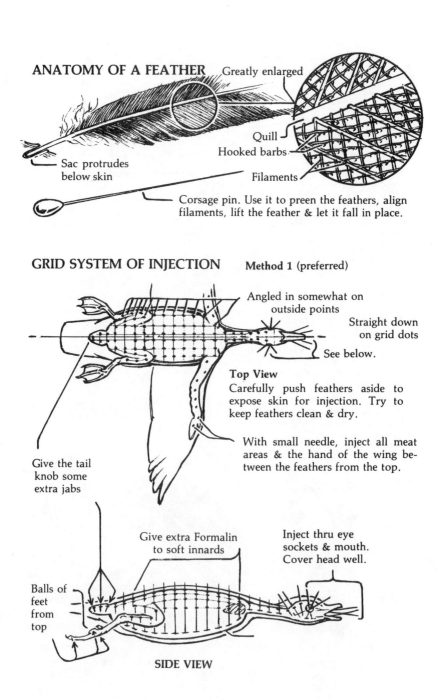

## ANATOMY OF A FEATHER

Greatly enlarged

Quill
Hooked barbs

Sac protrudes
below skin

Filaments

Corsage pin. Use it to preen the feathers, align
filaments, lift the feather & let it fall in place.

## GRID SYSTEM OF INJECTION

Method 1 (preferred)

Angled in somewhat on
outside points

Straight down
on grid dots

See below.

**Top View**
Carefully push feathers aside to
expose skin for injection. Try to
keep feathers clean & dry.

With small needle, inject all meat
areas & the hand of the wing between the feathers from the top.

Give the tail
knob some
extra jabs

Give extra Formalin
to soft innards

Inject thru eye
sockets & mouth.
Cover head well.

Balls of
feet
from
top

**SIDE VIEW**

# RADIATING SYSTEM OF INJECTION    Method 2

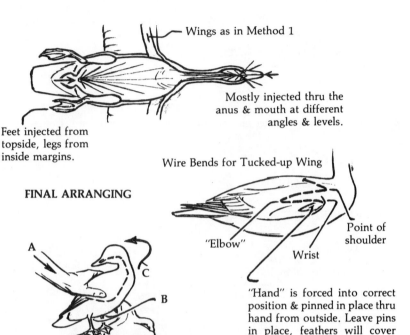

— Wings as in Method 1

Mostly injected thru the
anus & mouth at different
angles & levels.

Feet injected from
topside, legs from
inside margins.

Wire Bends for Tucked-up Wing

## FINAL ARRANGING

"Elbow"

Point of
shoulder

Wrist

"Hand" is forced into correct
position & pinned in place thru
hand from outside. Leave pins
in place, feathers will cover
them.

**Step 1.** Secure foot wires by inserting them
thru small holes drilled in base (driftwood) as
shown. Clinch wires tight under it before
attaching pedestal or board.

**Step 2.** Hold down (A) to keep wires positioned
in back as legs are bent to natural position (B)
at the natural joints. Do the same to twist head
around (C).

Suggestion: *Tape padding* around jaws of long-
nosed pliers to bend wires (jaws twisted in ½
open position) without damaging skin or
feathers.

Force Formalin
dampened cotton
down throat to
pad out crop.
Shape in place.

Study natural positions of
birds. Round out crop, but
don't exaggerate. Stuff crop
before wiring head & throat.

171

## T-PIN TAIL SUPPORT

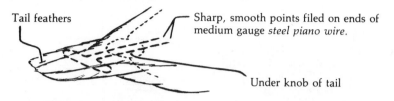

Tail feathers

Sharp, smooth points filed on ends of medium gauge *steel piano wire.*

Under knob of tail

**For Wing Decoration,** "inject" Formalin in all meat areas *from the underside* & let the curing take place *underside up.* Pin & wedge wing to keep the natural concavity of it during the cure. Feathers receive final preening after the cure.

## PREPARING THE CURE

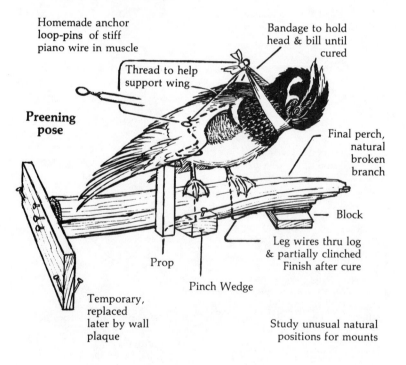

Homemade anchor loop-pins of stiff piano wire in muscle

Bandage to hold head & bill until cured

Thread to help support wing

**Preening pose**

Final perch, natural broken branch

Block

Leg wires thru log & partially clinched Finish after cure

Prop

Pinch Wedge

Temporary, replaced later by wall plaque

Study unusual natural positions for mounts

172

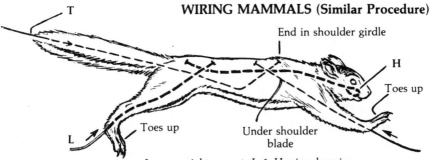

## WIRING MAMMALS (Similar Procedure)

T

End in shoulder girdle

H

Toes up

Toes up

Under shoulder blade

L

In an upright mount, L & H wires heavier

Start T, pointed annealed wire, *under the tail* as close to the end of it as you dare & carefully follow under the bone without piercing skin again.

Leg wires are pointed annealed wire. Keep legs pulled as straight as you can while inserting wires. Keep to inside.

Head wire (H) has a bent loop in end to be lost in the mouth cavity. Wire is annealed & pointed. It pierces neck inside & follows closely *under the backbone* ending in pelvic area.

Injections follow same patterns as those for birds given on p. 170 all from the top (recommended).

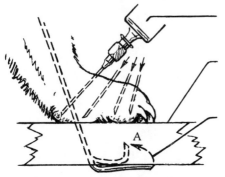

Feet with fat pads under the toes get injections *from the top* down thru or *between toe bones.*

Temporary base board drilled to receive wires with feet in proper positions.

Leave extra foot wire on the partial clinch while curing. Later, on final mount, the wire is cut at angle & clinched (A).

**Tails**     Inject *between* vertebrae

Loop end on tail wire to support tip

# SECTION V

# FISH FOR
# FUN & PROTEIN

CHAPTER 14

# FISHING COMES
# BEFORE THE DRESSING

The millions of men, women and kids who go fishing all are
loosely called fishermen, in spite of that chauvinistic title. Most
prefer the earned title of *sport-fisherman*, because fishing is
public recreation, and they know the courtesies and responsibilities that go along with the fun. Unfortunately, there are *spoilers*
in fishing, too.

The fishing virus singled me out at an early age. Even the
Great Depression and a very busy father who could spare little
time for play did not diminish the pleasant fever. There was only
one problem, and a big one — I hated to *eat* fish. But in those
days, kids didn't pick at their food, or make snide remarks
about it either.

But to prove I caught the fish, I had to bring them home, and
my straight-laced mother was adamant — if I killed it, I ate it—
or at least some of it.

My dad *never* filleted fish, and I swear my grandmother (the
one who drank tea while it was still boiling in the cup, or at least
I thought so), really enjoyed eating the bones. I soon learned to
dress my fish in self-defense.

A distant neighbor I knew only as Mr. Sprague seemed to find
a lot of time to go fishing, and he was there nearly every time I
went adventuring around a small pond not far from home. He
had a fancy casting rod and nice olive-colored hip boots (this at
a time when no one else I knew had any). He usually wore a

snap brim hat and an expensive, wool plaid shirt. A nifty net hung down his back. He didn't seem to take to kids and ignored me as I quietly watched from a distance.

Mr. Sprague caught a lot of fish, but he threw most of them back — and that was something new. One day I got up my courage to ask him why. He said, "No sense taking more than I can use." That made sense.

I just had to have a rod and a level-wind reel like Mr. Sprague's, and finally I got them from Sears Roebuck. Well, they looked like his, and I was happy.

I got so I could cast fairly well under low-hanging branches and into the pockets between the lily pads. My thumb got well-educated, but I had my share of backlashes or "bird's nests." I wasn't nearly so good as Mr. Sprague, but I took some nice fish — mostly bass, pickerel and perch. Trout fishing came much later — all brook trout and close to home. They didn't run very large.

I learned about fly fishing from magazines. It sounded like fun, and eventually a "split-bamboo" fly rod arrived from Sears too. I began to tie my own flies, and nothing with feathers on it was safe from my borrowing.

I'll never forget my first outing with that fly rod. Johnny Terrill and I went down to Mill Brook behind the old Weymouth Fair Grounds. I had a few of my homegrown flies, but mostly we used "garden hackles."

On our way home with good strings of brookies, a man stopped us and wanted to take our picture. That night it appeared in the newspaper, and then we remembered we had forgotten to go to school. I caught what for, and so did Johnny, whose father was the chairman of the school board. I still have that old rod, and I marvel that I could throw a line at all with it.

Gradually, I became used to eating fish. Cleaning and cooking them myself, I did not have to fight with the bones. Today I honestly look forward to fish — those from fresh water and salt — as well as shrimp, clams, scallops, lobsters, oysters and even squid. The only fish I don't really enjoy are mackerel — but I keep trying them.

Following the tradition of east coast ocean fishermen, I always killed and threw back spiney dogfish or sand sharks — but now I find I've been missing some fine eating, and I'll never throw them away again. Their flesh is as white as snow, and sharks have no bones, just cartilage. It is unfortunate the stigma against eating any of the sharks is so strong. Commercial fishermen on the east coast are missing a good bet. Don't knock dogfish until you try them yourself.

Fishing is a great family sport, of course, and when kids are fishing, they aren't getting into trouble. Go with them as often as you can. A lot more than fishing skills will be gained through fishing with youngsters; and if you do not have any children, take someone else's kid along.

Dress your fish in a way to make the eating easy and pleasant. Probably the major cause for people shunning fish on the menu, is the fear of getting bones stuck in their throats. Clean and prepare your fish properly, and there won't be any bone worries, if they are cooked properly. If you can get everyone to try eating just a little each time fish is served, eventually, I'll bet the whole family will learn to like fish as I did.

Fish not only taste good, they provide a fine source of protein. Furthermore, they are non-fattening and have no cholesterol. Now that combination is hard to beat.

CHAPTER 15

# EATING BY REGULATION!

## What Limits Mean

Most fishermen select the fish they keep according to length limits or other established laws or regulations — or according to their wants. No *sportsman,* however, keeps more than he can care for or use, unless the reduction of an overpopulated species is desirable and legal. It is important, therefore, that you not only know the law, but also are able to identify the different species and know how best to release a fish so it may survive. But before we get to that point, a word about keeping fish.

The well-intentioned "preservationists" should realize that most fish and game laws and regulations are set within known parameters and that if these regulations are obeyed, the species will not be jeopardized, either now or in the future. If a six-fish daily limit is established for a certain fish, don't worry about taking the full six allowed — *if* you can use them for your family or friends. (Giving away fish and game these days sometimes is legally difficult, so check out that point locally.)

What I am saying is that under normal fishing pressures for the area covered by the regulation, there will be no problem if everyone always takes his full daily quota, *and a good many won't be able to.* It is all figured by the numbers. The ones who can take a limit and the ones who will not are calculated on the average. A conservative number then is established as a limit for the species, to benefit people as well as to protect the future of that species.

180

Many times if sufficient numbers of fish (like game), are *not* taken, the future of that species and the benefit to the fisherman (or hunter) both suffer. Remember that fish and game are *renewable natural resources.*

Any given volume of water (according to its quality), at any given time can and will support only a certain maximum of life. It may hold one big fish, or several medium-sized fish, or dozens of small fish — but the total life support *will not be exceeded.* For this reason and others, a lot of fish that may never see a fisherman die every year. C'est la vie; *you cannot stockpile fish or wildlife.* So take your allowable limits when you are lucky enough to do so, and make use of them. You aren't being greedy or hurting someone else's sport.

Except under very high fishing pressure, "put-and-take" fishing or "fishing for fun" over the long term provides *no biological benefit.* And they can create a certain amount of waste, if enforced when it is not needed.

"Fly-fishing only" does little more. If a group of specialized fishermen wants a stretch of water open only to fly-fishing — to secure equal challenge or simply for the fun of fly-fishing with their own fraternity — there is no fault to be found, provided there is plenty of other fishable water around. But the fly-fisherman should not argue for the privilege on the biological benefits that will accrue because of their specialized sport. That reasoning simply does not hold up, as a good many careful studies have shown. This is just calling a spade a spade, for I thoroughly enjoy fly-fishing, tie my own flies (much better now), and consider "dry-fly fishing" the ultimate in the sport.

## Returning Fish

So we want to take some fish, and also may want to return some — with as little harm to them as possible. Any problems? You bet, especially regarding the fish being freed.

If a fish is badly hooked and its gills are ripped, it will die. Toss it back, if the law demands it, and some turtle, mink, raccoon or other wild passer-by will eat it. If the law allows it, and you are a *sportsman,* you will count that fish in your legal limit.

If the fish keep coming smaller than you want to keep, take steps to prevent the repeat performance. How? File the barb off the hook, change your location, or go to bigger lures or bait. Changing from treble or double hooks to single hooks also helps in releasing fish. Some waters are restricted solely to the use of single-point hooks to insure better survival of fish being released.

A built-in problem arises when a new species of fish is being introduced, and continues until they have become established. Small, sub-legal fish often are stocked because they adapt to their new environment better than mature fish, or perhaps economics demand such stocking. It is much cheaper to raise and plant small fish than to hold them to become larger fish at the hatchery, where they would demand a lot more space in the rearing tanks.

Unfortunately, these small fish almost always are more readily caught than the big ones. A good many will be caught until those waters achieve the varied age-classes needed to firmly establish the species. These small fish will have to be returned, and it is in the fisherman's best interest to release them *carefully*.

HOW TO RELEASE FISH

Unhook the fish and, if possible, release it without lifting it from the water. If you have to lift it out to disengage the hook, *wet your hands first*. Most fish are covered with a protective slime in their aquatic environment, and if they are handled with dry hands the continuous film over the fish becomes broken. Scales often will be disrupted and lost more easily. When a carelessly handled fish is returned to its natural environment, it is more susceptible to ever-present bacterial infection.

*Be careful how you lift a fish* you want to return to the water. Give it body support. If it is a large one, get some help, or pin it to the bottom in shallow water between the knees of your boots or waders as you work to release the hook.

Many times a well-intentioned angler lifts out a big fish just to have his picture taken with it. He intends to release it, but wants to take home bragging proof. The fish usually is held in the traditional pose: the smiling fisherman, one hand in the gills holding the fish up toward the camera to make it appear even larger than it is.

When this large fish is released, severe hemorrhaging probably already has started, and the fish will die. Large fish are not built to take lifting by a gill cover. If you must handle it, grab a fish around the tail ahead of the caudal fin or use *both* hands* to support its body for such pictures.

Another good solution for most big fish is the use of a net. Remove the hook while the fish still is in the net *in the water.* Then carefully lift the net with the fish well-supported in it, for a fast snapshot. Lower the net into the water, and help the fish* to get out and swim away. There will have been no excessive stress on any one part of the fish, and boy, will he look big as the net is swung toward the camera! That handle really helps.

## DEALING WITH THE HOOK

Most fishery biologists agree that when a fish is hooked deeply and you can't immediately withdraw it with a hook disgorger, its survival chances upon release will be greatly improved if the leader or line is cut off close to the fish's mouth. Thus, the hook or fly is left in the fish to pass along and perhaps be dissolved by strong stomach acids. Or the hook may become encysted, and chances are still good for the fish's survival.

When using a disgorger of the extended pincer or pliers-type,* don't try to withdraw the hook until it has been pushed down or backed out to expose the point. Then grab *the point* in the gripper and withdraw it.

I like the stick-type disgorger* with a different-sized grooved ball at each end. Use the ball that best fits the gape of the hook. Slide it down the leader to seat the ball in the bend of the hook. Push it in, and the groove in the ball will protect the hook point as the leader is tightened against it. The point, now hidden in the groove, will not snag anything when you withdraw it.

# CHAPTER 16

# THE FISH IS CAUGHT—
# THEN WHAT?

It is not enough just to know how to dress fish, for it may be well on the way to spoiling before you get to the dressing, even in winter.

Fish will never taste better than when cooked *fresh*, right off the hook, almost while they are still flopping. If you have tried this, you know. If not, give it a try, and I think you will agree. Being able to do this occasionally is one of the big pluses in catching your own fish. Time lost through handling and transporting fish caught commercially can and often does considerably lower their eating qualities. Don't blame the commercial fisherman, however, for he does his part well. And you should take a leaf from his book. On commercial fishing boats, a professional crew cleans and guts the fish as soon as they are brought aboard. Then they are packed in ice immediately. You cannot beat that system.

But many anglers arrive home with fish in poorer condition than necessary, often without even realizing what has happened. Most know that fish will deteriorate quickly, but they do little or nothing to prevent it. Here are a few basics:

The gills of the fish cause a lot of problems, for they go by the board in short order, even quicker than the innards. If you kill a fish, get rid of gills and guts immediately. (Sorry about that word, *guts*. It has been traditional with fishermen for centuries. *Innards* sometimes is used, but *entrails* and *viscera* are generally reserved for warm-blooded animals. It is only a word, and when I say *guts*, every fisherman knows exactly what I mean.)

Nothing is better than ice for keeping fish in good condition from the time of taking to final preparation for the table or freezing. There are things you can do, however, to improve your lot, even when ice is not available. I'll take these up as we go along.

## Warm Weather Fishing

The summer fisherman has several options, but the warmer the weather, the more consideration he must give to the care of his catch. If you are fishing and wading in water up to your navel, attach a good stringer to a suspender strap or belt. Choose a *stringer** that allows the fish on it to stay upright, so they can work their gills naturally to stay alive. Putting more than one fish on each snap of the large safety-pin-type* stringer usually kills the fish before long.

When the stringer becomes filled, or when you have to take the strung fish out of water to get around an obstruction or drop-off, it is wise to stop fishing long enough to field dress your catch.

Cut out the gills, and gut the fish by opening up the belly from the vent (anus) to the gills. Run a thumbnail along the backbone to remove the kidney — that dark red, brown or blackish material under the backbone. Wash out the cavity or wipe it clean with a cloth. *Handi-wipes* do a good job and rinse clean easily. Follow this same procedure when using a stringer over the side of a boat.

A **folding-mesh-wire basket*** with a spring-loaded cover can be used to replace the stringer. The basket keeps fish alive and natural in captivity for long periods of time, provided they are not crowded. Stream fishermen can use one too, since it packs well, folding compactly when not in use. It can be anchored in a cool, deep hole, and the fish you want to keep can be field dressed when it is time to move from your base of operation.

The basket also works fine when hung in the water or allowed to float over the side of a boat. A word of warning, however:

When it is time to move (even when you are rowing or paddling), take in the fish and field dress them, or most of them will die from water being forced through their gills, or from the crowding as the basket is pulled through the water.

I lost a good catch on Lake Champlain one day when I forgot to pull in the basket and headed out from Willow Bay at full bore. The tie chain quickly broke under the strain, and everything sank. I am sure all the fish died in their wire prison, but maybe some eels made use of them. I hope so, for I surely did not.

**Creels\*** also are good for temporarily keeping fish that are gilled and gutted. A ventilated canvas creel\* can be wet periodically, and resulting evaporation does an amazing cooling job, especially if there is a little wind blowing. It can be worn or hung in the shade from a branch. Don't forget, though, that lake shores and stream banks are favorite haunts of predators that are not above making away with your catch, creel and all.

If the traditional wicker type creel\* is carried, the fish also should be gilled and gutted as they are put into it. Place fresh, clean grass or ferns on the bottom of your creel before adding the fish. Not only are they great for color picture-taking, but they also keep the basket from becoming fouled with fish slime and help to hold the fish apart. They add a measure of insulation, as well, and provide space for air to circulate better through the bottom and sides of the basket for cooling by evaporation. More should be added to separate another layer of fish. Fish should never be allowed to press together in a mass. "Mass" usually means "mess." Wet the ferns or grasses occasionally.

Most anglers like to take trout and salmon home with the heads left on to show them off. There is nothing wrong with this if the gills are cut out completely and the guts removed through a regular belly cut, unless, of course, a mounted trophy is desired. Trophy fish are covered in the next chapter.

**Plastic bags.** Never dump your fish into a plastic bag unless they are going into the freezer immediately. As a general rule, *non-breathing plastic and fish do not go together.* The exception is an open plastic bucket with a locking mesh top that can be sunk into a pool of running water, or which has the water changed periodically to keep the water cool. Such an arrangement really is a small live-box, to keep the fish alive so they will stay fresh.


## REFRIGERATION

A simple refrigerator* for temporarily keeping dressed fish (and other perishables) in camp is described in fair detail later, should you wish to make one. It folds flat, dries quickly for trail packing, and maintains suprisingly low temperatures when it is wet and hung in the shade. Make your own variations to fit your needs. A square one is easier to load, holds more, and permits better organization of the items in it.

The boat fisherman has two solutions that he can provide for himself at small cost, if he plans ahead.

The first and easiest is to purchase a larger-than-normal portable picnic refrigerator. The cheap ones, made of expanded plastic pellets, can be purchased at tackle shops or department stores, but as a rule they do not stand up well under the normal wear and tear most fishermen demand. Double-walled types of smooth, rigid plastic or aluminum do better, if sturdy enough. With either material, you will be happier with a box having a rugged seat on top, doubling for a lid. It *will* be sat on or kneeled on, so get a good strong one, and it will last for years. A lasting, drainable, double-walled unit with rigid or foamed insulation between the walls is well worth the price, if you intend to do much transporting of fish or fishing from a boat.

The second option is to install a *permanent fish well/ice box* in your boat that also doubles as a seat.* Use paper masking tape to shape and hold sheets of cardboard in place while fiberglass mat* and/or ten-ounce boat cloth* is hand-laid with polyester or epoxy resin brushed into it. When cured, place the spacer blocks, making them slightly wider than the space needed to accommodate one-and-a-half to two-inch rigid foam planks. Tape more cardboard against the blocks to form the *inner wall*, putting the resin-fiberglass combination over the cardboard on the *inside*. Leave overage of about two inches around the bottom (inside and outside) so the fiberglass can be extended over the clean, sanded, floor of the boat. Make an oversized fiberglass cloth insert for the bottom inside, with the edges turned up slightly against the cured inside walls. Pull the spacer blocks and insert butted foam planks into the walls, but cut the foam to allow three-quarter-inch wooden cap strips to be fitted flush with the top of the walls. Secure the cap strips in place with adhesive made for attaching foam to cellar walls. Raw resin will melt most foam planks, so do not use it.

Now fit an overhanging cover (which is part of the seat) over the insulated walls capped with the wooden frame. Refrigerator welt or weather stripping is tacked or stuck in place around the underside of the cover, positioned to press against the wood cap-strips on top of the walls. Thus, the box is effectively sealed when the lid is closed. It can be locked by trunk latches or hooks and eyes.

The drain for the box should be planned before its construction. Many fellows let the water drain onto the floor when a stopper or plug is pulled. Then the water goes out when the boat's self-bailer clears the bilge under power. In dories or rowing skiffs, a bulb-type or other kind of siphon can be used.

Although some anglers will argue the point, I feel it is better to keep the water from melting ice at a minimum, especially if the fish have the heads cut off or are filleted when they are put in. If your box is watertight when plugged, as it should be, it also can be used as a live-box when partially filled with water.

The built-in or portable live-box is a good choice in areas that do not get too warm. In larger boats, a built-in live-box can have its water changed and replenished continuously or periodically by pump from the lake or ocean. If the box becomes crowded, start cleaning fish and packing them *in ice.*

Notice I did not say *on* ice. Follow the procedure of the commercial fishermen, and pack your rough-dressed fish *in* it — not just around and on top of a large chunk. In most fishing areas, you can find bagged ice cubes, which last better than ice chipped off a block. Pour in the cubes and work your fish into them, so they are more or less surrounded by ice. This is why I recommended at the start that you get a larger-than-normal picnic type refrigerator.

This follow-up recommendation will bring comments: *DON'T* put your beer in with the fish. If you want cold beer (and it certainly comes in handy if you don't overdo it), put that and anything else you may want to keep cold in a *separate* refrigerator. The ice for your fish will last much longer and will pack around the fish better — even if you don't mind a little slime on your can of beer.

**Take litter home.** Remember that empty cans weigh very little on the way back to a trash can. *Every boat should have an adequate trash bag or can* handy for you and your thoughtful friends. And then there's the "mini-litter." Many fish succumb each year to plastic cigarette filters and cigar tips, six-pack holders and other small pieces of indigestible or nondegradable litter carelessly tossed overboard. It flutters down, often attracting fish which gobble it up or become entangled. Keep it all aboard, okay?

## Winter Fishing

The winter fisherman in northern climates too often thinks he has everything going for him, as far as keeping his catch in good condition. He has, *if he thinks* a little about it, but as the song says, "It ain't necessarily so."

Many ice fishermen dress their fish right on the ice, leaving the trimmings for seagulls, crows and other scavengers on frugal winter diets to clean up — and they will. This is a good step toward saving quality food for the table, but later the cleaned fish are carried home, packed in a plastic bag or bucket in the back of a station wagon or van. What fisherman in his right mind is going to freeze on the way home, especially if he spent the day on the open ice? On goes the heat, and soon that nice catch is *really* a "mess of fish." You've got to do better than that.

Fish often are left beside the holes on the ice where they were caught, and some days they freeze solid in short order. On other days they only partially freeze. Periodically they are picked up and tossed into a bucket in various degrees of being frozen — guts and all. No problem yet, but again, where is the bucket carried on the trip home?

The gills deteriorate quickly in the warm temperatures of a heated automobile, and the protective coating on the fish still will soak into the flesh of rough-dressed fish. In addition, the final dressing at home will be much more difficult, if not downright unpleasant.

Many problems can be avoided if the winter fisherman carries some cotton rags with him (old turkish towels are great). Tuck an end of one under your belt and use the free end to dry off cold, wet hands, which are a hazard of the sport. *Then* put on your mittens.

Clean cotton rags also absorb excess moisture and slime when put in the bottom of your fish bucket. Another towel can be used to quickly wipe most of the slime off fresh-caught fish, which then can be tossed into the bucket. The excess water and slime are most easily removed as soon as the tip-up is reset. If the fish already has frozen on the outside, dip it in the water again, and then wipe it. Just a quick wipe is all that is needed — no big deal.

AVOID REFREEZING

Repeated freezing and thawing doesn't help the eating qualities of anything — much less fish — so you will have to adjust your fishing habits to the problem. Pick up your fish often on days with well-below freezing temperatures. Keep the bucket in the cold trunk of the car between collections. Or a trick that can work for you when there is plenty of snow on the ice: Sink your bucket entirely into a pile of snow, which is good insulation. A boat cushion or thick wad of newspapers over the top of the bucket gives top protection from deep freezing, and it assures easy access, too. The same idea can be used to keep minnows from freezing in the bait bucket, if you are fishing on the open ice.

*An ice tub* works as well today as it did a hundred years ago, when there is no adequate amount of snow, or even when there is, to keep your fish alive when temperatures are 20 degrees Fahrenheit or above. Chip out an ice tub big enough to hold the fish you think you will catch. It always can be enlarged. Depending on the weather and the thickness of the ice, make it deep enough so when it fills with water, it will cover the backs of fish swimming in it maybe with an inch to spare.

An average, rectangular tub should measure about two feet by three feet and be four to six inches deep. Use an axe or ice-spud to chip out the tub, and a skimmer to clean out the chips. Some ice fishermen cut an intake hole down to water right in the tub, but they soon learn. Don't do it. Chances are good the intake hole will melt out, and by the end of the day you may find half your fish have disappeared.

Time and effort are saved and fish will not swim free if the tub is located only two or three feet from a centrally located fishing hole. A *very narrow* channel from the hole to the tub safely supplies it with water. If a fish tries to sneak down the channel, you'll see it.

## ROUGH-DRESS YOUR FISH

If the day is bitter cold, and you are one of those hardy souls who fish the open ice no matter what, you should at least rough-dress your fish. Cut partially down from the back behind the head of each fish to the pectoral fins. Grab the head in one hand and pull it down and back toward the tail, ripping off the head and pulling out most of the guts. You can do that with rubber gloves over your regular gloves, and rubber mitts work even better, if you can find them. Then toss the rough-dressed fish into a pail, knowing full well it will freeze solid. When it comes time to go home, lash your fish in a suitable container on the roof, if you own a wagon or van, or make provisions to carry them outside somehow. Put them in the cold trunk if you have a sedan.

When you get home, divide the frozen beauties and put some into burlap or mesh onion bags to allow them to drain as they thaw somewhat. Put the bags in a warm place (60–70 degrees F.) and get to work. The first batch can be placed in a collander or on burlap tacked to a frame. When the skins become wet and while the fish are still mostly frozen, finish the cleaning job. When you have enough for one meal, immediately proceed with whatever method you have chosen for final freezing. Or put them outside until the lot is ready for taking to the locker.

Fishermen making use of a comfortable fishing shanty or bobhouse need only use common sense and the methods recommended earlier when warm temperatures are encountered. A good cutting board, however, should be in every shanty.

*Rectangular milk cartons* work well for freezing and insure against freezer burn (dehydration): Put the dressed fish or fillets into a plastic bag. Fold the top diagonally, leaving the top corner for air evacuation. Work the air out by pressing the bag to the fish, working from bottom to top. Then put the upper corner in your mouth, and you can easily suck out most of the remaining air. Fold over the corner a couple times and tape-seal it. Shape the package to fit easily into the milk carton and drop it in. Fill the carton only about a third full so the fish will not float. When this has frozen, top off the carton to cover the fish by at least a quarter inch, but not too full. Allow space for freezing expansion, and freeze it. The cartons stack well in the freezer, and the fish keep top quality for a long, long time.

Large, baking-type fish can be handled in bitter cold weather a special way when you fish from a shanty. Dress the fish, take its head off, and wash or wipe out the body cavity carefully. Then put it outside on top of a sheet of plastic or flat plastic bag until the fish partially freezes, which seals the exposed, fleshy end. When that end is hard, pour water over it or dip it, and let another layer freeze. Repeat the operation to build up a thick glaze of ice over it all. Leave the fish outside to freeze solid. As soon as you get home, wrap the ice-encased fish in freezer paper or put them into individual plastic bags, and put them into the freezer.

**Smelt** fishermen just gut their fish, leaving the heads attached (to prevent water from soaking into the exposed flesh). They cut a milk carton's top off around the top, square-edge fold. Then they drop the fish into it. Things work even better if you lay them out straight first to partially freeze. Then they line up vertically with fewer voids when they are placed in the milk carton. When the fisherman gets home, water is poured into the carton with the smelt to within a half inch of the open top. The cartons then are put into the freezer as is. Later, when the fish have thawed and are ready for cooking, they are washed and the heads are taken off.

**An alternative** is to cut off the heads and gut them on site, if the weather is well below freezing. Spread them outside, flat and straight, on a plastic bag, and let them freeze. About a half hour before you plan to leave, collect them (well frozen) and stack them *tails first* in the milk cartons. Pour in only a couple of inches of water and let their tails freeze into it. *Don't* let them thaw on the way home.

Once home, top off the carton to within a half inch of the top and immediately put the carton into the freezer. (The raw, cut head ends, being already frozen, will not soak up the water.) When the fish are being thawed for cooking, rip the carton off the block of ice with the fish in it and place it, *tails up*, in a collander in the sink to thaw. The water will run off and gravity take it away. Again the exposed flesh will not soak up excessive amounts of water and the fish will cook better.

# Tips on Cleaning
# and Dressing Fish (General)

Few people of ordinary means have to worry about taking giants from ocean depths, unless they own the charter boat. Then they know how and what to do. The skipper, his mate or the crew take care of the giants, and most of these fish taken are sold on the dock. After the weigh-in and the picture taking, the professionals make the sale or take over the dressing chores.

If you should luck into a big sturgeon and manage to keep your gear intact to land him — or have the same luck with an ocean monster — the dressing goes much the same as it does for smaller fish.

In fishing, as in hunting, the *sport* has ended after the challenge is met. I don't know anyone who thinks cleaning and dressing fish is fun, even though fishermen are well-known for the lies they tell from time to time. It isn't that we really lie — we just forget the details in reliving the excitement of the sport.

**Knives** are important for cleaning and dressing fish, and opinions about them often vary with the user and the particular kind of fish being dressed. As a general rule, however, a heavy, stiff, relatively hard (but not brittle) steel blade is used for beheading, cutting thick planks through heavy bone, and cutting through the tough skins of some monsters. Because this is a heavy-duty knife*, the blade should have more of a wedge edge than one with a fine, long taper.

A second *filleting knife*\* is very useful. It has a long, narrow, flexible, tough steel blade, and for my money should be neither stainless nor too sharp. How sharp? Sharp enough to cut through the skin, flesh and small bones along the sides of the backbone without tearing the flesh or lifting the grain of it, yet *not* so sharp that it slices through the skin continually from the inside.

**A good splinter-free cutting board,**\* big enough to handle the fish you plan to dress and with surface to spare, is a must for most fishermen-at-work. Fine end-grain, hardwood blocks, cemented with epoxy to a piece of marine-grade plywood is best.

A similar board* often is built into the rail or on the fantail of serious fishermen's boats. Low, solid boards at each side of the working surface keep things neat. The guts, trimmings and wash-down go over the side. A portable dressing board can be clamped or hinged to the rail and stowed out of the way when it isn't needed.

On the way back to the dock, the person cleaning the fish usually takes them from the live-box, strikes the fish on the head with a billy-club and removes the head and guts. The offal pushed overboard feeds the gulls, eels, turtles, crabs and other aquatic scavengers.

How do you hold these slippery fish for easy dressing? There are all kinds of ingenious devices to assist, and some work better than others. A large spring clamp at one end of the board often is used to securely hold the tail of the fish. These cleaning boards can be purchased ready-made, or you can make one fairly easily.*

A sharp, strong metal peg or spike fixed at one end of a board,* or on the side of a shed, is used to good advantage by some eel, catfish and bullhead fishermen to help in dressing their catches. The spike, angled toward one end of the board, pierces the head and keeps it in place. The board below it provides a smooth, hard working surface for skinning and dressing.

Another type of work surface (and it should not be pooh-poohed) is several layers of ordinary newspaper spread on a table or counter top. The blotter characteristics of the paper soak up the wetted skin surface and slime to securely hold such fish as pickerel, northern pike and muskelunge, which demand special handling for bone-free fillets.* As each fish is finished, the top sheet or two of newspaper is folded over the head, guts, bones and remaining skin, and put to one side, exposing new, fresh paper for the next fish.

**Scaling fish.** Many fishermen use the clamp board to secure the tail while they scrape away the scales against the grain, but the scales fly in all directions. Try scraping them at about a forty-five degree angle to the axis of the fish, and you will wear fewer scales. Some roller-type scalers work well too.

I do most of my final dressing of fish right at the kitchen sink — even the scaling of big bass. No, I don't have scales all over the floor and up the walls. I fill the sink about half full of cold water first and sometimes add ice to it. Then I scale the fish with a knife or serrated scraper. The fish is pressed to the bottom of the sink under at least two inches of water. The scales don't fly at all. They just settle to the bottom, and I catch them in the strainer when I let the water out.

One reason I like to work in the kitchen rather than outdoors when doing final fish dressing is that I don't enjoy flies and hornets, which are quickly attracted to fish-dressing operations.

Many fish, such as yellow perch, trout, salmon and bullheads, can be completely dressed in hand with little chance of cutting yourself, once you have the method down pat, but the practice is not recommended for youngsters. As a general rule, cuts are made away from and in front of the hand holding the fish. The belly cut is made upward from the hand holding the back of the fish. Other cuts are made downward, away from and beyond the hand holding the fish, such as the head cut on the yellow perch.*

You will find many professional fish strippers ignoring safety precautions, cutting heads toward a hooked thumb, as many housewives cut vegetables. In time, both of these pros shed some blood. One young professional fish-stripper I know had a moment of carelessness. Twenty or thirty stitches and two weeks later, Bill went back to work, still partially incapacitated. While he had been recuperating, his boat had brought in fantastic hauls, and Bill received a percentage of the catch money in addition to a regular salary — when he worked. He paid dearly for that brief lapse of respect for a sharp knife.

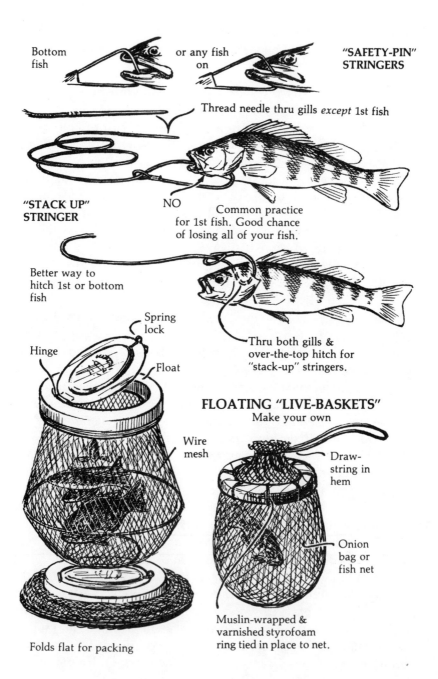

Bottom fish

or any fish on

**"SAFETY-PIN" STRINGERS**

Thread needle thru gills *except* 1st fish

**"STACK UP" STRINGER**

NO

Common practice for 1st fish. Good chance of losing all of your fish.

Better way to hitch 1st or bottom fish

Spring lock

Hinge

Float

Thru both gills & over-the-top hitch for "stack-up" stringers.

**FLOATING "LIVE-BASKETS"**
Make your own

Wire mesh

Draw-string in hem

Onion bag or fish net

Muslin-wrapped & varnished styrofoam ring tied in place to net.

Folds flat for packing

## ON RELEASING FISH

Wet hands first

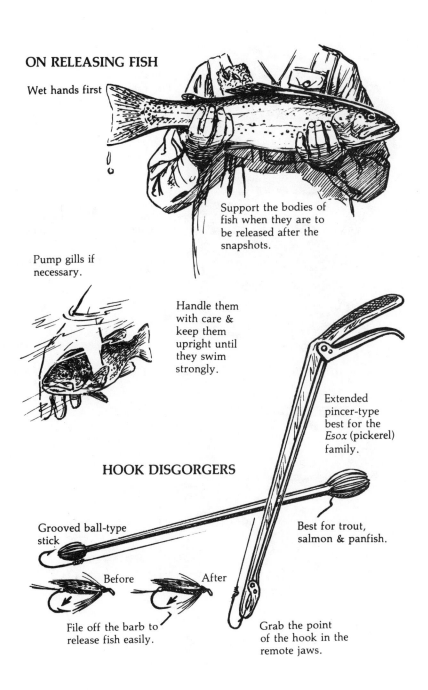

Support the bodies of fish when they are to be released after the snapshots.

Pump gills if necessary.

Handle them with care & keep them upright until they swim strongly.

Extended pincer-type best for the *Esox* (pickerel) family.

## HOOK DISGORGERS

Grooved ball-type stick

Best for trout, salmon & panfish.

Before    After

File off the barb to release fish easily.

Grab the point of the hook in the remote jaws.

# CREELS

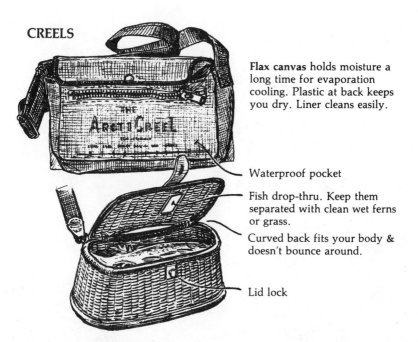

**Flax canvas** holds moisture a long time for evaporation cooling. Plastic at back keeps you dry. Liner cleans easily.

Waterproof pocket

Fish drop-thru. Keep them separated with clean wet ferns or grass.

Curved back fits your body & doesn't bounce around.

Lid lock

**Traditional Split Willow** or durable plastic facsimile, well ventilated & cleans well.

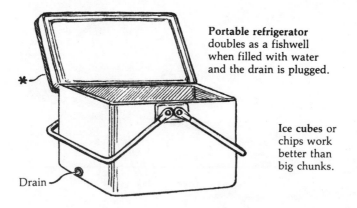

**Portable refrigerator** doubles as a fishwell when filled with water and the drain is plugged.

**Ice cubes** or chips work better than big chunks.

Drain

**✻** The best is even better when it has smooth, finished plywood epoxied to the lid to double for a seat.

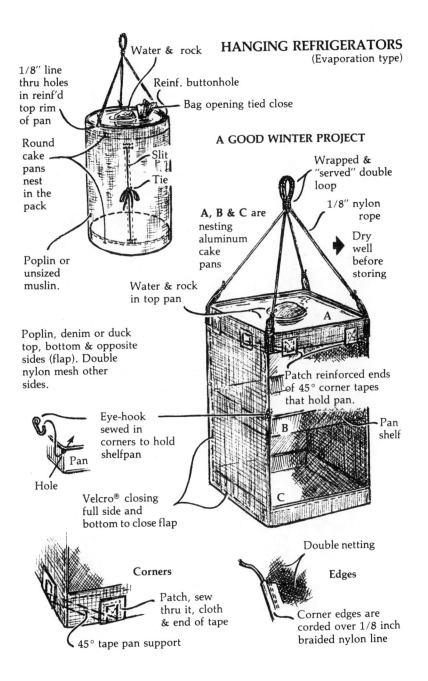

# HANGING REFRIGERATORS
(Evaporation type)

Water & rock

1/8" line
thru holes
in reinf'd
top rim
of pan

Reinf. buttonhole

Bag opening tied close

**A GOOD WINTER PROJECT**

Round
cake
pans
nest
in the
pack

Slit

Tie

Wrapped &
"served" double
loop

1/8" nylon
rope

A, B & C are
nesting
aluminum
cake
pans

Dry
well
before
storing

Poplin or
unsized
muslin.

Water & rock
in top pan

A

Poplin, denim or duck
top, bottom & opposite
sides (flap). Double
nylon mesh other
sides.

Patch reinforced ends
of 45° corner tapes
that hold pan.

Eye-hook
sewed in
corners to hold
shelfpan

Pan
shelf

B

Pan

Hole

Velcro® closing
full side and
bottom to close flap

C

Double netting

**Corners**

**Edges**

Patch, sew
thru it, cloth
& end of tape

Corner edges are
corded over 1/8 inch
braided nylon line

45° tape pan support

## BOAT SEAT REFRIGERATOR/FISHWELL

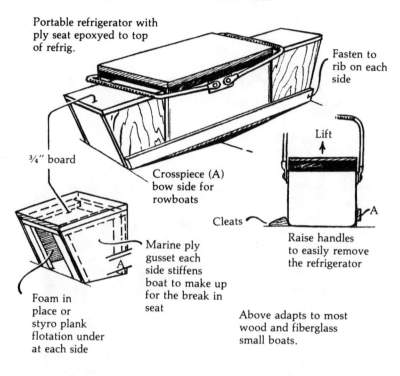

Portable refrigerator with ply seat epoxyed to top of refrig.

Fasten to rib on each side

¾" board

Crosspiece (A) bow side for rowboats

Cleats

Lift

A

Raise handles to easily remove the refrigerator

Marine ply gusset each side stiffens boat to make up for the break in seat

Foam in place or styro plank flotation under at each side

Above adapts to most wood and fiberglass small boats.

## A REFRIGERATOR/WELL FROM SCRATCH

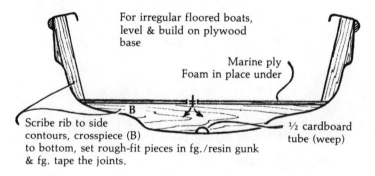

For irregular floored boats, level & build on plywood base

Marine ply Foam in place under

B

Scribe rib to side contours, crosspiece (B) to bottom, set rough-fit pieces in fg./resin gunk & fg. tape the joints.

½ cardboard tube (weep)

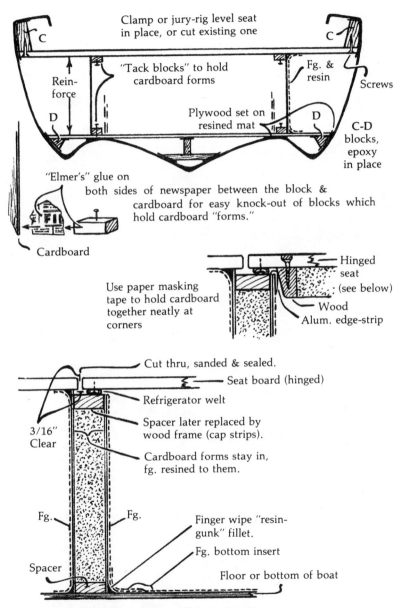

Clamp or jury-rig level seat
in place, or cut existing one

C

C

"Tack blocks" to hold
cardboard forms

Fg. &
resin

Rein-
force

Screws

Plywood set on
resined mat

D

D

C-D
blocks,
epoxy
in place

"Elmer's" glue on
both sides of newspaper between the block &
cardboard for easy knock-out of blocks which
hold cardboard "forms."

Cardboard

Use paper masking
tape to hold cardboard
together neatly at
corners

Hinged
seat
(see below)

Wood

Alum. edge-strip

Cut thru, sanded & sealed.

Seat board (hinged)

Refrigerator welt

Spacer later replaced by
wood frame (cap strips).

3/16"
Clear

Cardboard forms stay in,
fg. resined to them.

Fg.

Fg.

Finger wipe "resin-
gunk" fillet.

Fg. bottom insert

Floor or bottom of boat

Spacer

**Details of section thru wall & seat top**

## FISH KNIVES

**Heavy knife** for skinning monsters & planking (steaks), also beheading big fish. Note recessed holes in handle for hanging both of these knives.

Trout knife

A comfortable **fillet knife** that *floats*, orange tipped handle up. A good idea.

Length of blades dependent on fish expected to be dressed. Use stainless or wash down and oil (in the sheath) around salt water.

## SCALERS

Old standby

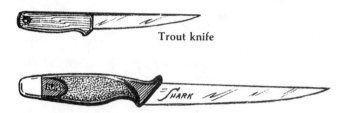

Scaler-combo knife

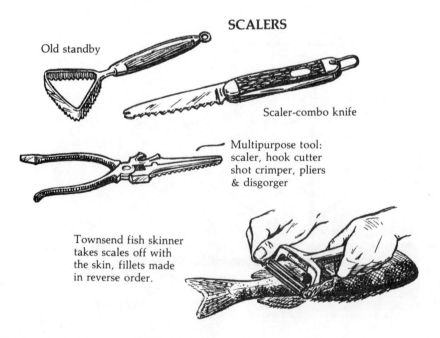

Multipurpose tool: scaler, hook cutter shot crimper, pliers & disgorger

Townsend fish skinner takes scales off with the skin, fillets made in reverse order.

## DRESSING BOARDS

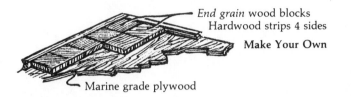

*End grain* wood blocks
Hardwood strips 4 sides

**Make Your Own**

Marine grade plywood

**Step 1.** Use marine waterproof glue or epoxy to stick blocks & side strips to plywood base.

**Step 2.** Seal all except working surface with oil based sealer & varnish.

**Step 3.** Treat topside with 50-50 linseed oil/turpentine, several coats after sanding all flush. Final steel wool rub for top.

**Step 4.** Provide for hanging storage.

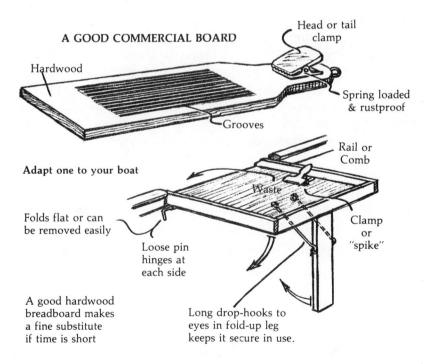

**A GOOD COMMERCIAL BOARD**

Head or tail clamp

Hardwood

Spring loaded & rustproof

Grooves

Rail or Comb

**Adapt one to your boat**

*Waste*

Clamp or "spike"

Folds flat or can be removed easily

Loose pin hinges at each side

A good hardwood breadboard makes a fine substitute if time is short

Long drop-hooks to eyes in fold-up leg keeps it secure in use.

CHAPTER 17

# DRESSING FISH

The methods for dressing the selected species of fish shown here will adapt to other, quite similar species, and cover the whole gamut of both fresh and salt water fish. An understanding of basic fish anatomy* will help you do a better job when the end goal is fine eating.

Check the drawings: The line of *hemal or dorsal ribs*, sometimes called *false ribs*, above the *ventral* ribs (rib cage) vary considerably in different species. They are almost negligible in some species (like yellow perch) and very well developed in others (such as the herring and pickerel families). The latter are fine tasting but almost impossible to eat unless special methods for dressing them are understood and carried out well. It's not difficult.


TROUT AND SALMON*

Perhaps the easiest of all fish to prepare for the table are the salmonids. Some innovations for you to try are shown in the illustrative supplement immediately following this section.


YELLOW PERCH* *(Perca flavascens)*

The how-to for this very popular table species, step-by-step illustrated, works exactly the same for many other species. Also see "Bass," p. 226.

204

## PICKEREL FAMILY*

The most notable species in the *Esox* family are the chain pickerel, northern pike and muskellunge. All provide great sport with light tackle. They make fine table fare, too, once you learn to cope with their special bone problems.

## BULLHEADS AND OTHER CATFISHES*

Preparing these "meat-fish" for the table is covered on pages 223-225. The live catfishes require special handling* to avoid painful puncture wounds.

## BASS — AND OTHER FISH FOR BAKING.

The method shown is adaptable to many other fish, several noted by species names. Procedures for yellow perch (p. 219) and bass (p. 226) can be adapted to most of the common fish destined for the table.

## THE AMERICAN SHAD (BONE-FREE)*

American shad *(Alosa sapidissima)* is the largest herring we have on the east coast and is now fairly common, from introductions, on the Pacific coast. Mature shad, eighteen inches to two feet long, are average on most runs.

In New England, fishways are being created or improved up the Connecticut River to accommodate passage of shad and salmon above barrier power dams. The four states — New Hampshire, Vermont, Massachusetts and Connecticut — that border on this big river are working with federal agencies and the power companies in a cooperative program for restoration of anadromous fish in the river. It is hoped that Atlantic salmon will be the prime species, but thousands and thousands of American shad already are running the river each spring. It won't be many years until the shad, a fine fighting fish on light tackle, will be back in all of its historical waters and maybe beyond them. These powerful, silvery herring run the river each year to spawn in the main stem and tributaries to it. Thousands of sport fishermen line the banks and bridges, and flotillas of boats can be found below the dams each spring as anglers try to get some shad with "darts," flies and lures.

*Shad roe,* the egg mass, often is the main appeal in the eating of these big herring. A large mature female has enough tiny eggs to fill the two hands of a big man. Individual eggs are about the same size as those of the very much smaller yellow perch, and are a similar dull yellow-orange.

Inland fishermen hardly make a dent in the shad population, and even the offshore commercial fishermen have no more than a healthy effect on their numbers. The teeming hordes in the river attest to that.

When it comes to eating the fish itself, however, there is one horrendous problem — bones! Rows of bones radiate in all directions through the pinkish-white flesh. There is, of course, an organized pattern for them,* but hemal ribs are extensive, and curve around the flesh in addition to lacing it thoroughly. The flesh is somewhat oily, like most of the salt water fishes, but when it is cooked the flesh turns pure white. It is fine-grained and surprisingly dry, not unlike that of a pan-fried freshwater trout. The taste is a little stronger than a trout, but much milder than most ocean fish, especially if the dark colored "side-straps" are removed. (I remove the dark colored flesh down the sides of bluefish, too, because I like the resulting milder taste much better.)

Some anglers, often those with old-country backgrounds, smoke herring and find that the bones, many of which are more like hard, fine tendons, become somewhat less obnoxious. Partial deterioration may be the cause. At any rate, they eat the bones along with the fish, and they claim the bones are more cooperative. The texture of the flesh is changed, and the smoke gives it a different flavor as well.

Others pickle herring, and the vinegar acts on the bones to make them soft. They are good, but I rarely make a meal of pickles. Pickled anything always tastes pickled, and I like the natural flavor of meat and fish (though I admit to camouflaging strong-tasting fish and sea ducks). And shad, once free of their bones, are really delicious.

Most of you have heard of cooking the larger herring on heavy brown paper or a board — and when they are done, you throw away the fish and eat the paper or board. Well, the bones in the herring family do make things almost that bad.

In the smaller sizes, everyone eats herring bones — as in kippered herring and sardines — and in the latter you eat more than the bones. But if the larger herring are fried or broiled, you do not eat the bones by choice. You just eat very slowly and very carefully. You also can be sure of eating cold fish.

Finding a practical solution* for shad that an average person could handle was as much an obsession for me as learning to work a pickerel into four delicious, bone-free fillets.* Too many of both fishes are being wasted needlessly.

**Getting rid of shad bones.*** I believe my solution for shad in particular and large herring in general is completely practical — and different. They are filleted,* but that is only part of the procedure, not the end product. Perhaps someone will come up with a knife shaped like a corkscrew to easily fillet a shad bone-free, but I cannot imagine even a Rube Goldberg doing that job. A few oldtime shad fishermen in the New York-Connecticut area traditionally have boned shad for the select New York restaurant trade, but they are a vanishing breed. Even the best of them can only do a couple dozen in an hour, so what are the odds for the casual shad fisherman? Pretty bad! This is why a good many fishermen are taking the roe and wasting the fish or using it for organic fertilizer. I hope this "Candy-dandy" will show that you can have delicious, bone-free eating of big shad and alewives without becoming a "herring choker" — unless you want to. The secret is "fish cakes," although once the flesh is bone-free, there is a variety of other ways to prepare delicious meals from it. I much prefer my shad fishcakes to codfish cakes. I like cod fillets, but not the texture of codfish cakes. My shad cakes are all fish and have fine texture, but you can mix in roe, mashed potato or anything else you would like to try. Once you have the main ingredient, the choice is yours. I like them plain, with a little lemon juice or a thin tartar sauce dip. Most people use the roe in one way or another whenever shad is served.

I'll try to describe what has to be done, step by step. Probably you've never used a "bone-clamp."* At this writing, I also doubt that you can buy one, but I'm sure there will be one on the market soon. Nevertheless, if you will jury-rig a clamp, the job will go amazingly fast with very satisfying results. The tool is a very high-class, expensive item. All you need is a fine-toothed, *used* hacksaw blade and a small piece of wood cut to your own hand dimensions. (It also is a great tool for holding down the edge of skin when removing flesh from the skin, as in dressing flounders.)

To get the makings for your shad cakes on ice quickly in warm weather, catch one or two shad, fillet them with a sharp knife, *leaving the skin and scales on the flesh.* Ice the roe and the fillets. Bury or dispose of the rest *thoughtfully,* for a shad is a pretty big fish! The bones can be removed from the fillets later, leaving only clear flesh for the cooking.

I urge you first to study the anatomy drawings* so you will understand the reason for the different steps.* You can take my word for it: the Y-bones of a pickerel or pike are nothing when compared to the bones of a herring. Herring have combinations of bones that are hard to beat — no, *were.* See page 227.


SHARKS

Many sharks not only are edible, they provide very fine eating. Some are sold as one kind or another of swordfish and though that's dishonest, the lie is seldom discovered. Their flesh is about the whitest, most appealing and tastiest of ocean fish. Species that are readily eaten in many areas of the world all too often are shunned like the plague in other places. Probably the best eating of the more than a hundred species are the great white shark, mako, parbeagle, thresher, and the spiny dogfish (sand shark locally — *Squalus acanthias).* You are on your own exploring any of the others. Some contain considerable urea, and should be avoided. To learn more about the various sharks, find a copy of Patricia Pope's *Dictionary of Sharks,* Great Outdoors Publishing Co., St. Petersburg, Florida.

Shark skin generally is very tough and rather valuable, as is the liver, depending on market availability. Actual skinning is accomplished much the same as that for any large animal. Then the skin is fleshed, salted and rolled or folded similarly.

**Shark steaks.** I suppose you could use a Samuri sword to cut steaks or planks from the big sharks, but since sharks have no bones, a heavy butcher knife is sufficient. For my size shark, the spiny dogfish, the one with the "spike" on its dorsal and no anal fin, a good fillet knife will do. When this dogfish is skinned, it looks like a clean, white tapered log about the size of a good zucchini squash. Cut it crosswise as you do the squash, making slices about three-quarters of an inch thick. Dip them in milk and put them in a bag with dry, "Shake and Bake" commercially prepared for fish — or make your own. Shake the slices to accumulate a coating of seasoned crumbs, and then put them into a shallow pan. Bake at 400 degrees F. until browned and the flesh readily pulls apart with a fork. You'll be pleasantly surprised.

## EELS

Eels have long been considered a great delicacy in Europe, and there is a growing demand for them in the Boston, New York and Montreal markets. Fine restaurants frequently make hors d'oeuvres of them or serve them creamed or en casserole.

The American eel *(Anguilla bostoniensis)* has a broad range along the Atlantic and Gulf coasts of North America. It extends all the way to Greenland and Labrador and south even to Brazil, though it is quite rare there. Thus just about all river systems emptying into the Atlantic usually get their share of migrating American eels. Some become impounded, but they will not establish populations even though they live long lives, since they must go to the ocean to spawn — and perhaps to find the opposite sex — another oddity of nature. The Pacific coast of North America, strangely enough, has no members of the eel family.

Although American eels can grow to five or six feet, most anglers catch eels only half that size or smaller. They *appear* to be scaleless — like the bullhead and other catfish — but such is not the case. The eel's unique scales are imbedded in the skin and can be seen under a magnifying glass. "Slippery as an eel" is an old but well-founded cliche. Their skin is covered with heavy protective slime, and certainly lives up to the expression. This condition gives a lot of people a bad time when it comes to skinning eels, the first step when preparing them for cooking.

**Skinning eels.*** I've seen people cut off the eel's head (to stop it from wiggling) and then proceed to gut it like a regular fish by slicing it down the belly. They nail one or both ends of the eel to a board, and cut and pull off pieces of skin with pliers, making a lot of work out of a very easy job. See page 230.

A nail through the head is not a bad idea, but if you have many to skin, the sharpened spike, suggested earlier — in one end of a board that can be washed and put away for the next time — is much better. Drive a 10-penny nail at a forty-five degree angle away from where the body of the eel will hang or be worked on the flat. Then file the head off the nail and sharpen it. Make a good protecting sheath for it, that will cover the point when it is not in use.

A pair of cotton work gloves helps in handling the slippery critter, but wipe it off first with a cotton rag or paper towel.

Grab the eel by the head and cut a ring all around it *just through the skin* behind the head. Then force the sharpened end of the spike up through the underside of the jaw and the skull.* Now you have a firm anchor point.

The second cut can best be accomplished by pinching the point of the knife blade at an angle forward, *sharp edge down,* between a thumb and index finger. The exposed point should extend out between the thumb and finger* only far enough to make about an eighth-inch-deep cut along the back. The thumb and finger act as a depth gauge for the cut. Cut through the skin beginning in the ring-cut at the top of the back, and slide the blade along to the tip of the tail. Hold the eel straight with your free hand by pulling the body away from the spike holding the head.* Keep the pulling or guiding hand a few inches behind the blade between it and the tail. Make the cut the full length, staying close along one side of the dorsal fin when it is reached. Then cut along the other side of it the same way.

A stiff injector razor blade also does an excellent job, too. It is *pulled* along the back with the guiding hand close to and behind the blade,* between the anchored eel's head and the cut being made.

Once these cuts are made, slip the point of the knife under the corners of skin at either side of the juncture of the head and back cuts. Pressing the corner of skin flat against the blade with your thumb, rip *both corners* back and down until the skin starts to pull away at the belly. Then slip the head off the spike and grab it in your free hand, gloved or with a rag in it. With the free hand firmly gripping the head, peel the skin off from the belly side in one continuous motion, pulling it out and away from the body. The skin will invert over the body parting at the back cut. It will peel like a banana.

Take out the soft-rayed fins against the grain with thumb against a flat blade as you do for the removal of the dorsal fins on the yellow perch (see page 219).

You can grab the belly skin and flesh under the body cavity in the jaws of pliers when pulling back the skin, if you find it easier, but the knife alone works fine with a little practice, and one tool is then adequate for the whole job. The dorsal and belly fins also are removed like the dorsal fins of the yellow perch.

The flesh of the eel is white when cooked and of fine flavor. I had always heard they were greasy before I tried them. The flesh may be oily when you skin it, and even this appears to vary — perhaps depending on length of time from the ocean. When cooked, the flesh is dry and flaky. The back meat can be filleted — well, sort of. See below. Since the ribs and backbone hold together quite well, I find it easier to break the long body into chunks of a length best suited to your pan. Cut *between* the ribs and spines of the backbone, parting it *between the joints*, and there will be no loose bones. When cooked, you will find the flesh easily rakes from the bones with the tip of a fork pulled parallel to them. If the eel is cut into short chunks, you will encounter less resistance from those not accustomed to eating eels. They soon forget that long, slithering, snake-like fish it once was, and think only of the pleasant taste.

There are a dozen or more species of eels found around the world, but at this time, I do not know how many are edible. Check this point locally if you are a world traveler. The next time I pull in a sand- or orange-colored "conger" eel from the ocean, I may give it a try. The same general procedure should be applicable to any of them, but you are on your own, with all but the American eel.

The parasitic *lamprey*, incidentally, is *not* an eel. The head of an eel has a fish's mouth with normal jaws, and pectoral fins further distinguish it from a lamprey, which has an ugly, sucking disc mouth with concentric circles of rasping, cone-shaped teeth.

Seven external ports or openings on each side of the parasite give final proof it is no eel. But "Dairyfield Beef" reputedly was eaten during the 1800's in substantial quantities — lampreys!

**Fillet an eel AFTER it is cooked!** If you are making a casserole or hors d'oeuvres from eels, do your filleting after poaching them. Now, maybe that isn't technically correct, but then again it might be. It is the result that counts, so skin and gut the eels. Cut them into lengths according to the pan you plan to cook them in. *Part the backbone by wiggling the knife blade between the vertebrae.* Don't slash through and get loose bones or chips.

A large, rectangular cake tin works fine. Cut each eel in lengths about an inch short of the pan when they are laid in straight, side by side. Don't pack them together tightly. Cover them with water — "spiked," seasoned or *au naturel* — and keep them just under the boiling point, about 200°, for approximately 10 minutes, (400° if done in the oven, but watch it. Don't let them boil).

Drain and lightly pull the flesh from the bones on one side. It should slide off easily when you use the side of a fork. Then lift out the backbone intact. The flesh should be in chunks if not in just two pieces for each length of eel cut. Now you can finish the cooking, eat as is, or doctor it for hors d'oeuvres without worrying about bones.

*Note:* The same reasoning and principle of poaching first can be used for learning where the bones lie in many fishes. Just cut a fillet off one side,* poach the remaining side, then lift up and remove the backbone for study. Now you can *see* how the bones are arranged. Once you understand this, about 80 to 90 percent of the battle is won for obtaining boneless fillets thereafter.

Another thing you can do that helps is to run a fingertip over the fillet, feeling for the butt ends of the bones cut off during the filleting process. Run the fingertip from *tail to head* to line them up. Often a slice *to the skin* at each side of the line of bones will suffice — pinch the head end between the cuts and lift it to rip back. Usually the strip comes out with all the offending bones in it.

The pickerel* and herring* families need a little more thought. They are more complicated to say the least!

## THE FLAT FISHES

Flounders come in many shades and sizes, and they're all delicious. They're easily caught at the right times of the year in the right places (which are usually accessible to the average fisherman). You owe it to yourself to know how to dress them for the table. They *are* different.

The tiny flounder comes into the world a pretty normal-looking fish, but when about a half-inch long things happen. His right eye, the one that would have been on the white or bottom side of the fish in later life, gradually migrates to join the other eye on the dark top or left side of the fish. When adult, the *topside*, as it swims along the ocean floor or scuttles under loose sand or mud to hide, is really its *left* side, and the bottom side is its *right* side. Some flounders are "lefthanded," but this is generally what happens. The clean, white side that is down also loses its gill opening, which probably would only fill with sand or mud if it didn't defer to the one on the topside.

To many, flounders* and "sanddabs" may seem to be screwed-up fishes, but all agree they are delightful on the table with their fine mild taste and clean white cooked flesh. They usually are filleted,* so there are no bones to contend with either.

The halibut is the granddaddy of this clan, and in large sizes it usually is planked, like other monsters such as bill fish and sharks.

## SNAKES

While snakes are reptiles and not fish, they seem to fit best in this section. Snake skins sometimes are used for novelty accessories such as small decorative boxes, belts or hat bands. Needless to say, poisonous snakes should be handled carefully, even when they are dead. Their heads should be cut off and sealed in a can for disposal or for venom sale where legal. Keep them close to freezing temperature in storage.

Rattlesnake meat has long been a delicacy, tasting and looking much like chicken. Canned rattlesnake can be purchased in some gourmet shops. Most of the snakes, however, get short shrift from too many people. But once dead and made into beautiful and practical items, all is forgiven. Snakeskin cemented as a partial inlay in a regular oak-tanned leather belt will last for years and bring a lot of "ohs" and "ahs." The skin is tough, but it needs backing for strength. Perhaps the hate all began in the Garden of Eden. Nevertheless, snakes do help man immeasurably through rodent and insect control, and they *are* an integral part of the checks and balances needed in the healthy wildlife community.

**Skinning.** The snake usually is ring-cut behind the head and then spiked to a board through its head, *belly up.* Hold the tail of the snake under stress pulling against the nail, while the other hand draws a sharp knife or razor blade through the skin in a straight line down the belly, opening it full length. Then loosen the corners and strip the skin off the body from head to tail. The knife will be little needed. Check to see that the inside of the skin is clear of meat or membrane.

Then stretch it evenly, *inside up,* tacking the edges to a board in a straight line. Place tacks closely together (every inch or two) working from the head end. Place the tacks alternately across from one another, as you proceed to the tip of tail. Leave the rattle of a rattlesnake attached until you decide what you will do with it.

When dry, the snake skin will be almost like parchment. Roll it up and keep it dry. Warm a covered can or wide-mouth screw-top bottle to dry the air in it. Put the roll of skin into it, replace the cover while the container is still warm, and tape-seal it.

*Alligators and lizards* are skinned and handled much the same as "open-skinned" furbearers.

**RAINBOW TROUT**

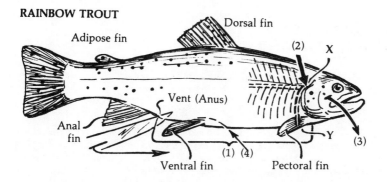

## DRESSING THE SALMONIDS

Formerly called "salmon*oids*," now salmon*ids*, they include all of the trout and salmon, and as a group, they're about the easiest of all fish to dress.

**Dressing them (whole) in hand.** (See above)

**Step 1.** Hold the trout on its *back* in one hand & open the belly from vent (anus) forward to throat. Just cut thru the flesh, not the innards. Skirt ventral fin.

**Step 2.** Rotate wrist (fish belly down). Cut across the back behind the skull *between* backbone spines down *to the backbone* at X. Now slip blade up inside the body cavity at one side of gut, sharp edge against flesh & its point thrust out at X. Cut *outward* & down thru belly cut at Y following a rib. Repeat other side.

**Step 3.** Break down head & guts will go with it.

**Step 4.** Cut around base of remaining ventral fin to free it.

**Step 5.** Thumbnail the kidney from under the backbone, rinse it all well, and it's ready for the pan. (You may want to lightly scale a big one.)

## A BRIEF LESSON
## IN THE EATING

There is a proper & practical way to eat fish, cooked whole, which insures warm food without fighting troublesome loose bones.

Split back skin of cooked fish with an outside angled tine of a table fork (head to tail). Then slip table knife in flat next to backbone to hold fish on the plate while the tines of the table fork are inserted between the long top back muscle of the fish and the smooth upper surface of the table knife. Lift the fork at right angles to the knife toward you rolling the flesh up & away from the knife holding down the backbone. Continue with the fork pulling the flesh from the ribs. The whole upper half of the fish should pull away free of bones if it is cooked properly. (Hemal bones should hold to the backbone in most fish.)

Now grasp the head end of the exposed backbone and lift it up and away from the flesh of the fish held down by a fork in the back muscle close to the end of the backbone.

The backbone and hemal bones on the remaining side will pull out cleanly. Push away the fins and you're in . . . bone free!

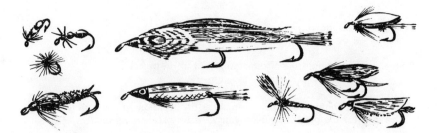

## DRESSING FOR
## "POACHED" COOKING
**(Not to be confused with taking fish illegally)**

### With Special Fish-poaching Pan

When a narrow fish-poaching pan with cover and lift-out, raised bottom is available, I dress the salmonid(s) for it as shown on pg. 215.

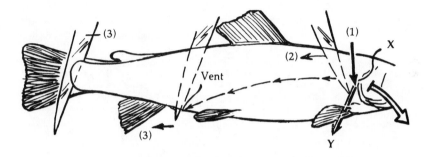

### Using Efficient Substitute Pans

Various bread pans may be used. Dress fish to fit them. Cover with aluminum foil, edges turned down 1" or so over the pan.

**Step 1.** Remove head by cutting across & down to X, then slice thru each side (X-Y) join underneath. Avoid guts, most of which pull out with head.

**Step 2.** Instead of a belly cut, open up the fish from the *back* following closely along the backbone (edge angled in toward it). Cut just *through the ribs* to vent. Avoid any remaining guts but don't worry about that, it will all be washed out at once.

**Step 3.** Knife point comes out at vent, and fillet is freed from vent to tail.

**Step 4.** Clean out any remaining guts. Thumbnail the kidney and wash all well. Skin & flesh at belly makes hinge for the "butterfly" (4) next page.

**Step 5. Alternate method:** Cut head off & remove guts exactly as outlined above. Then completely remove one fillet (skin on), knife all the way across from tail to head (one side only).

(continued)

**Note:** The "butterflied" partial fillet works great when poaching in a square broiling pan or cake tin. It also works best if a fish is to be broiled on a plank or split log tipped up as a reflector by the fire.

"Alternate" dressing for best placement of fish in a variety of pans, foil-lined with edges *turned up* all around to facilitate removing and draining the fish.

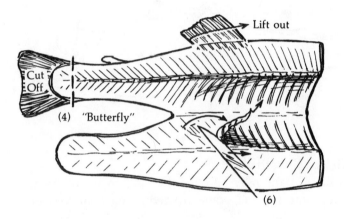

**Step 6.** Skin off ribs on the side without the backbone rolling them forward. All bones on the other side will lift out with the backbone when the fish is cooked.

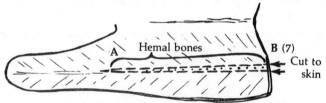

**Step 7.** Run finger tip over flesh from A to B. If tips of hemals are felt, cut each side to skin. Pinch flesh between cuts at B and lift out the strip containing the bones.

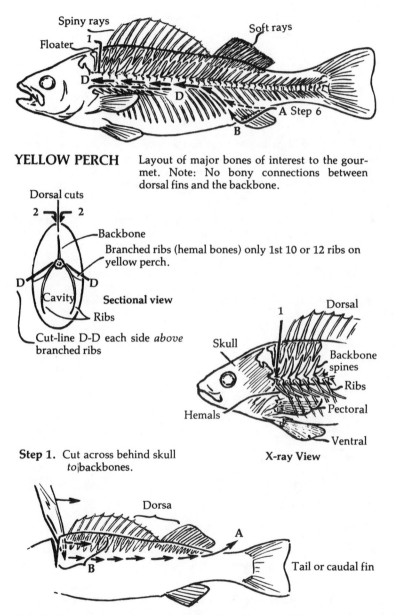

**YELLOW PERCH** Layout of major bones of interest to the gourmet. Note: No bony connections between dorsal fins and the backbone.

Dorsal cuts

Backbone

Branched ribs (hemal bones) only 1st 10 or 12 ribs on yellow perch.

**Sectional view**

Cut-line D-D each side *above* branched ribs

**Step 1.** Cut across behind skull *to*|backbones.

**X-ray View**

**Step 2.** Cut close to backbone *at each side* of the dorsal fins, coming out at (A).

219

## REMOVING SOFT RAYS

Soft rays

Dorsal fins

**Step 3.** With knife blade angled (edge forward) tight behind rear of dorsal fin, press thumb against the fin holding it firmly against the blade and pull up & forward removing the whole dorsal fin. (Soft ray fins of any fish may be removed by the procedure in steps 2 & 3 shown here.)

**Step 4.** Loosen corners of skin from flesh at each side (head end) and pull skin down & back to about (B), diagram Step 1, with tip of knife sliding just under the skin.

**Step 5.** Hook thumb into body cavity grasping flesh at same time from the top and with other hand break down head and pull everything to the tail pulling against fish held firmly. Head, guts, pectoral and ventral fins all pull free.

**Step 6.** Hold perch body cavity up, head end toward you.

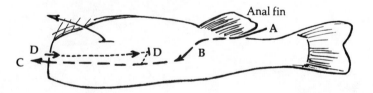

Anal fin

A

D

D

C

B

Make cuts D-D (slice angled in *on each side* just dorsally of the "hemal" ribs). Compare with 1st two diagrams. Skip cuts D-D & you'll eat a few bones.

**Step 7.** As in Step 3, pull anal fin forward & cut down following the rear rib of the body cavity. Now pull with blade edge angled forward along underside of backbone (B-C). Push kidney off backbone with thumbnail & wash well.

## DRESSING THE PICKEREL FAMILY (Bone-Free)

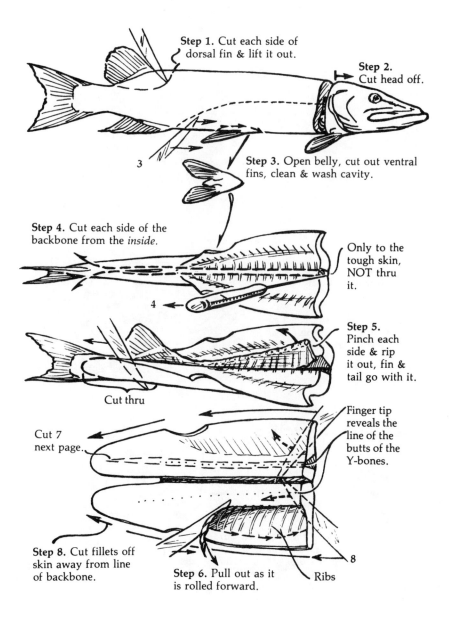

**Step 1.** Cut each side of dorsal fin & lift it out.

**Step 2.** Cut head off.

**Step 3.** Open belly, cut out ventral fins, clean & wash cavity.

3

**Step 4.** Cut each side of the backbone from the *inside.*

4

Only to the tough skin, NOT thru it.

**Step 5.** Pinch each side & rip it out, fin & tail go with it.

Cut thru

Finger tip reveals the line of the butts of the Y-bones.

Cut 7 next page.

**Step 8.** Cut fillets off skin away from line of backbone.

**Step 6.** Pull out as it is rolled forward.

8

Ribs

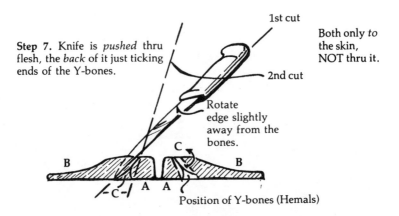

**Step 7.** Knife is *pushed* thru flesh, the *back* of it just ticking ends of the Y-bones.

1st cut

2nd cut

Both only *to* the skin, NOT thru it.

Rotate edge slightly away from the bones.

B                    C                    B

-C-   A   A

Position of Y-bones (Hemals)

After the Y-bone cuts (above) are made on both fillets (still on the skin) pinch under front of piece (C) containing the Y-bones and lift it up, ripping it out to the rear similar to (5). Now proceed with (8) on the previous page. You're done — four bone-free fillets!

### For Baking Whole

Sew

*Scale the fish first*, then proceed with steps 1-7 only. Then spread stuffing on the fillets working it into the voids between the strips of bone-free flesh. Sew the edges together along belly to close the pocket.

### ⌣ or My Favorite Way

Cut into strips

B        A   — then —

Make the pinwheels from the strips, dust in a bag with dry *Shake 'n Bake®* according to the directions. They're all done at the same time, bone-free & delicious.

Wooden hors d'oeuvre toothpicks.

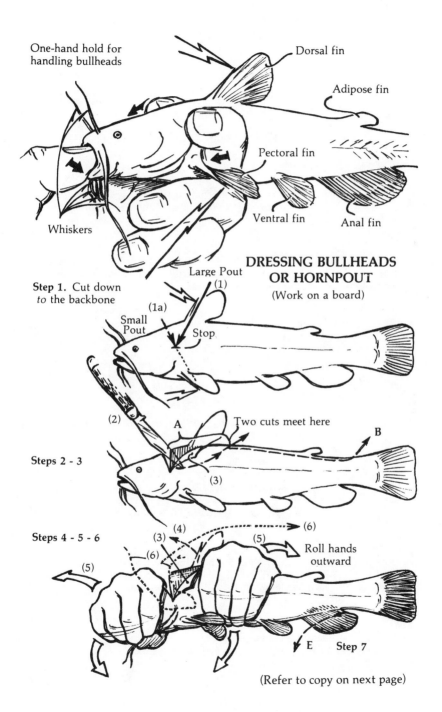

One-hand hold for
handling bullheads

Dorsal fin

Adipose fin

Pectoral fin

Ventral fin

Anal fin

Whiskers

**Step 1.** Cut down
*to* the backbone

Large Pout
(1)

## DRESSING BULLHEADS
## OR HORNPOUT

(Work on a board)

(1a)

Small
Pout

Stop

(2)

A

Two cuts meet here

B

**Steps 2 - 3**

(3)

**Steps 4 - 5 - 6**

(4)

(6)

(3)

(5)

Roll hands
outward

(6)

(5)

E     Step 7

(Refer to copy on next page)

223

# DRESSING BULLHEADS & OTHER CATFISHES

All of the catfish clan have a sharp stiff spine as the first ray of pectoral & dorsal fins. The whiskers don't hurt, but the spines DO! "Cats" rate high on the American menu. We eat 30 to 40 million pounds of them every year.

**Step 1.** Cut from back of skull on a line angling to behind pectoral fins. STOP at the backbone. On large bullheads, *cut behind* stiff dorsal spine. Follow it down to backbone and cut into backbone.

**Step 2.** Cut deep from the first cut at the top of the backbone back & up behind the dorsal fin (A), at one side of it. Do the same on the other side, then continue a single cut just under the skin to (B).

**Step 3.** Peel back top corners of skin at each side.

**Step 4.** With the blade flat across the soft rays of dorsal, press them forward to the spine which is held at the front by the thumb. Pull the fin out forward, only possible on small to medium bullheads.

**Step 5.** Place a hand each side of cut (1) and snap them down & in, breaking the backbone. On big ones do it across your knee making sure pectoral spines are kept *flat*. The top spine stays *between the hands* and separates with the backbone on the forward section.

**Step 6.** Shift rear hand to hook its thumb inside the body cavity under the backbone. Pull hands apart, holding the fish's head steady as the body is ripped out thru the cut skin on the back. Head, guts, skin & fins (except anal & tail) come off as a unit.

**Step 7.** Pull anal fin (E) out as in (4) or leave it. Rub out the kidney under the backbone and rinse the fish. It's ready to cook whole.

(continued next page)

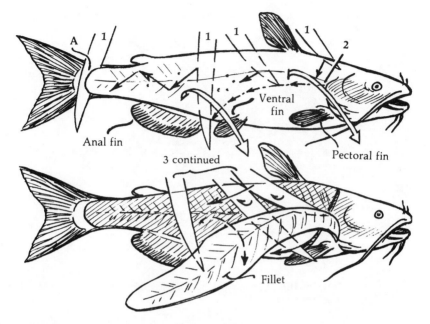

Anal fin

Ventral fin

3 continued

Pectoral fin

Fillet

## FILLETING A CHANNEL CATFISH

Hold the fish on its side. Put pad of the thumb of your free hand against the top of the skull with the index finger hooked over the top cheek and into the mouth, thus gripping the top of the head firmly.

**Step 1.** Cut down & back from the skull close to backbone. When ribs are felt, follow *on top* of them. When vent is reached, cut all the way thru to (A).

**Step 2.** Cut in from the side behind gill-cover to backbone, then rotate blade edge outward, guiding *the flat* of the blade on the ribs.

**Step 3.** Let it come thru skin above pectoral & ventral fins freeing the fillet.

**Step 4.** Flop fish (exposed backbone down) & repeat.

**Step 5.** Slice the flesh off the skin (head to tail) holding fillet (flesh side up) at front end, skin held by thumbnail pressed hard on it against the board.

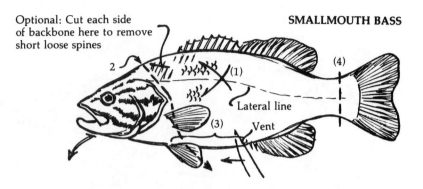

Optional: Cut each side of backbone here to remove short loose spines

SMALLMOUTH BASS

2

(1)

(4)

Lateral line

(3)

Vent

## BASIC FOR MOST BAKING FISH

Also for largemouth & striped bass, walleye, snappers, haddock, cod, salmon, large trout, carp and many others.

**Step 1.** Scale the fish (if necessary) at an angle to the lateral line. Try doing it under water (see text).

**Step 2.** Open up belly from vent forward just thru skin and flesh. Avoid cutting into the guts.

**Step 3.** Cut across behind the head, parting the backbone. The head can be broken down, but a neater job results from cutting along a forward rib bone at each side from the backbone thru the belly.

**Step 4.** Pull off head and guts will come with it.

**Step 5.** Thumbnail the kidney off the backbone & rinse the fish inside & out.

**Step 6.** Salt the cavity & fill it with stuffing. Then skewer or sew the belly up to keep it all neat and together.

226

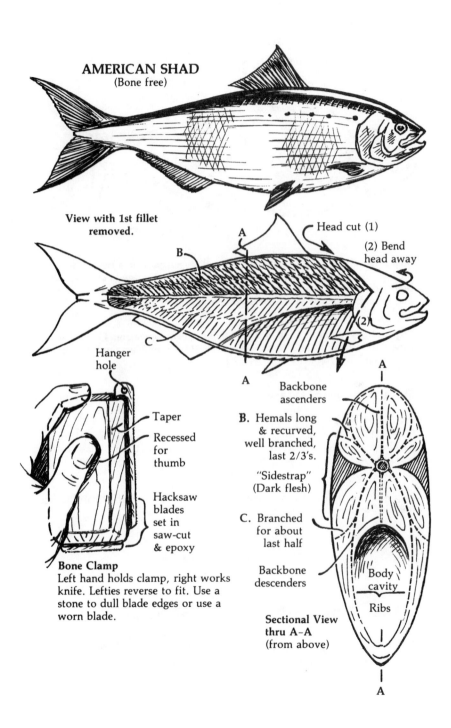

# AMERICAN SHAD
(Bone free)

**View with 1st fillet removed.**

Head cut (1)

(2) Bend head away

A

B

C

A

A

(2)

Hanger hole

Taper

Recessed for thumb

Hacksaw blades set in saw-cut & epoxy

**Bone Clamp**
Left hand holds clamp, right works knife. Lefties reverse to fit. Use a stone to dull blade edges or use a worn blade.

Backbone ascenders

**B.** Hemals long & recurved, well branched, last 2/3's.

"Sidestrap" (Dark flesh)

**C.** Branched for about last half

Backbone descenders

Body cavity

Ribs

**Sectional View thru A–A** (from above)

A

**Step 1.** Cut across straight in to backbone following ascender line.

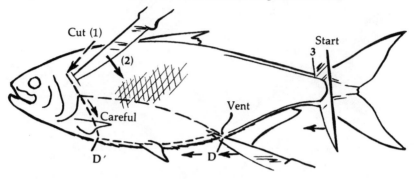

**Step 2.** Angle blade to rear to get under gill cover, pick up a rib on the tip of the knife & follow it down (between it and the next rib) as you cut. When the body cavity is reached, hold blade tip up to avoid cutting the mass of roe & the guts. Complete cut at D´. Repeat on the other side.

**Step 3.** Insert point of knife into vent and cut belly open from D to D´ being careful to just cut thru the thin belly muscle. It is easier when the fish is held in hand, head away & belly up.

**Step 4.** Break down head and remove roe & guts. (Put the roe on ice.)

**Step 5.** Fillet from *tail to head end.* Keep blade close and parallel to the backbone, cutting "dorsal ribs" and regular ribs at butt ends close to the backbone.

**Step 6.** Rinse well and pack these bony fillets in ice until the final dressing (detailed on next page).

**Shad Hardware for Spinning**

**Step 7.** Stripping the fillet off the skin.

Hold skin with thumbnail or bone clamp.

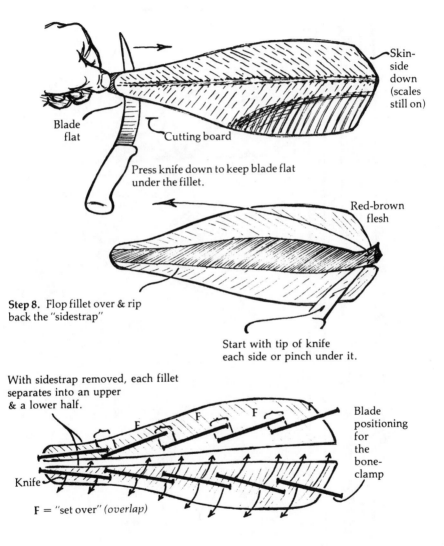

Skin-
side
down
(scales
still on)

Blade
flat

Cutting board

Press knife down to keep blade flat
under the fillet.

Red-brown
flesh

**Step 8.** Flop fillet over & rip
back the "sidestrap"

Start with tip of knife
each side or pinch under it.

With sidestrap removed, each fillet
separates into an upper
& a lower half.

F     F     F     F

Blade
positioning
for
the
bone-
clamp

Knife

**F** = "set over" *(overlap)*

**Step 9.** Work from tail to head on each half-fillet, holding the bone-clamp
firmly down on bones crossing under it. Keep knife blade angled quite flat.
*Press* flesh down and *push* out to edges in the direction of the bones. Only the
bones will be left under the clamp. Refer back to text.

229

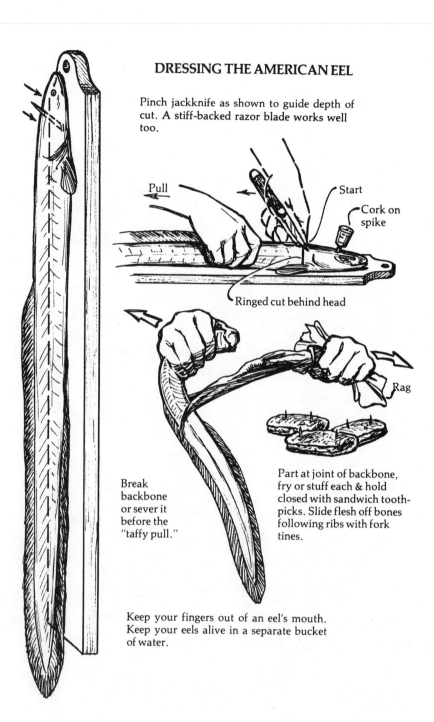

## DRESSING THE AMERICAN EEL

Pinch jackknife as shown to guide depth of cut. A stiff-backed razor blade works well too.

Pull

Start

Cork on spike

Ringed cut behind head

Rag

Break backbone or sever it before the "taffy pull."

Part at joint of backbone, fry or stuff each & hold closed with sandwich toothpicks. Slide flesh off bones following ribs with fork tines.

Keep your fingers out of an eel's mouth. Keep your eels alive in a separate bucket of water.

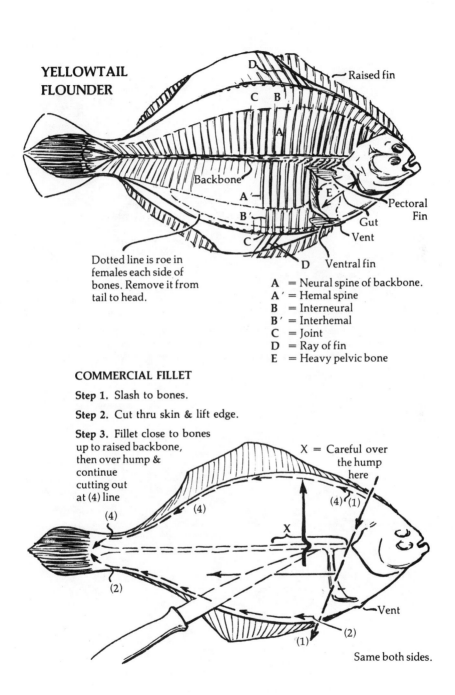

## YELLOWTAIL FLOUNDER

Raised fin

Backbone

Pectoral Fin

Gut

Vent

Dotted line is roe in females each side of bones. Remove it from tail to head.

D Ventral fin

A = Neural spine of backbone.
A′ = Hemal spine
B = Interneural
B′ = Interhemal
C = Joint
D = Ray of fin
E = Heavy pelvic bone

## COMMERCIAL FILLET

**Step 1.** Slash to bones.

**Step 2.** Cut thru skin & lift edge.

**Step 3.** Fillet close to bones up to raised backbone, then over hump & continue cutting out at (4) line

X = Careful over the hump here

Vent

Same both sides.

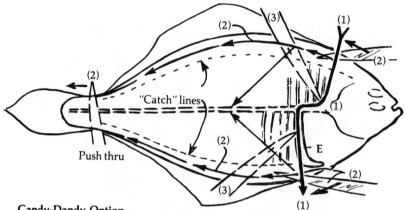

"Catch" lines

Push thru

**Candy-Dandy Option.**

**Step 1.** Slice thru to bones, angling off just above the backbone then down over pelvic bone, thus avoiding gut cavity.

**Step 2.** "Pie-plate" it, just thru skin.

**Step 3.** Grasp edge of skin, lift & cut close to bones only up to the backbone at each side of it, blade flat to avoid "catch lines" where interneurals & inter-hemals go between spines. Stop each side when ridge of backbone is felt.

Note: Study "white side" & you can readily see how the fish is put together.

Edge view, vent toward reader

Cut tendons if needed

**Step 4.** Run index and 2nd fingers under fillets, one finger each side of back-bone, pinch & lift, cutting tendons if necessary until past area (X) in diagram on p. 231. Then just rip back to the tail. Flop fish over & repeat on the other side.

(Continued next page.)

Remove skin from fillets (unless you scaled both sides first). The pros fillet in *one* piece usually, but I like 2 neat pieces that fit the pan better.

## REMOVING FILLET FROM THE SKIN

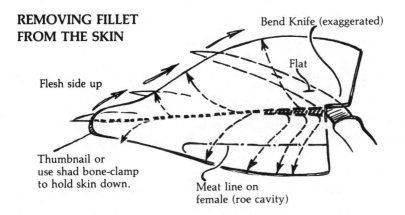

Bend Knife (exaggerated)

Flat

Flesh side up

Thumbnail or use shad bone-clamp to hold skin down.

Meat line on female (roe cavity)

**Start** at line of backbone, roll edge of blade down and out from line. When blade is flat on skin under flesh, press down hard keeping bend in knife as it is worked from tail end to head end.

## STUFFED SOLE

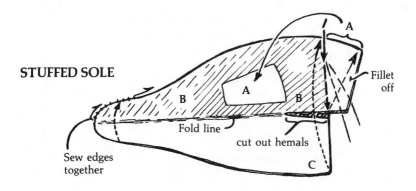

A

Fillet off

B

A

B

Fold line

cut out hemals

Sew edges together

C

Scale the dab or flounder both sides. Do it under an inch of water if you haven't tried it before.

(Continued next page.)

**Stuffed sole (continued)**

Proceed as you would with dressing any flounder, but **leave fillets on the skin.**
Refer to diagram at bottom of the previous page.

**Step 1.** Cut (1) only to the skin, then fillet off piece extending (A) and put it
and vegetables or any stuffing of your choice on the shaded area (B).

**Step 2.** Fold lower portion (C) over stuffing to match outside edges of upper
piece. Sew or skewer the two edges together from tail end to head.

**Step 3.** Flap of skin from (A) can be brought up and over head end to hold
stuffing in the pocket and the corners sewed or pinned in place.

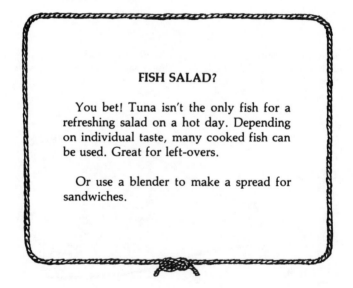

### FISH SALAD?

You bet! Tuna isn't the only fish for a
refreshing salad on a hot day. Depending
on individual taste, many cooked fish can
be used. Great for left-overs.

Or use a blender to make a spread for
sandwiches.

# CHAPTER 18

# YOU WANT THAT FISH IMMORTALIZED?

To have a traditional fish mount you will want to keep around later, demands certain care in the field. You can't blame the taxidermist for your mistakes, and he cannot do much with a damaged or half-spoiled fish. The same dangers that apply to the fish you plan to eat, apply to the once-in-a-lifetime trophy. And even more problems are generated by the fact it is a trophy.

## Preparation for the Taxidermist

Your trophy must show one *good side* after the long-remembered battle. Broken fins quite often can be repaired, but scars and lost scales cannot. Of course, the fish can be so reconstituted that it is practically a "scratch original" when completed, but then it is *not* that big trout you took from Judge's Pool. You might as well pick up a plastic trade model.

So take good care of that prize fish. Keep it alive as long as you can without damaging it. Leave it by itself, tethered on a stringer in a quiet pool and in the shade. Or if you have a fair-sized fish basket or live box available, put your fish into that and keep it dark so it won't thrash around. And don't load the basket or box with other fish. When it comes time to move your prize, kill it quickly to avoid its doing damage to itself.

NETTING AND HANDLING A BIG ONE

If you net a big fish from a boat, the best equipment you can have along is a friend to help. Have him handle the net while you remove the hook and secure the stringer. Put the stringer on *from the poorer side*. Use the stringer even if you intend to keep the fish alive in a well in the boat. It will help later when you want to take the fish out. If no well is available, put the fish back into the water to keep it alive. And don't use that stringer for other fish.

On shore, when alone and a net is used, or if the fish is too big for the net, you will have to do the best you can. If you have cotton gloves along, the job will be much easier, but *be sure to wet them* before handling the brute. Once the fish is grabbed, take it (with both hands holding only the head) to a wet, marshy spot, or kick water onto the grass where you will have to put it down. Kneel down with your back to the water and the fish trapped between your wet legs, its head between the knees of your wet boots or waders. Remove the hook, secure the stringer, and ease the fish back into the water. Be darned sure the free end of the stringer is well tied when you leave it.

Many fine tropies have been ruined at streamside when the angler backed up onto the shore. In his panic to get the fish out of the water, he dragged the flopping fish over dry rocks or gravel. That one would make a good eating fish, and provide a good model for photographs — but forget having it mounted.

You may know that when your prize fish is mounted, it will be a dull brownish gray all over. Its life-like color is gone and will have to be recreated by the taxidermist. His talent and skill as an artist determines how beautiful the end product will be.

It is not the purpose of this book to circumvent taxidermists who perhaps have provided more pleasant memories by their work than all of the photographs ever collected by hunters and fishermen. Unfortunately, many of them should concentrate only on species they do well and know best. Too many will take on anything that comes into their shops. The few who have studied (and will continue to study as long as they live) probably *can* do just about anything well. As true artists, their prices are up accordingly — and should be.

## KILLING AND GUTTING

Use a wet glove or folded handkerchief to grip only the fish's head, or "eye-ball" it, to hold the head steady. Slip a pointed, long blade of a knife in behind the gill cover on the *selected poorer side,* and thrust it upward and forward through the thin bone of the underside of the skull.* Make a deep cut through it, then twist the knife 180 degrees, drawing it toward the tail through the skull before withdrawing it. If done right, the fish will tremble noticeably and then hang quietly.

Still holding the fish by its head, cut out the gills,* working *only from the poorer side,* being careful not to cut or damage the throat below, nor the gill cover on the good side. Make all cuts downward from the hand holding the fish by its head. (Small heavy scissors do a fine job if they are available.)

Cut along the length of the body cavity *on the poor side,* a third of the way down toward the belly from the lateral line along the fish's side,* angling the cut toward the vent (anus), but ending it short of and *above* the vent. The guts can be removed from this cut, which will be through the ribs. The belly itself will be untouched. Carefully wash it all out and put the trophy on ice, cut side down. Wet paper toweling packed into the cavity will keep the body shaped.

Rainbow trout shed their scales at the least provocation, while bass and other relatively large-scaled fish usually hold their scales much tighter, and they can take a limited amount of careful handling, even with the good side down on a pad of wet cloth.

For the fragile rainbow and others like it, a special holding peg* can be readily made for the task at hand. Look for a fairly stout live branch (about a half-inch in diameter at the tree trunk) at shoulder height. Cut it off about a foot out from the tree trunk. Hang the fish on the stub from its gill opening *on the poor side.* The length of the branch keeps the body of the fish hanging free from the trunk of the tree.

With a wet glove, or folded wet handkerchief grasp only the thick membrane of the caudal fin, the tail. Pull down lightly but steadily on it against the opposition of the branch holding the head.* One hand stretches the fish and holds it away from the tree. The other hand with knife or scissors cuts open the poorer side for removal of gills and guts, as just described. Gut it first. The job can be completed without letting the good side touch anything in the process.

I like the green branch peg best, but with care, even a ten-penny nail can be used after driving it into a post. Remember to make all cuts *downward* to avoid lifting the fish off the peg with the chance of its falling to the ground.

When the body cavity has been emptied and wiped out, it can be stuffed loosely with clean grass or ferns to keep the general shape of the fish and to aid the circulation of cool air into the cavity as it lies, *cutside down*, supported on ice. A *wet* cloth can be carefully laid over the fish's good side, uppermost in the ice box. Then a layer of ice chips or cubes can be placed around and over it. If the container holding the fish and ice can be put inside another larger box also packed with ice, the trip to the taxidermist can be made without worry.

## An Exact Replica of Your Trophy

With the foregoing attitude to taxidermy understood, here is an easier-than-you-think way* to get an exact duplicate of your fish, down to the last, minute detail. The operation can be done streamside, but better perhaps at camp. You won't have to worry about long transportation of the fish or getting the right size or set of the eye. Every scale and tooth will be in its proper place. Furthermore, it will never smell or deteriorate. And you can eat the fish, too, which puts it all in balance with the intent of this book. All you have to do is make sure the needed materials are packed in the car or at camp, so they will be available when the trophy is caught.

USING PLASTER OF PARIS

You will need a twenty-five pound bag of plaster of Paris for an eight- to ten-pound fish, about a dozen common pins rolled up and taped in paper, some paper towels, a couple of old cotton handkerchiefs, a large mixing bowl, a cup, tablespoon and a filled salt shaker. An old blanket also is advisable to wrap and provide padding for your work of art on the return trip home.

The plaster, which must be kept dry, can be stored in clean (washed and dried) potato chip cans, which are available from restaurants. Pour the dry plaster into a dry, warmed can. Put on the cover and seal it with tape.

Practice this procedure on a small fish or two first, so you will be confident when the big one shows up. Place the fish *au naturel* (guts and gills in) in the pose you want* on level bare ground in the shade, the *poor side down*. Then take a pencil or stick and make a rough outline* of it in the dirt or sand below. Set the fish aside with a light *wet* handkerchief or two over it.

Scoop out the earth or sand* inside the outline to accommodate *half* the thickness of your fish in the desired pose. If a more interesting background is desired, place dampened grass or leaves naturally in and around the depression, keeping them fairly flat.

Remove the wet cloth and lay the fish in the shallow depression, making adjustments to it as needed. When your fish is resting half in and half out of the depression,* lightly tamp the soil, sand, or leaves snugly and naturally to it, making a fairly even junction line around your prize. Arrange the fins naturally.* You can use a few common pins pushed through the fins into the ground or the fish, keeping the pin heads snug to the surface of the fin. Later, the bump of the pin's head can be scraped off the final production.

If the mouth is to be open, it is a good idea to pack it* smoothly with wet paper towels or cleansing tissue to a level closely following the tooth line to the inside.

Now mix up a good batch of plaster by pouring it into a half-filled bowl of water. Ease the plaster in until a hill is formed* with an inch or two of water surrounding it. Then carefully and thoroughly mix in the plaster, trying not to introduce air bubbles. You will have to work steadily, but make haste slowly to avoid excess bubbles. When the mix is the consistency of heavy cream, sharply tap the sides of the bowl and drop it on its bottom from a height of an inch or two a couple times to bring any bubbles in the mix to the top. Wipe the bubbles off with a sheet of newspaper or paper towel.

Then immediately and steadily pour the plaster over the fish, *starting at the eye.* Keep a steady pour over the fish until it is all covered and the plaster extends out from it all around evenly for two or three inches. Pour enough on the ground around it to form a pleasing shape for the background* when it is trimmed later. When all is to your satisfaction, *lightly* and evenly sprinkle table salt over the plaster.

Clean the bowl out thoroughly to prevent a "quick-set" in the next batch. Mix a new batch and pour again all over the first plaster that now is setting. You want to build the thickness of the plaster up to at least a half inch everywhere. It will settle some and be heavier where it should be — where the fish meets the ground. Again, lightly salt the exposed plaster and shade it. Leave it for a couple hours. The plaster should feel hard when you return. Take a stick or shovel and dig up the earth deep *around* the plaster, starting at some distance from it. Then carefully dig deep under the plaster.* DON'T pry up on the plaster itself. When all is loosened, lift the plaster up and turn it over, exposing the fish. Do not try to clean any of the dirt or debris from the plaster at this time.

Carefully lift the tail of the fish out of its plaster prison. Then slowly lift the head, pulling it forward away from the plaster in line with the spines of the pectoral and ventral fins that may be mostly encased in plaster. Take it easy! As soon as the fish is free, wash it well in cold water. Gut and clean it normally, and put it on ice immediately. Don't freeze this fish. Plan to eat it that night or the next day.


THE DRY MOLD

Let the plaster mold dry in the shade. That is what you have now, a female or negative plaster mold. Allow it to dry hard before attempting to clean it. Depending on its thickness, this may take a few days. Once you are sure it has thoroughly dried, gingerly rub, brush or pick off the debris on the outside. If some slime has adhered to the inside, *carefully* pick it off, but do not worry about a little here or there.

Dust *all of the inside* carefully with a soft, clean, dry paint brush and blow any dust away. Note the minute detail around the eye and the fine detail of the scales. If a few small bubbles show, they can be filled with a little wet plaster now, or just leave them. The round bumps which will form in them on the end product can be cut or filed off later. You can wrap and store the mold for finishing the project at your convenience or proceed with the finished product.

## READYING THE MOLD

Mix a half cup of acrylic paint (can or tube type), which can be thinned with water, and the brushes just washed out. Dilute the paint almost to water consistency. Mix it well. A cheap, mouth-blown sprayer made of two straight tubes held at right angles to each other can be purchased at an art supply store. It will be perfectly adequate for the job. Spray if possible, or use a very soft brush *lightly* and *quickly* to avoid any scrubbing action, to completely cover the inside of the mold with paint. Cover the surface of the flanged background too. Leave no spot untouched, but do not put a second coat over any of it at this time.

The thin paint should sink right in. Let it dry overnight, and then give the mold a second light coat. If the thin paint should accumulate in a puddle in any area, blot it out with a corner of paper towelling immediately. Let it dry *thoroughly*.

Pour about a third cup of self-polishing floor *wax, not acrylic* or any other kind of polish. Spray it if possible, or carefully wipe the inside of the mold and the flange with a soft cloth soaked with the wax. Keep it to a *thin*, continuous film. It should not be allowed to build up and obliterate the fine detail. Don't scrub it in — wipe it over. Again, if any puddling occurs, wipe it out immediately. It is better to give two light coats than one heavy coat. Just be sure to cover all of the surface, and let it dry well.

Your "negative" or "female" mold now is ready for the casting of your trophy. Undercuts are no problem since the mold will be carefully broken away from your "positive" or "male" model that will go on the wall. It is a one-shot deal. Nobody else will have a trophy exactly like yours.

## THE RESIN-FIBERGLASS REPLICA SHELL

The "positive" is made by the hand-lay-up method for handling resin-fiberglass, much in the manner of boat building. It will make a beautiful, durable trophy. Liquid polyester resin is the binder penetrating between the glass fibers and filling the voids.

When mixed with the catalyst, it cures quickly to a hard, strong homogeneous mass that picks up every detail of your fish. When cured without added pigmentation, the cast shell is a translucent, dull blue-green that adapts well to later decorative coloring. Check when you buy your resin to see whether or not a primer is needed to coat or wash down the cured resin before painting it.

Buy or borrow some scrap fiberglass mat* and ten-ounce boat-cloth* from a boat yard or a do-it-yourselfer. No scrap or strip will be too small to use, and *get more than you think you will need.* A quart of polyester resin should suffice for an eight- to ten-pound fish.

If the fish is to be painted in life-like color, white or neutral gray (special paste) pigment can be mixed into the liquid resin, but that finishing is too ambitious for everyone. I'll describe a way that anyone, with a little care and common sense, can produce a beautiful, exact replica of that fish, even though it will not be naturally colored.

First, cut some small patches of mat from a larger piece and pull a handful of threads from the scrap material. Then cut some strips and patches of varied larger sizes that will fit inside the mold. Have a good supply of usable scrap ready. Trim away any hardened resin that may be on the scrap material to be used.

Now pour into an unwaxed (hot drink) paper cup enough resin to fill about two thirds of it. Add the correct amount of catalyst — you don't have to be exact — and mix well. Then paint the whole inside of the mold and the flanged background with it. This is the "gel coat." It should take fifteen or twenty minutes to cure. Wait until it feels smooth and hard; not sticky anywhere.

Give it another complete coat, and while that is still wet or tacky — the tack coat — push short resin-wet glass fibers into the small voids of the fins, the tooth line of the jaws, eyes and behind the gills. (Make a "gunk" putty of fine-cut short fibers in resin in another cup for this.) Then use the larger pieces over the broad surfaces of the mold and flange, resin-wetting them thoroughly in place, pressing them onto the wetted surface. Tamp them with the tip of a resin-loaded brush. Let this cure. Next mix scissor-cut fibers and threads into more catalyst and resin, wetting them thoroughly. Lift out a gob of this gunk and more or less spread it carefully over the "lay" to even up the inside surface. Force out any air bubbles by again tamping the lay into the mold with the tip end of a nylon varnish brush. Keep the fiberglass wet with the resin, for too much pressing can squeeze it dry. Overlay strips of cloth where edges come together. You should try to build a continuous shell about an eighth-inch thick over all of the fish and the background. Resin-coat the excess fiberglass cloth and mat to extend beyond the edges of the flange. When it becomes rubbery during the cure, trim it off neatly and quickly with a sharp knife or ordinary scissors. Don't wait for it to harden or it will require a lot more work. When all appears to be thick enough, let it cure to a hard finish.

Rough-cut two pieces of pine or bass wood to fit loosely inside the fiberglass shell from top to bottom toward the head and tail ends. These pieces hold the hangers. Set the wood in resin gunk, flush with the flange of the background. Once they cure in place, drill the holes to receive hangers or screw eyes. Or you can just drill holes angled upward in those two pieces of wood, and the mount will stay tight to the wall when hung from properly spaced nails or screws in the wall.

## BREAK OUT THE CAST FISH

Now it is time to free the cast fish. Care is needed to keep fins and thin undercut areas from breaking off. Soak the plaster in a pan of water, and soon it can be easily cut and scraped with a knife, chisel or saw. *But do not cut all the way to the fiberglass.* Make deep grooves* across the plaster and break loose the pieces of plaster between them. Make several close cuts around the fins.* They require extra care. Once the fiberglass fin can be seen, the plaster trapped between the fin and the body of the fish can be picked out or brushed away. Keep the plaster wet. Before long you will have a complete one-piece fiberglass fish and molded background free of all plaster. Little bumps from pin heads used to hold fins or resulting from air bubbles in the plaster can be scraped or cut off carefully to blend in. Lightly scrub away any dried slime adhering to the cured plastic or it will stain the finish later. Trim the edges of the fiberglass background with hacksaw, rasp and file to get the final shape right and smooth the edges.

Avoid breathing in the dust from sanding. Wash the molded casting thoroughly with laundry detergent in warm water. Rinse it well and let it dry.

You don't think a dull green or gray fish is very attractive, and you say you're not an artist? Don't worry.

Use bronzing paints — silver, gold or copper — to evenly and quickly coat the fiberglass model. Keep the paint thin. Avoid filling in the tiny crevices that give detail to the fish. If you use a brush, paint all strokes across the width. Work quickly from the wet edge, and *don't go back over it.* Working fast is the secret. Let it dry thoroughly. A second coat may be needed.

Once the replica is hard and shiny, you can give it added quality by antiquing it. Take a small soft rag and smear a little oil paint directly from a tube of artist's paint — black for silver, burnt umber for gold, and terre verte (dull green) for copper. Lightly wipe it *across* the lines of scales and other details. A little paint catches in the fine lines and sets off the whole fish. A happy blending of polishing and touching a little of the dull oil paint here and there proves your artistry. If the mouth of the fish is open, paint the filler to the tooth line carefully with flat medium dark paint of a color complementary to the metallic paint used. It is even better to carefully cut out the filler. A final thin coat of urethane varnish can be used if a real shine is desirable.

It is done. Hang it. Do you think I exaggerated? The maid won't have to worry much when she dusts the fins on this fish, for they are tough. Even if it gets bounced off the floor, it usually won't be damaged, and if it is, you can repair it easily.

## TROPHY FISH

Hold fish firmly on peg.

(1) "Sticking" the trophy.

Best side. All work done from opposite (poorer) side.

Thrust knife point up, then draw it back & twist it.

**Step 1.** Kill the fish quickly by sticking.

½"

(2) Incision on *poor* side to remove innards.

Stop ½" up above belly at rear of body cavity.

**Step 2.** Remove gills & guts. Stuff cavity loosely with clean wet ferns or grasses while still on peg.

Pull down steadily as work goes on.

**Step 3.** Remove carefully from peg and pack in ice.

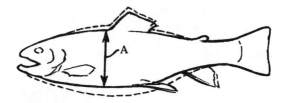

Tell your taxidermist you want it mounted *naturally* (solid line) not "stuffed" (dotted line). Give him the natural *half-girth* (A) measurement.

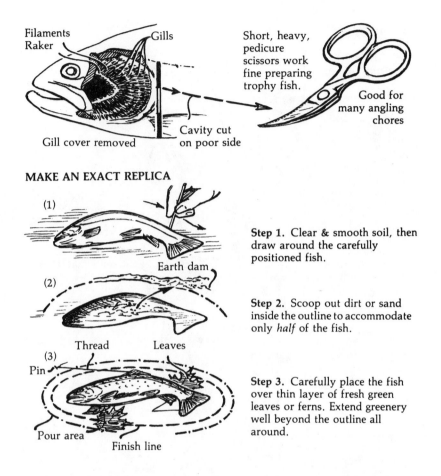

Filaments
Raker
Gills

Short, heavy, pedicure scissors work fine preparing trophy fish.

Good for many angling chores

Gill cover removed

Cavity cut on poor side

## MAKE AN EXACT REPLICA

(1)

Earth dam

(2)

Thread    Leaves

Pin

(3)

Pour area

Finish line

**Step 1.** Clear & smooth soil, then draw around the carefully positioned fish.

**Step 2.** Scoop out dirt or sand inside the outline to accommodate only *half* of the fish.

**Step 3.** Carefully place the fish over thin layer of fresh green leaves or ferns. Extend greenery well beyond the outline all around.

**Step 4.** Press or lightly tamp the greenery in close around the fish to establish a relatively even flat juncture with the body.

**Step 5.** Arrange fins with pins or sewing thread to pins beyond the "pour area."

Thread to pin

loop

Dorsal fin pulled forward

(Continued next page)

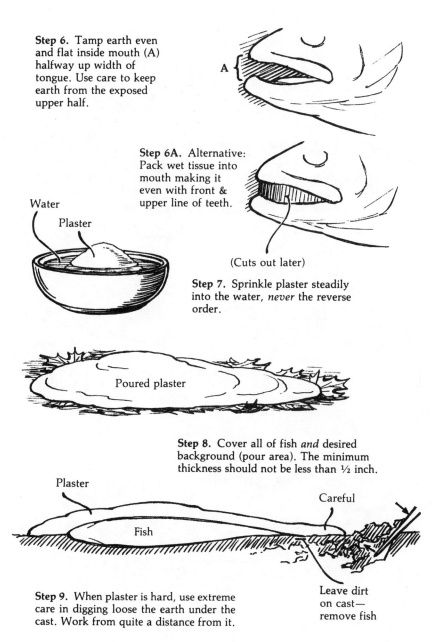

**Step 6.** Tamp earth even and flat inside mouth (A) halfway up width of tongue. Use care to keep earth from the exposed upper half.

A

**Step 6A.** Alternative: Pack wet tissue into mouth making it even with front & upper line of teeth.

Water

Plaster

(Cuts out later)

**Step 7.** Sprinkle plaster steadily into the water, *never* the reverse order.

Poured plaster

**Step 8.** Cover all of fish *and* desired background (pour area). The minimum thickness should not be less than ½ inch.

Plaster

Careful

Fish

**Step 9.** When plaster is hard, use extreme care in digging loose the earth under the cast. Work from quite a distance from it.

Leave dirt on cast— remove fish

247

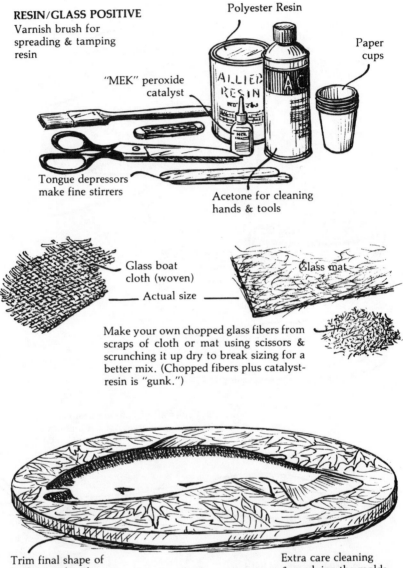

### RESIN/GLASS POSITIVE

Varnish brush for spreading & tamping resin

Polyester Resin

Paper cups

"MEK" peroxide catalyst

ALLIED RESIN

Tongue depressors make fine stirrers

Acetone for cleaning hands & tools

Glass boat cloth (woven)

Glass mat

—— Actual size ——

Make your own chopped glass fibers from scraps of cloth or mat using scissors & scrunching it up dry to break sizing for a better mix. (Chopped fibers plus catalyst-resin is "gunk.")

Trim final shape of background with plaster *wet*.

Extra care cleaning & readying the molds pays big dividends.

Work wet (fine chopped ) "resin-gunk" into these areas. Use stiff paper edge to force it into voids of the fins.

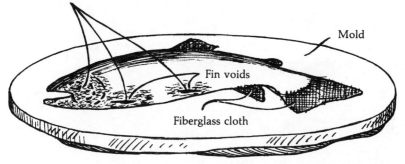

**Step 1.** After preparing mold according to the text give all exposed top surfaces of the fish and background a "gel coat" of resin (catalyst added in all cases).

**Step 2.** While gel coat is still wet, smoothly put in "gunk" (top of page). Then let it all cure.

**Step 3.** Follow text to completion. Let cure.

**Step 4.** Break away *well-soaked* plaster by carefully grooving sections (below) almost down to fiberglass. Leave sections F & F ' to last, these contain the thin pectoral and ventral fins (undercut).

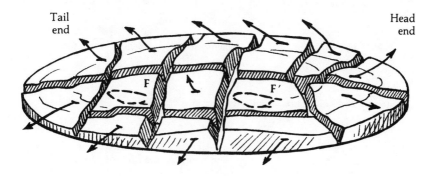

Carefully chip away wet plaster from head toward tail on F & F′ sections.

Exposed cast fish, plaster removed.

Head end ⟶

**Step 5.** Work gingerly until fin is located and lay of it determined. If fin should break off, it can be stuck on with resin later. But if you follow the above suggestions, this should not happen.

## ONLY FOR THE ARTISTIC

If natural colors are to be restored with oil or acrylic paints, it is best to replace the cast eye with a glass fish-eye of correct size.

**Step 6.** Center spot the eye in the cast (fg) with the point of a knife.

**Step 7.** Use drill *smaller* than diameter of eye and drill through shell at this point.

**Step 8.** Use knife to pare out circumference of the eye.

**Step 9.** Set glass eye when it arrives. (All added color must be painted on *back side* of the eye.) Set it in resin gunk or adhesive and fill around exposed edges with wax.

# SECTION VI

# KITCHEN TIPS

# CHAPTER 19

# KITCHEN TIPS

While this book does not pretend to be a documentary on cooking, much of it leads up to that end result. To be sure you get the most from your wild game and fish, the following suggestions touch on basic matters which most cookbooks fail to mention.

1. The eating quality of most small animals, whether mammal or bird, is improved if, after the dressing and washing or wiping it clean, the meat is *refrigerated* for a day before cooking.

2. Commercial meat tenderizers also work for wild game, if you don't mind holes being poked all over your meat.

3. Don't overlook marinating meat overnight to help tenderize it, along with providing exotic taste.

4. Soaking squirrels and rabbits overnight in salt water is pretty standard procedure in some parts of the country, and sometimes vinegar is added to tenderize the meat. It usually is a good idea also to salt the body cavity before adding stuffing.

5. I strongly recommend parboiling or steaming all *mature* birds and small game mammals before attempting to roast them.
Steam your bird on a rack *above* a half-inch of water in a covered roasting pan. Bring it to a boil, then lower the heat to just keep the steam coming. Aluminum foil can be placed over a racked bird in a large pan. Crimp the foil under the edge of the pan and let it steam. Some will escape before pressure builds.

Parboiling partially cooks and tenderizes the bird. Cover it with water and let it boil. It takes less time than steaming, but some of the taste may be lost — with sea ducks this liability becomes an asset.

6. Diving ducks, especially mergansers and sea ducks, are best soaked overnight in water with salt and baking soda added: 1 tablespoon salt, 1 tablespoon soda to each pint of water, before adding the bird. Stir well. Keep the meat covered and weigh it down. A well-scrubbed rock can be used.

7. Exact times for cooking wild game are hardly possible to give. There are too many variables and no USDA standards. While no housewife in her right mind purchases a "fowl" if she wants to fry or broil the chicken, she would find very few wild birds flying around labelled "fryer," "broiler," "roaster" or "fowl." So what do you do?

Try to determine whether the bird or animal is a juvenile, young of the year, or a yearling (one year old). (See the charts at the end of this section for determining the young of different species.) They present no problems and you can cook them any way you choose. Trouble comes when the game is mature. You know it is old, but how old? With a little luck a wild goose can live fifteen to twenty years, and an exceptional few a good deal longer.

As a general rule, young mammals and young birds usually are in good coat or feather. There is a "young" look to them. Juvenile birds usually have a load of pin feathers and mature plumage is either lacking or incomplete. For the young of small game generally, feathers, toenails, teeth and coat show little wear. Look for these indicators.

Some species are easier than others to age by observation. If in doubt, choose a method of cooking for older birds or mammals — parboil or steam them first and braise the meat. Stews are great, and so are casseroles. Extend the cooking time and test for tenderness. If you think your subject is pretty old, and it will fit whole or cut up inside a pressure cooker, use that instead of parboiling it.

When a rare antique comes along, one that has been living on borrowed time, you probably will know it. Unfortunately you may know too late — but maybe the dog will eat it, or you can give it a good burial, spices, wine and all.

Use common  sense, work to improve your odds by selecting an appropriate method of cooking, interpolate on the cooking time a little, add a shot of luck, and you will do just fine in the kitchen — or at least you will make an excellent coach.

8. The suggested time chart that follows is *averaged.* Smaller birds, you will note, are cooked *longer per pound* than larger birds, and as you think about it, that makes sense. The smaller bird is done much sooner, but the larger one takes less time per pound because of heat retention once the heavier meat begins to heat.

The chart provides rule-of-thumb timing. The meat of a mature bird will have to be tested for tenderness. Pierce the meat with a fork *in a hip and the breast.* When tender, it has probably cooked enough.

9. The accompanying chart gives comparative *average* times for roasting birds of different size by species. Degrees are in Fahrenheit.

| | |
|---|---|
| Dove | ¾ hr. @ 375° |
| Quail | 1 hr. @ 375° |
| Grouse | |
|   (Juvenile) | 1 hr. @ 375° |
|   (Mature) | Steam 20 min. Drain, stuff, and roast ½ to ¾ hr. @ 375° |
| Wood Duck | ½ hr. @ 400° (desirable to keep on rare side) |
| Mallard | ¾ hr. @ 400° (desirable to keep on rare side) |
| Goose | 6-8 lbs. (juvenile) 20-25 min./lb. 10 lbs. and up (mature) parboil ½ hr. Drain and stuff, then roast at 350° until tender and brown (15-20 min./lb.) |
| Wild Hen Turkey | |
|   (Juvenile) | 20-25 min./lb. @ 350° |
|   (Mature) | Steam ½ hr. Drain and stuff, then roast at 350° until tender and brown (20 min./lb.) |

Wild Tom Turkey (Gobbler)
   (Juvenile)      18-20 min./lb. @ 350°
   (Mature)      350° until tender and brown (20 min./lb.)

10. When young, whole birds are to be roasted in the oven or broiled on a spit over an open fire of hardwood coals, stuff the body cavity and the crop cavity in front of the breast to keep the meat moist and tender. In the dressing, ring-cut the neck, push the neck skin down to the body to expose the neck, which is cut off close to the body. This leaves the skin to sew or skewer together up front, to hold the stuffing in place. Dampened, torn pieces of bread with chunks of apple or whole cranberries work great over a campfire.

11. Different kinds of stuffing take different times to cook, whether the carcass is actually stuffed or pieces of it are placed on top of the stuffing. Times needed for properly tenderizing and cooking the meat have to be considered totally; time spent par-boiling, time for basic cooking, plus time needed to brown and glaze the bird to a fine finish. Check often until you gain experience with different species.

12. I like to  partially press the breast "unit" of ducks into a mound of one of the *pre-cooked* stuffings now available, and then broil them to a medium-rare finish. You also can concoct your own stuffing by making use of *pre-cooked* packaged rice. With pre-cooked stuffings everything is assured of being done at the same time. Medium-rare to rare is the preference of most people for wild duck. Plan accordingly. (The cooked meat is more like roast beef than chicken.)

13. I leave the legs and wings attached on small birds like quail and dove and usually roast them, trying to get the most possible from them. The flavor is good, even if the wing and leg meat does require more chewing. Besides, I like to see them all in a circle on the platter, browned and looking like tiny stuffed chickens, fit for a king.

14. Most small game has but little fat on it when compared to domestic animals of similar species. But recipes for cooking

domestic animals can be used for wild game if the differences are considered and adjustments made to compensate.

Added fat often is needed. One good way to hold and evenly distribute the spread of fat, grease, cooking oil or basting liquid in the roasting of young small game is to put a "shirt" on the meat. Spread a double layer of cheesecloth over the critter and put your grease, oil or basting mix on that. The cloth soaks up the hot liquid and keeps it from running off too quickly. Take the shirt off for final browning.

15. You might think cooking small game without skin or fat would present a problem. It doesn't. Grease or oil the meat first, or drape bacon strips over the meat, held in place by toothpicks. Occasional basting with margarine, butter or cooking oil does a fine job. A damp stuffing mix, with diced apples or cranberries or raisins added (or regular stuffing with spices and onion), can be molded around it to keep it moist.

16. I ask your indulgence to give you this jury-rigged recipe I worked out with my wife. It is terrific for any small game *when rare meat is not a goal* — thus anything but ducks. In fact, you can make a potpourri with rabbit, squirrel, partridge and wood-cock all in the same pan if you wish. It's hard *not* to have it come out right. And it can be cooked in the coals of a campfire or in the oven at home.

First we spread margarine evenly over the inside of a sheet of foil as in greasing a pan. That really is what we are doing. The foil is made into a shallow pocket with its edges pulled up some, and gently tucked here and there. The job goes easier without spilling if the foil pocket is formed inside a pan of appropriate size to accommodate your prize. You have to wash only one mixing bowl and a spoon later. I like that part, too.

This is a recipe you can play with, adding spices if you like zesty Mexican fare, or substituting tomato soup thickened with tomato paste for an Italian flair. Try beer or white wine in place of sherry. Arithmetic is not critical. The important thing is to keep wet/dry relationships close to the basic proportions given for the cooking of a quartered snowshoe hare in three foil pack-ages by the campfire. The three units make for easier serving when tent camping, but the ingredients can be mixed and the whole hare cooked in one 9 x 13 x 2 inch cake pan, or a comparable roasting pan covered with foil. The aluminum foil over the top should be crimped firmly under the edges of the pan all around. Take your choice.

Continuing with the campfire effort, the hare can be divided* this way: a front leg and a hindquarter (including the hip with the backbone removed). That takes care of two packages. The third package is scheduled for the meaty saddle ahead of the hips.

Ingredients needed are as follows: 1 can each of condensed cream of celery and cream of mushroom soup, 1 cup of hard raw rice, ½ cup of cooking sherry, ⅓ cup of water, a package of dried onion soup, and about a ½ cup of mushrooms (drained if canned, or soaked if carried dry and then drained before adding). Mix all but the onion soup in any order you want. Put a third of the mix into each foil pocket. Grease the pieces of meat thoroughly with bacon fat, butter or margarine and place them on the mix. Sprinkle the dry onion soup liberally over them. Then pull the edges of the foil together,* folding them over a few times to seal them. Allow some space at the top of the package, but make no holes in the top. When steam builds up, the foil will loosen enough to let it escape before it explodes.

Cook the whole disjointed hare in the foil-covered pan in the oven at 325°. At fireside, turn the packages end for end every fifteen to twenty minutes, keeping them at the edge of the fire, with new coals pushed around them from time to time. Don't peek, either at home or in camp, *for two hours.* Some additional fireside time may be needed, depending on how well you know your fire. You'll be pleasantly surprised with the final result.

The same amount of mix required for the snowshoe hare (or a western jack) also will take care of four squirrels, two cottontails, three partridges or five woodcock.

17. *Juvenile/Adult Aging Charts* for ducks, geese, squirrels, quail, grouse and turkey are given (starting on p. 261) so the cook can better choose an appropriate method of cooking.

18. *Reflector broiling* by the campfire can be done quite satisfactorily with a folding aluminum reflector oven. Place the object to be broiled (heat from the top only) on the *bottom* of an

*inverted* shallow pan resting on the cooking shelf. Adjust distance of the reflector from the fire so the heat will bounce off the inside *angled top* onto the exposed meat or fish to be broiled. The angled bottom reflector can remain fairly cool.

19. *Split-log broiling* by the campfire works fine too, and is especially good for broiling "butterflied" fish fillets or single fillets that have the skin left on.

The meat or fish is pegged onto the clean split surface of the log. (The face may be shaved with a large knife or axe to smooth it.) Work the sharp point of a knife through the meat or fish (skin side down) into the log to create a correctly placed slit (with the grain of the wood) on the smooth, flat face. Whittled, flat-sided pegs replace the knife and are forced through the flesh into the slit in the log. The pegs keep the object to be broiled in place when the log is stood on an edge to catch the radiant heat of the fire. The face of the log is held at the desired angle with rocks or stakes placed behind the log near the ends of the curved back side. Heat is controlled by the proximity of the fire. Push in coals or pull them back.

Bacon strips can be held straight or criss-crossed over the meat or fish by the same pegs, or insert a few additional ones. If bacon is lacking, baste periodically with butter or oleo and drip lemon juice on the fish. (Plan ahead and you will have what you want on hand.)

20. *Poaching fish* is a far cry from *boiling* fish and should not be confused with it. The fish is placed in a pan and just covered with water. Put the pan on a grill at the campfire. Watch for tiny bubbles forming inside the pan. Move the pan or the fire to just keep the bubbles forming but *not rising,* which would be *boiling.* Keep the water just *under* boiling temperature.

At home *in the oven,* set the temperature at 375°. Fifteen minutes is usually enough for a 1- to 2-lb. fish. Drain and eat with butter and lemon juice.

A *recommended* variation is to cut the water 50–50 with dry Vermouth or other wine. It adds that extra oomph! A melted cheese sauce instead of lemon juice is great, too.

21. *Reasons for bones in filleted fish.*

a. Wrong angle behind head in cut-off severs a few spines of the backbone. Pick these out or check for them at the top of the back at the head end.

b. Hemal bones vary with the fish. They are cut off at the butt ends in the filleting. Run a finger tip (tail to head) over the flesh where you expect to find them. Check earlier diagrams. When you feel them, study the line, cut each side of them to the skin. In most fish the strip between these cuts can be pinched at the head end and lifted out of the raw fish.

c. Overcooked broiled or baked whole fish dry out, and hemal bones then separate from the backbone to become lost in the flesh. They should hold to the backbone so flesh can be pulled from them on one side, and on the other side, they should come out with the backbone as it is lifted — *if the fish is cooked properly.*

d. Pickerel family, a special hemal bone situation, see p. 222.

e. Shad and alewives are nearly impossible to bone short of taking a good deal of time and skill, *but the job is very easy* if you will settle for a variety of cooking methods possible after following directions on pp. 228-229.

# CHECKING OUT THE OLD BIRDS—the *young ones* are tender.

## WATERFOWL

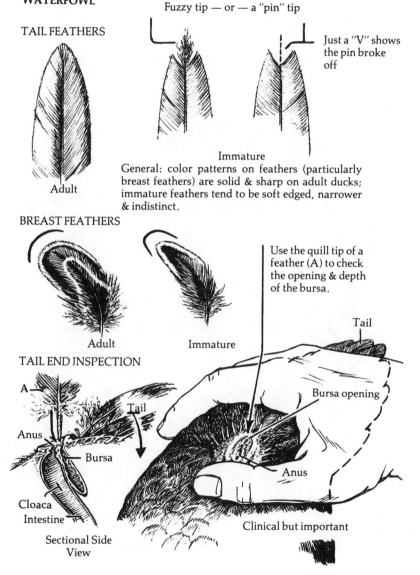

**TAIL FEATHERS**

Fuzzy tip — or — a "pin" tip

Just a "V" shows the pin broke off

Adult

Immature

General: color patterns on feathers (particularly breast feathers) are solid & sharp on adult ducks; immature feathers tend to be soft edged, narrower & indistinct.

**BREAST FEATHERS**

Adult

Immature

Use the quill tip of a feather (A) to check the opening & depth of the bursa.

**TAIL END INSPECTION**

A

Anus

Bursa

Cloaca
Intestine

Sectional Side View

Tail

Tail

Bursa opening

Anus

Clinical but important

261

## AGING BY THE BURSA

Canada geese: bursa is *closed* at 3 years of age and older, designating maturity. Closing varies during first 3 years for they do not all mature at the same time. *Both sexes of immature geese* have the bursa. Closed bursa, think about tenderizing.

**Ducks:** a mature female (♀) duck has a *closed* (sealed) *bursa.* Immature females have a relatively deep bursa.

X-rated but factual: a mature male (♂) duck has a *noticeable sheath* over the penis that shows when the anus area is pressed in at each side simultaneously; an immature male shows a twisted penis *with no sheath.*

**Grouse:** for determining best cooking methods relative to age, the following *applies to all grouse.* Males tend to be heavier bodied. Juveniles look like females.

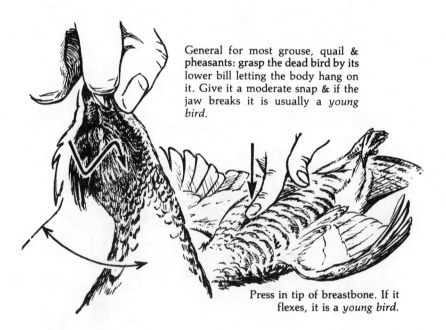

General for most grouse, quail & pheasants: grasp the dead bird by its lower bill letting the body hang on it. Give it a moderate snap & if the jaw breaks it is usually a *young bird.*

Press in tip of breastbone. If it flexes, it is a *young bird.*

**GROUSE & QUAIL** (except Coturnix)

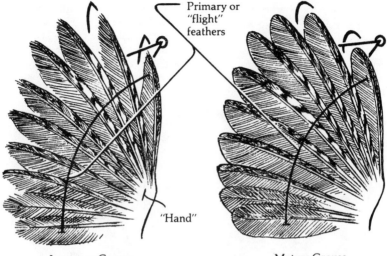

Primary or "flight" feathers

"Hand"

Immature Grouse                    Mature Grouse

The outer two *pointed* primaries of an immature quail or grouse are kept through the bird's *1st winter.*

**RING-NECKED PHEASANT:** Hens are difficult to age for the primaries can vary. There's no difficulty in determining sex by plumage, and spurs of the male are good indicators of maturity of the cock in fall hunting seasons.

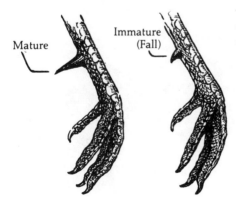

Mature

Immature (Fall)

The jaw test can be used as a check on the hens, but it isn't too accurate for them (p. 262).

**WOODCOCK:** Outer primaries of immatures show *uneven wear & V'ed tips;* adults show even wear & *squared off tips.*

**WILD TURKEY:** Restoration efforts & an abundance of mature hardwood forests have combined to make wild turkey hunting one of the fastest growing sports with a prize to put on the table. In but eight years, 31 wild turkeys trapped from a New York flock & transferred to Vermont created a flock of thousands for the Green Mt. State. And now they are overflowing into eastern N.Y., as well as N.H. and Mass. *Spring and fall hunting seasons* only help to keep a healthy flock of these super wary birds. The 1977 fall harvest in Vermont, a mere 9,000 square miles in size (only one-third of it suitable wild turkey habitat) was 1,043.

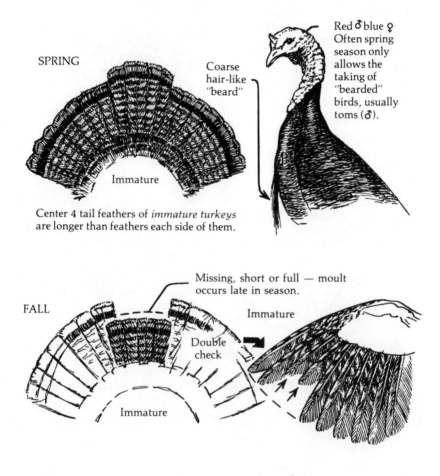

SPRING

Coarse hair-like "beard"

Red ♂ blue ♀ Often spring season only allows the taking of "bearded" birds, usually toms (♂).

Immature

Center 4 tail feathers of *immature turkeys* are longer than feathers each side of them.

Missing, short or full — moult occurs late in season.

FALL

Immature

Double check

Immature

# AGING THE MAMMALS — Tough or tender?

**Bear:** if your bear is a big one, chances are it is at least approaching tough conditions. *All bear meat*, like pork, should be thoroughly cooked anyway, so plan for pressure cooking & braising.

**Deer:** most states in the U.S. have *young* herds these days. Few deer live to old age. For most purposes, especially when cooking the meat is of prime concern, tooth wear is the best indicator of age.

Check the 3rd premolar for moderate wear, outside cusp (ridge) smooth, rear outside of 2nd worn too. Indicative of a typical 2½ yr. old, still tender, but when more wear is evident plan cooking accordingly.

This 2½ yr. whitetail — 130 lbs. He could have weighed 155 lbs. Normal cooking was sufficient for taste & tenderness.

A good turning point

Incisors
Canine
Only slight wear

1  2  3  4
5  6

11/18/75

130 lbs.    4 pts. Ferdinand Vt.

1 - 2 - 3 are premolars
4 - 5 - 6 are molars
White-tailed & mule deer's teeth are comparable enough to determine aging for cooking needs.

You may have heard of biologists aging deer by tooth *replacement* patterns. Until they get their full set, don't worry. Before they do, you can be sure they'll be tender.

If teeth all show moderate wear or if all flattened & shiny you've got *an old one*. Plan for a lot of venisonburg, stews & braising. See page 75 for aging venison.

Note: All deer have matching back teeth upstairs for "roll-around" chewing, but no front teeth on upper jaw.

# While We Are on the Subject of Deer

**Moose, caribou & elk:** the same general wear on the teeth holds true with larger deer too for our purposes, but more wear usually shows on their 2nd premolar (2) & the 1st molar (4) than on smaller species of deer (based on 2½ yr. old animals).

Liver.   It is normal for a fresh liver to change color on first exposure to the air—deep maroon, blue, gray & don't worry about a bluish or grayish cast to it later.

Spleen.   Your deer has only one liver. That thing that looks like a small liver is its spleen — the blood factory.

Warts.   *(palatoma)* A skin virus that once in a while puts a deer in horrible shape. I've seen deer with eyes completely masked & others with warts like black or bloody eggs hanging scattered over their bodies. Warts do not harm the meat, they say, but they do ruin my appetite. And I'm not squeamish!

**Squirrels:** Tails.  Check tip, *under skin* exposed & pattern.

Immature      Skin                          Mature
              shows

X-rated check: *Adult* ♀ has large nipples lacking hair around them; adult ♂ has large scrotum & not much hair on it.

**Rabbits & Hares:** They're tough to sex & age. Check wear on teeth & general condition. If in doubt treat it like an old one. You can't go far wrong with a stew or hassenpfeffer. *Young cottontails,* when quartered, show the top of the hip bone (humerus) looking like the cap hasn't really hitched to the bone. You'll see a line all around under it. An *adult has a smooth head* on the humerus & no line showing under the cap.

**Woodchucks:** if the chuck has light, grizzled hairs around the head & shoulders, it is getting along in age. See p. 128.

**Porcupines:** not just a survival food. You'll be safe going by size. A *big porky* makes fine stew & you might try parboiling a hind leg and hip, followed by draining & roasting over the coals of an open fire.

**Bobcats & coyotes:** don't knock them until you try them. The only cat I ever tried was an *old tom* from New Hampshire & weighed 46 lbs. His round steaks were fine grained, tasty & even tender. I've yet to try the canids, but I do know, you rarely see dogs in China. The Chinese consider the dog a delicacy — coyotes?

**"Four & twenty blackbirds?"**

Cooked this way, they'd all be tender.

**Survival food:** In a pinch, I guess any meat is nourishing & most of it probably tastes good, if prepared half decently. In parts of the world, monkeys are for gourmets. I tried some once on a survival course. It tasted good, but went down hard. I kept seeing a friend I had in India. It is the hang-ups in the head that make the stomach reject a lot of nutritious food.

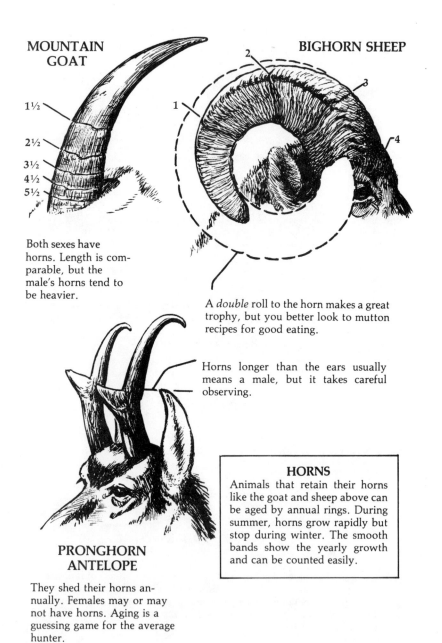

## MOUNTAIN GOAT

1½
2½
3½
4½
5½

Both sexes have horns. Length is comparable, but the male's horns tend to be heavier.

## BIGHORN SHEEP

2
1
3
4

A *double* roll to the horn makes a great trophy, but you better look to mutton recipes for good eating.

Horns longer than the ears usually means a male, but it takes careful observing.

## PRONGHORN ANTELOPE

They shed their horns annually. Females may or may not have horns. Aging is a guessing game for the average hunter.

### HORNS
Animals that retain their horns like the goat and sheep above can be aged by annual rings. During summer, horns grow rapidly but stop during winter. The smooth bands show the yearly growth and can be counted easily.

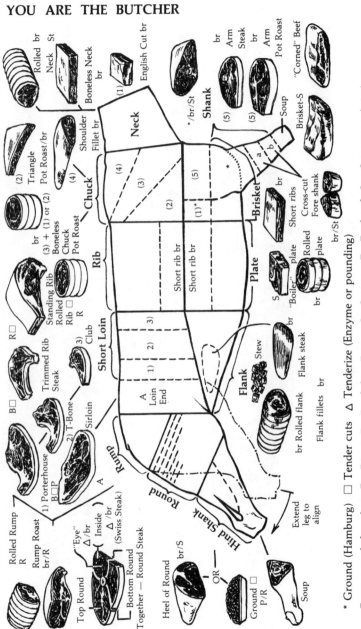

* Ground (Hamburg)  □ Tender cuts  △ Tenderize (Enzyme or pounding)

Recommended cooking  R—Roast  B—Broil  br—Braise  S—Simmer  P—Panbroil  St—Stew meat (trim)

• Major Cuts & Some Retail Cuts  Suitable for Elk, Caribou, Moose & Buffalo

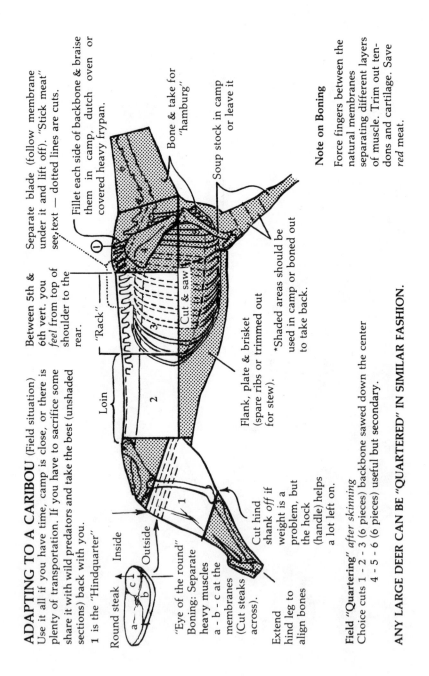

## ADAPTING TO A CARIBOU (Field situation)

Use it all if you have time, camp is close, or there is plenty of transportation. If you have to sacrifice some share it with wild predators and take the best (unshaded sections) back with you. 1 is the "Hindquarter"

Round steak — Inside

Outside

"Eye of the round" Boning: Separate heavy muscles a - b - c at the membranes (Cut steaks across).

Extend hind leg to align bones

Cut hind shank off if weight is a problem, but the hock (handle) helps a lot left on.

Between 5th & 6th vert. you *feel* from top of shoulder to the rear.

Loin

"Rack"

Cut & saw

Flank, plate & brisket (spare ribs or trimmed out for stew).

*Shaded areas should be used in camp or boned out to take back.

Separate blade (follow membrane under it and lift off). "Stick meat" see text — dotted lines are cuts.

Fillet each side of backbone & braise them in camp, dutch oven or covered heavy frypan.

Bone & take for "hamburg"

Soup stock in camp or leave it

### Note on Boning

Force fingers between the natural membranes separating different layers of muscle. Trim out tendons and cartilage. Save *red* meat.

**Field "Quartering"** *after skinning*
Choice cuts 1 - 2 - 3 (6 pieces) backbone sawed down the center
4 - 5 - 6 (6 pieces) useful but secondary.

**ANY LARGE DEER CAN BE "QUARTERED" IN SIMILAR FASHION.**

**LAMB CUTS** can serve as guidelines for butchering any small deer. Study both beef & lamb charts, then interpolate between. That way you'll get good cuts & meals from any deer, goat or sheep. Or you can study the next (Deer) page. Take your choice.

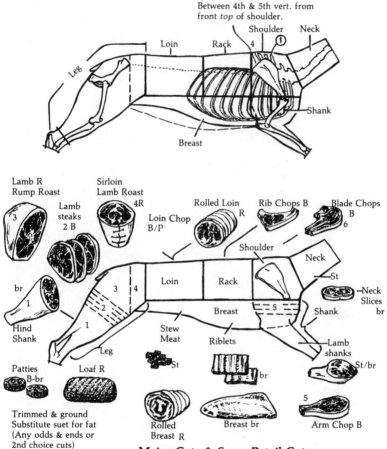

**Major Cuts & Some Retail Cuts**

*Drawings on this & next page keyed same as page 264.*

**Note on Boning**
Pare around bones with long knife parallel to them.

Cushion
Roast
R
(stuff)

Take blade, bones & cartilage from the shoulder & sew the 3 sides together.

**KNOWING THE BONES** helps to cope with them

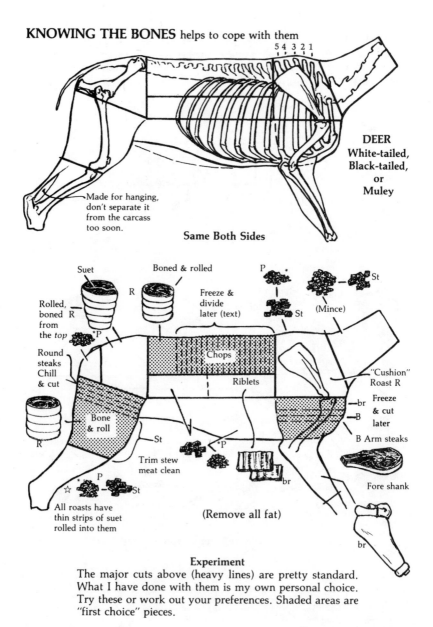

5 4 3 2 1

**DEER**
White-tailed,
Black-tailed,
or
Muley

Made for hanging,
don't separate it
from the carcass
too soon.

**Same Both Sides**

Suet

Boned & rolled

R

P   *

St

Rolled,
boned   R
from
the *top*

Freeze &
divide
later (text)

St

(Mince)

*P

Round
steaks
Chill
& cut

Chops

"Cushion"
Roast R

Riblets

br   Freeze
& cut
B   later

Bone
& roll

R

St

B Arm steaks

*P

Trim stew
meat clean

br

Fore shank

☆   *   P

St

br

All roasts have
thin strips of suet
rolled into them

(Remove all fat)

**Experiment**

The major cuts above (heavy lines) are pretty standard.
What I have done with them is my own personal choice.
Try these or work out your preferences. Shaded areas are
"first choice" pieces.

# REFERENCE SOURCES

In addition to those credited in text:

Arnold, Walter L. *Professional Trapping,* 4th Ed. Guilford, Maine. 1947.

Bishop, Clarence F. "Lake Champlain's Globe Trotting Eel," *The Vermonter* section of *The Burlington Free Press.* August 28, 1977.

Candy, Robert. *Nature Notebook.* Boston, Mass.: Houghton Mifflin Co. 1953.

Candy, Robert, and John Hall. *News and Notes.* Vermont Fish & Game Department, Montpelier, Vt. 1961-1978.

Kortright, F.H. *Ducks, Geese and Swans of North America.* Wildlife Management Institute, Washington, D.C., Harrisburg, Pennsylvania: Stackpole 1967.

Madson, John. *Gray and Fox Squirrels.* East Alton, Illinois: Conservation Department, Winchester Western Division, Olin Corporation. 1964.

Madson, John. *Ruffed Grouse.* East Alton, Illinois: Conservation Department, Winchester-Western Division, Olin Corporation. 1969.

Madson, John, and Ed Kozicky. *Game, Gunners and Biology.* East Alton, Illinois: Conservation Department, Winchester-Western Division, Olin Corporation. 1971.

Mosby, Henry S. *Wildlife Investigational Techniques,* 2nd ed. revised. Printed for the Wildlife Society by Edwards Bros. Inc., Ann Arbor, Mich., 1963. Washington, D.C.: The Wildlife Society. 1963.

Peterson, Roger Tory. *The Birds.* New York: Life Nature Library, Time-Life, Inc. 1963.

Scarola, John F. *Freshwater Fishes of New Hampshire.*Concord, N.H.: New Hampshire Fish and Game Department. 1973.

*National Geographic.* 1925–1978 personal library. Washington, D.C.: National Geographic Society.

*The Trapper* (periodical). Box 337, Sutton, Nebraska.

*Trapping and Wildlife Management,* 7th printing. Lilitz, Pennsylvania: Woodstream Corporation. 1975.

Interviews and field trips with many fish and game biologists, conservation officers and wardens, especially those of the New Hampshire and Vermont Fish and Game Departments (1946–1978). Their friendships as well as the information gleaned from these associations probably have had the greatest single impact on my outdoor career. (The Author)

# INDEX